George Hawley
The Moderate Majority

George Hawley

The Moderate Majority

Real GOP Voters and the Myth of Mass Republican
Radicalization

DE GRUYTER

ISBN (Hardcover) 978-3-11-147096-2
ISBN (Paperback) 978-3-11-146778-8
e-ISBN (PDF) 978-3-11-146972-0
e-ISBN (EPUB) 978-3-11-147040-5

Library of Congress Control Number: 2024941909

Bibliographic information published by the Deutsche Nationalbibliothek
The Deutsche Nationalbibliothek lists this publication in the Deutsche Nationalbibliografie;
detailed bibliographic data are available on the Internet at http://dnb.dnb.de.

© 2025 Walter de Gruyter GmbH, Berlin/Boston
Cover image: bee32 / iStock / Getty Images Plus

www.degruyter.com

For Nick. Rest in peace, brother. We'll continue our debate on the other side.

Contents

Chapter 1
Introduction

Many well-known pundits and journalists unfortunately promote mistaken ideas about American voters. This has always been the case, and it is a bipartisan problem. Beginning with Donald Trump's election to the presidency in 2016, however, the narratives promoted by some influential media voices became increasingly disconnected from reality. This is concerning, because mistaken ideas, to the extent that they are accepted by the public, can have unfortunate consequences. Much of the anger about politics among Americans is driven by misperceptions.[1] This does not mean political polarization is a myth. Republicans and Democrats do intensely dislike each other. Political partisans believe that their opponents are radicalizing, perhaps in dangerous ways, and it makes them angry. In response to their opponents' apparent growing radicalization, partisans are more willing to excuse the worst behaviors of their own side, turning a blind eye to the small number of genuine extremists in their own ranks. After all, one might reasonably conclude that, if the other side is willing to ally with extremists, perhaps my side should do the same. The problem, however, is that partisans on both sides overestimate their opponents' radicalism. They are, in effect, angry at each other for views they do not even hold.

One recent study, titled *The Perception Gap: How False Impressions are Pulling Americans Apart*, makes this point well.[2] The researchers on that project found that both Democrats and Republicans misperceive each other's views, overestimating their political and cultural differences. They found that misperceptions were particularly sizable among Democrats, who consistently exaggerated Republican racism and nativism. In other words, although this problem cuts across party lines, this study suggests Republicans understand Democrats better than the reverse. This does not seem to be something we can resolve with more education. Among Democrats, having more years of education was associated with even greater misperceptions about Republicans – there was not a similar education effect for Republicans.

Partisan hyperbole sells books. This is true across the partisan divide, and it can be a problem regardless of who is doing it. I am not here defending conserva-

---

1 Victoria A. Parker, Matthew Feinberg, Alexa Tullett, and Anne E Wilson, "The Ties that Blind: Misperceptions of the Opponent Fringe and the Miscalibration of Political Contempt," Working paper.
2 Daniel Yudkin, Stephen Hawkins, and Tim Dixon, *The Perception Gap: How False Impressions are Pulling Americans Apart* (New York: More in Common, 2019).

https://doi.org/10.1515/9783111469720-001

tive commentators like Ann Coulter, the late Rush Limbaugh, or Sean Hannity, who have each made enormous sums of money writing and speaking about liberals using uncivil, unfair, and often conspiratorial language. They have unquestionably contributed to the problem of partisan polarization. This does not excuse progressives – including progressive scholars and respected journalists – who do the same thing. The commercial success of books like *White Rural Rage: The Threat to American Democracy*, by Tom Schaller and Paul Waldmen,[3] and *American Psychosis: A Historical Investigation of How the Republican Party Went Crazy*,[4] by David Corn, shows that there is a large audience for progressive works promoting alarmist claims about large swaths of the US population.

Although this is an unfortunate trend, it is also comical, in an absurdist way. Republicans and Democrats, to a great degree, are mad at each other for extremist attitudes that they do not possess. That is, Republicans think Democrats are far more unhinged, radical, and violent than they are, and *vice versa*. In the minds of many Republicans, the typical Democrat is a gender-bending, religion-hating communist who wants to abolish the police – the type of person showcased on the popular right-wing X (formerly Twitter) account, "Libs of Tik Tok." According to many Democrats, the typical Republican is a Proud Boy, a revanchist Christian nationalist, an Alt-Right white supremacist, a QAnon conspiracy theorist, or a January 6th rioter. Such people exist, of course, but they are not the norm in either party.

Politics is an ugly business, and I am not so naïve as to believe progressive activists and commentators are going to change their approach to discussing Republican voters. I should therefore note that I am also concerned by changes I have noticed among elements of conservative media and some Republican politicians, and I would like them to rethink their attitude to politics. Student groups like Turning Point USA have recently exhibited a shift to the far right, which is an odd development, given that a few years ago they proudly rejected this approach.[5] Leading conservative commentators such as Tucker Carlson have moved toward conspiratorial, right-wing populism. Less responsible Republican legislators such as Rep. Marjorie Taylor Greene from Georgia seek to pull the party in a more right-wing direction. The American conservative movement has always had far-

---

3 Tom Schaller and Paul Waldman, *White Rural Rage: The Threat to American Democracy* (New York: Random House, 2024).
4 David Corn, *American Psychosis: A Historical Investigation of How the Republican Party Went Crazy* (New York: Twelve, 2022).
5 George Hawley, "The "Groyper" Movement in the US: Challenges for the Post-Alt-right," in *Contemporary Far-Right Thinkers and the Future of Liberal Democracy,*" edited by A. James McAdams and Alejandro Castrillon (New York: Routledge, 2021), 225–241.

right elements, but this has historically been tempered by conservatives' understanding that the American political tradition is at least partially rooted in classical liberalism, and this is one reason for the nation's extraordinary success. Some leading conservative pundits and intellectuals have concluded that it is time to reject that tradition. A superficial look at the Republican party in the electorate seems to indicate that ordinary Republican voters are happy with this shift, and they want to continue moving in the country in a far-right direction. I argue here that this belief is mistaken, and most Republican voters are not clamoring for the party to take a hard right turn. In fact, following such a policy may alienate a large part of the party's base. A potential long-term problem is that the "radicalization" of the GOP in the electorate may prove to be a self-fulfilling prophecy. If partisan and ideological elites rush toward extreme positions and messaging, moderates may disaffiliate, leaving a party that is smaller but more radical and cohesive.

Some of my own thinking on this matter was influenced by a project I completed for The Brookings Institution several years ago. I contributed research to a larger project on the status of Muslims in Western countries. My research focused on Trump supporters in the US and their attitudes toward Muslims and Islam.[6] For many years, right-wing extremism has been one of my primary areas of research. I admit that, within this milieu, I am one of the less alarmist scholars. For example, I have always argued that claims about a rising "fascist" threat in the United States are overstated. But I was surprised by what I found as I conducted that research.

Like most people my age or older, I remember the way Americans felt about Muslims during the George W. Bush Administration – I was in high school when the 9/11 attacks occurred. President Bush, for all his faults and mistakes, deserves credit for not personally fanning those flames, but plenty of other Republican leaders and conservative pundits embraced irresponsible anti-Muslim rhetoric, and a huge swath of the public followed suit. If you were reading right-wing blogs at the time or listening to the more bombastic talk-radio hosts, you learned that Islam is inherently violent, and that Muslims believe they have a sacred duty to slay the infidels. Although not all Muslims personally engaged in violence, even the so-called moderates, we were told, were unwilling to condemn the violence of their more extreme co-religionists.

When Donald Trump pursued the presidency, he rejected Bush's approach to Islam, openly calling for a complete end to all Muslim immigration. The Republican

---

6 George Hawley, "Ambivalent Nativism: Trump Supporters' Attitudes Toward Islam and Muslim Immigration," The Brookings Institution, July 24, 2019, https://www.brookings.edu/research/ambiv alent-nativism-trump-supporters-attitudes-toward-islam-and-muslim-immigration/.

base seemed, from what I could tell at the time, delighted with that kind of rhetoric. When I began my research on this subject, I expected to find that Islamophobia among Republicans was as strong as ever. Furthermore, because hatred of Islam was still, at least for many people on the right, considered an acceptable prejudice, I assumed Trump's most devoted supporters would have no problem echoing their president's remarks on the subject. As I began interviewing Trump supporters across the country on this issue, I expected to hear the same tedious, bigoted remarks about the Islamic threat to America. This was not what I found.

A political progressive listening to those interviews would have many reasons to be appalled. Compared to progressive Democrats, these MAGA Republicans were unquestionably far more nativist and suspicious of racial and religious out-groups. However, they were less intolerant and reactionary than I anticipated. I understand that social desirability bias – the tendency to withhold certain opinions a person believes are unpopular – is a major problem in both survey research and qualitative interviews, especially when dealing with hot-button issues like race and religion. I nonetheless had experience with this kind of research and had come to expect that, especially when guaranteed anonymity, after a sufficiently long conversation I could usually get honest answers from people. Despite the very recent anti-Muslim remarks from Trump, the men and women I spoke with were clearly ambivalent about this issue. No one I spoke with was enthusiastic about large-scale Muslim immigration, but they did not express the more extreme Islamophobic sentiments that were so common in conservative media at the peak of the Global War on Terror.

A bit surprised by my findings, I wanted to see if empirical data aligned with my personal observations. They did. For political scientists studying the US electorate, the American National Election Survey (ANES) is one of the more useful tools. Although it changes based on the issues and personalities of the election cycle, it also recycles questions, asking many of them year after year, allowing us to see changes over time. According to the 2016 dataset, which was the most recent ANES survey at the time I was working on that project, Republicans had colder feelings toward Muslims than toward most other groups, but their attitudes had not become more negative compared to previous years. In fact, compared to 2012, they were noticeably warmer. When I revisited this question after the 2020 ANES became available, I found that Republican attitudes toward Muslims had become warmer still. If Trump's presidency had prompted a growth in anti-Muslim attitudes among Americans, I was not seeing it in the data.

Examining other groups and issues, I saw this pattern repeat. Republicans remain more right-wing than Democrats on every issue that matters, and similarly, compared to Democrats, express more negative feelings toward most religious, ethnic, and racial minority groups. They have not, however, been moving farther right. In fact, on many issues they have been moving left, and their attitudes toward demographic out-groups have either remained consistent with historical norms, or they have become more tolerant.

The concept of the "Overton Window" has received a lot of scholarly and popular attention in the last decade.[7] This refers to the range of what is considered possible and acceptable in the political arena. In every democratic nation, there will always be certain ideologies and policy agendas that are simply off the table. In the twentieth century, for example, neither communism nor fascism ever stood a real chance in the realm of partisan politics in the United States. Today, we hear from concerned progressives that right-wing radicals, inspired by Trump, have dragged the Overton Window dramatically to the right, making fascism, or something like it, a genuine possibility. Some people on the radical right agree, crowing that the American people are slowly "waking up," coming around to their way of thinking. They are wrong.

In this book, I will show that claims about Republican extremism have been overstated. The notion that the Republican Party in the electorate is dominated by crazed radicals has little empirical backing. To be clear, the typical Republican voter has many opinions that would make a left-wing progressive apoplectic, but those opinions are within the current American mainstream, which is no more right-wing than it was 20-years ago. If polarization is increasing, it is not because Republican voters are becoming more reactionary.

I seek to provide a sober analysis of Republican voters, noting their demographic traits, geographic distribution, policy preferences, religious identities, ideological constraints, and cultural attitudes. To be sure that I am not overstating my case, I also note that the party does contain genuine white supremacists and conspiracy theorists completely disconnected from reality. Using a variety of methods, I show that these groups are a small minority within the party, and I argue that exaggerating their influence can only serve to strengthen their position. American democracy requires two functional, competitive parties. The Republican Party remains a vital part of American political life, but unfortunately some of its prominent voices are trying to drag it down a dangerous path. It is not inevitable that they will succeed.

Political scientists studying political parties usually consider three major components: the party in government (elected officials carrying the party label, for in-

7 Derek Robertson, "How an Obscure Conservative Theory Became the Trump Era's Go-to Nerd Phrase," *Politico*, February 25, 2018, https://www.politico.com/magazine/story/2018/02/25/overton-window-explained-definition-meaning-217010/.

stance), the party in organization (the Republican National Committee, state-level parties, etc.), and the party in the electorate (people who identify with the party and vote for its candidates). The latter group is my entire focus here. Other elements of the Republican Party are of course important, perhaps, in terms of policy, even more important than the voters. Whether or not these other aspects of the GOP are radicalizing is a question outside the scope of this book. Trends within the organized conservative movement (magazines, television personalities, think tanks, grassroots organizations, etc.) are also not considered in this volume. I have written other books on these topics, if readers are interested in my thoughts about them.[8]

Republicans are my focus, but in my quantitative analysis of public policy preferences, demographic attributes, and cultural trends, it was also necessary to discuss Democrats and independents. After all, without knowing how they differ from other Americans, even an exhaustive understanding of Republicans provides little value. I will therefore also consider the extent to which Republicans are different from other Americans on key issues.

While working on this project, I combined two skillsets that I rarely use in the same project. Like my doctoral dissertation, most of my peer-reviewed articles, and three of my previous books, I focus primarily on quantitative data. I examine public opinion and demographic data, using both new and old data sets. Quantitative data is an indispensable tool for making sense of social trends. There are limits to what we can learn from such analyses, however. Public opinion polls typically rely heavily on multiple choice questions. Again, these are extremely useful, but their usefulness depends strongly on question wording, collecting a sample that reflects the total population, and subjects answering the questions honestly. The accuracy of such polls was recently called into question when public opinion experts, for the most part, failed to predict Donald Trump's victory in the 2016 presidential election.

It is my view that pollsters were unfairly maligned in the immediate aftermath of that contest. In the aggregate, the polls were not that far off from the result. Donald Trump did lose the popular vote – as the polls suggested. It is nonetheless also the case that qualitative approaches, in which scholars leave their social and ideological bubbles and personally interact with people from many different walks of life, can result in insights that they would miss from looking at numbers alone.

---

8 For example, see George Hawley, *Right-Wing Critics of American Conservatism*, (Lawrence, KS: University Press of Kansas, 2016) and George Hawley, *Conservatism in a Divided America: The Right and Identity Politics*, (Notre Dame, IN: University of Notre Dame Press, 2022).

For this reason, after developing a plan for ensuring the security of my data and anonymity of my subjects, and receiving permission from my university's institutional review board, I began interviewing Republicans of varying levels of political interest and activity across the country. Unlike my qualitative research on the radical right, for this project I did not actively seek out political radicals – though I did not disqualify subjects if they expressed extremist attitudes. Several of my early interviewees were students I recruited from conservative organizations at the University of Alabama. I recognize that this group is not representative of the Republican Party overall, and this book includes few quotes from this group. These interviews were useful largely because they helped me fine tune the questions I used throughout the process. They were additionally helpful because several of these students introduced me to other Republicans of different ages and backgrounds who also agreed to be interviewed.

I also reached out via email to political activists I had previously never met, and I found many were eager to speak with me and make additional introductions. I was worried that my plan to use a "snowball sampling" approach to this study would prove challenging. This fear was unwarranted. Many interviewees offered to make further introductions, without even being asked.

I owe a special debt of gratitude to the pastor of a small-town evangelical church in the Midwest I reached out to early in this project. Despite having no reason to do me a favor, he went out of his way to gather a large group of men and women from his congregation who graciously gave me a day of their time. That group was especially helpful, in part because of how closely its members matched the demographic profile of the typical Republican, but also for the many blunt conversations that occurred during that meeting. Of all the groups I met with, that was the most illuminating.

I was eager to speak with a wide cross section of Republican voters throughout this process, with one prominent exception. I intentionally avoided Republicans working in politics in Washington, DC, whether directly for politicians or the many conservative non-profits in that area. From personal experience, I find that they are distinct from other GOP supporters throughout the country. A large, qualitative study of professional conservative activists in the DC area would be very helpful and important, and I hope someone is working on such a project. That would be distinct from this book, however.

During these interviews, I sat with municipal politicians and professional activists, but also many people with only a high school diploma who identify with the Republican Party but usually do not bother to vote. I spoke with affluent lawyers who could give me a few minutes of their time in between international business trips, as well as retirees on a fixed income. I met college students whose interest in the GOP was tenuous, and stay-at-home mothers concerned about the direction of

American culture. Whenever possible, I held these discussions in person, which meant travelling across the country, visiting people in or near Seattle, St. Louis, Birmingham, and Nashville, as well as rural communities on the West Coast and Midwest.

I met an evangelical African American who believed the free market represented the most viable path for black advancement, as well as a conspiracy theorist who wanted to educate me about satanic pedophiles who dominate the nation's elite. I spoke with people who thought the "culture war" stuff was a stupid distraction from real issues, and those who cared about nothing else. The diversity of opinion within the Republican Party demonstrates just how hard it will be for a politician to satisfy its many constituent groups. Libertarians who care deeply about criminal justice reform, evangelicals who base their foreign policy preferences on their strongly-held beliefs about end-times prophecies, old-fashioned isolationists, economic conservatives delighted that mass immigration provides inexpensive labor, antisemites who believe the Trump presidency was derailed by his Jewish daughter and son-in-law, wealthy Americans who just want lower taxes and less regulation, open nativists, and conspiracy theorists with weird ideas that do not neatly fit anywhere on the ideological spectrum are all elements of the Republican Party in the electorate.

Not all these groups represent equal shares of the Republican Party, however. Both the policy wonks and the white nationalists receive a disproportionate share of media coverage. The former understandably have a large sway over the actual policies that Republican politicians seek to implement. The latter provide endless fodder for breathless coverage from progressive pundits. The overwhelming majority of Republican voters are neither. They are ordinary people with ordinary concerns. They are not radicals, and they often do not have a coherent ideology. Although, more often than not, they will call themselves 'conservatives,' this label often seems to have little substantive meaning for then. Many self-described conservatives do not seem to possess what political scientists call ideological constraints. This book attempts to sort through all these groups, providing a complete a picture of the Republican Party in the electorate.

In Chapter 2, I provide an overview of the Republican Party's demographic attributes. The GOP is associated with certain individual characteristics: white, evangelical, rural, older, etc. The percentage of people that perfectly match that profile is relatively small. If these were the only people that consistently supported the Republican Party, it would not be able to compete at a national level. This chapter examines the demographic attributes of the Republican Party in the electorate, noting how it differs from the Democratic Party and the adult population more broadly, and how it has changed over the last several decades.

A key finding we see throughout the available data is that the Republican Party is performing very well among demographic groups that are shrinking as a percentage of the total population. This finding suggests the party's days are numbered, and it will inevitably be swept aside by a coalition of ascendant diverse groups. In the long run, this may be true, and the US may enter a period of one-party dominance. To the Democratic Party's frustration, however, the Republicans have continued to grow in strength among these declining groups, which continues to offset the Democratic Party's advantage among other demographic categories. The GOP is likely approaching a ceiling on its support among white evangelicals and white rural Americans, and it will need to expand its support among non-whites, the highly educated, and non-religious Americans to remain competitive. In the meantime, however, its current demographic makeup remains sufficient to be competitive in national elections, and dominant in many states.

Chapter 2 does contain some hopeful information for Republicans, noting the degree to which they remain much more likely than Democrats to form large families, which helps the party in the long-run because of the degree to which partisanship tends to run along family lines. I also consider the evidence indicating that Republicans in the last presidential election made some important inroads among Latino voters, and consider the possibility that this group may be more amenable to Republican appeals than many observers once expected.

In Chapter 3, I examine what Republican voters want from government. When people speak of political polarization, they usually suggest that the policy platforms of the Republicans and Democrats are moving farther apart. After all, changing public policy (or resisting changes) is presumably the entire point of political activism. If Republicans really are radicalizing, it should manifest itself in the kinds of policies they want to see enacted. In this chapter, I examine Republican attitudes on some of the most contentious policy issues, with a special focus on the trends in these attitudes and the direction of recent changes. I consistently find little or no evidence of a turn toward the right within the Republican electorate. I also discuss the debates within political science about public attitudes toward policy, noting that some scholars remain skeptical that significant portions of the electorate have meaningful and consistent opinions on most matters of public policy.

Throughout the chapters on Republican attitudes, I examine trusted sources of public opinion data, such as the ANES, the General Social Survey (GSS), the Cooperative Election Study (CES), and the Baylor Religion Survey. I supplement my analysis of these data with knowledge I gained from long-form interviews conducted with Republicans across the country, as well as an opinion survey I commissioned that asked Republicans which policy issues they personally considered most important. This survey took place during the summer of 2022, at a time when culture war issues, such as the new right-wing fight against Critical Race Theory and the Supreme Court's decision to overturn *Roe v. Wade*, were at the center of national discussions. Despite the countrywide focus on these kinds of issues, I found that Republican voters overwhelmingly prioritized economic concerns such as inflation.

Chapter 4 considers ideology among Republicans. I show that, if we are just looking at trends in ideological self-identification, it does appear that Republicans are moving to the right. Over the last several decades, the number of Republicans that define themselves as conservative or very conservative has increased. This may be misleading, however, if Americans do not attach very much ideological or policy content to these ideologies. That is, calling yourself conservative or liberal may be little more than an expression of political tribalism.

I attempted to make sense of Republican ideological orientation by commissioning a survey of Republicans, asking them to describe conservatism and liberalism in their own words. I supplement what I found from this survey with a discussion of how Republicans described these ideological terms during my long interviews.

In Chapter 5, I turn my attention to cultural attitudes, which do not always directly relate to issues of public policy. Most political observers take it for granted that the US is experiencing a 'culture war.' The stakes and dividing lines of this war are too infrequently defined. I nonetheless concur that cultural antagonisms are at least as central to American political life as wonkish policy debates. In this chapter, I discuss Republican cultural attitudes, especially as they relate to the major cultural and demographic changes that are presently occurring in the US. Is the Republican Party a vehicle for a white Christian backlash? Is that what the party's voters want?

This chapter shows, unsurprisingly, that Republicans are far more conservative than Democrats when it comes to cultural attitudes, and that the gap is growing. The two parties are not becoming more distant because Republicans are moving to the right, however. The growing cultural gap is largely the result of the Democratic Party's recent movement to the left, especially on questions related to race and gender. Survey data indicate that, on most issues, Republicans have held steady in their opinions for the last several decades, and in some cases have moved slightly to the left.

In Chapter 6, I examine some of the more concerning claims about the contemporary GOP, especially the idea that the party has become more overtly racist and conspiratorial in its thinking. Voices on the political left and center have been understandably alarmed by what they perceive to be a strong rightward turn by the Republican Party. The events of January 6th, 2021, and the failure of Republican leaders to appropriately condemn the Capitol rioters, seems to underscore the GOP's rejection of basic democratic norms. Some pundits have even begun describing the Republican Party as nothing more than a stalking horse for white Christian nationalism. The world of political commentary is currently dominated by hyperbole and cherry-picked examples, making it possible to present almost any narrative one wishes.

Throughout this book, I argue that most Republicans are moderate in their policies and not especially ideological. That is not to say that the Republican electorate does not include strange, bigoted, and sometimes dangerous elements. In Chapter 6, I attempt to quantify which parts of the Republican electorate are seemingly aligned with racist movements in the US. I also discuss what the latest research tells us about conspiratorial thinking among the GOP electorate, especially QAnon and related conspiracy theories. I discuss the various ways scholars measure racism, noting that each measure has downsides. Using multiple surveys, I attempt to measure the percentage of the electorate that can accurately be described as white supremacist, finding that the label does not fit most Republicans.

This raises an important question, however. If Republicans have not become more nativist or prejudiced, what explains their recent anger about politics? As other scholars have documented, partisan hostility, sometimes called 'negative partisanship' or 'affective polarization,' is very real and it is growing. Republicans may be less likely to express negative views toward ethnic or racial minorities, but they are happy to declare their hatred of Democrats and liberals. This is itself a disturbing trend, one that makes bipartisan compromise difficult, but partisan animus is not the same as overt racial and religious prejudice, and we should be cautious before conflating these phenomena.

Although I rely heavily on survey data in this book, I did not make use of any advanced statistical techniques. The purpose of this book is to give a broad overview of the Republican Party today, and filling the text with regression tables would be more likely to confuse than clarify.

I hope readers of all political persuasions will find something useful in this book. People from all sides will likely find things in the forthcoming pages they find heartening or disturbing. Conservatives may be alarmed by the degree to which the typical Republican is moderate when it comes to policy positions – doctrinaire economic conservatism is actually quite uncommon among Republican voters. Liberals may be frustrated to see that Republicans continue to hold many positions they consider reactionary and intolerant. This book should not be interpreted as a defense of those views, nor am I suggesting that there are not real and important differences between the parties. I do believe, however, that a clear-eyed analysis of the state of the electorate shows that the most alarmist claims about American politics are based on mistaken information about the public. A more accurate understanding of the US public may help diminish some of the unhelpful hyperbole that has become so prevalent in the nation's political discourse.

Chapter 2
The demography of the Republican Party today

The Republican Party's obituary has been prematurely written many times. Two decades ago, important scholars were declaring the arrival of a new Democratic majority.[1] The logic of this prediction was sound. The Democratic Party attracted majorities of young people, minorities, residents of big cities, and highly educated professionals. Given the demographic profile of the United States, that looks like a winning coalition. Yet the Democrats' unstoppable electoral behemoth never seems to make its appearance. Or, when it does look like it has taken hold, the Republicans have had a habit of returning with a vengeance, dashing hopes that a new era of left-wing liberalism has finally arrived. For many progressives, these repeated periods of Republican resurgence must feel akin to a horror movie franchise in which the villain, thought convincingly defeated, implausibly rises, again and again, to threaten the beleaguered protagonists.

The argument that Democrats perform well among demographic groups that are large, influential, and growing is correct. It has been correct for decades. That narrative is incomplete, however. In the 1990s, it was already the case that Republicans performed very well with older, white, rural, Christian Americans, and Democrats consistently won a majority of younger voters, secular voters, and racial and ethnic minorities. However, the Republicans had not yet hit a ceiling of support among its base demographic groups. Furthermore, although Democrats win the majorities of many different demographic groups, there is no sizable group that is universally Democratic in its vote choice. Marginal improvements among certain groups can go a long way to keeping the Republican Party competitive, even when the opposing party seems to have the demographic wind at its back.

The Republican conquest of rural America

The Republican Party dominates most of rural America, and it has for many decades. Donald Trump secured the presidency in 2016 largely based on his overwhelming support from rural areas. He performed even better in rural America in 2020, though it was not enough to secure the Electoral College a second time be-

---

[1] John Judis and Roy Teixeira, *The Emerging Democratic Majority* (New York: Scribner, 2002).

https://doi.org/10.1515/9783111469720-002

cause of large turnout in more urbanized parts of the country.[2] Democratic strength within major metropolitan areas is similarly well documented.[3] Indeed, the Republican Party has done well in many rural regions of the country through-out its history. It could not have become a national political player in the nine-teenth century without widespread rural support. Even during periods of Demo-cratic dominance, such as the New Deal era, Republicans enjoyed significant support in many rural areas.[4] However, Republican support from rural voters once varied wildly by region. From the period following Reconstruction until the Civil Rights Movement, Republicans performed poorly in the rural South, for example. William Jennings Bryan's populist movement was built largely on an im-poverished rural base.

Even relatively recently, there were rural, majority-white counties in the US where Democrats typically performed very well. In Figure 2.1, I show those coun-ties in the lower 48 states where Republicans were overwhelmingly dominant in both the 2000 and the 2020 presidential elections. The shaded counties on these maps are those in which the Republican presidential candidate won more than three-fifths of the total vote.[5] Examining the two maps, the significantly greater number of dark-red counties in the latter election is the first thing that stands out. In both elections, the Republicans lost the popular vote (though George W. Bush narrowly won in the Electoral College), yet in the more recent election, a much larger geographic swath of the country voted Republican in overwhelming numbers. We see this most pronounced in the Upper Midwest, where, 20 years ago, Republicans were not so dominant in rural counties. It was not long ago that Democrats performed well in places like rural Minnesota and rural Wiscon-sin.[6] Increasingly, however, rural Northerners are becoming like rural Southerners

---

2 Don E. Albrecht, "Donald Trump and Changing Rural/Urban Voting Patterns," *Journal of Rural Studies*, 91(2022): 148–156.

3 Ron Johnson, David Manley, Kelvyn Jones, and Ryne Rohla, "The Geographical Polarization of the American Electorate: A Country of Increasing Electoral Landslides?" *GeoJournal*, 85(2020): 187–204; David F. Damore, Robert E. Lang, and Karen A. Danielsen, *Blue Metros, Red States: The Shifting Urban-Rural Divide in America's Swing States* (Washington, DC: Brookings Institution Press, 2020).

4 Seth C. McKee, "Rural Voters and the Polarization of American Presidential Elections," *P.S.: Political Science and Politics*, 41(2008): 101–108.

5 I chose this cutoff because it is the same standard Bill Bishop used in his book, *The Big Sort: Why the Clustering of Like-Minded America is Tearing Us Apart* (New York, Mariner Books: 2009). It is also the standard I used in my own book on voter migration, George Hawley, *Voting and Migration Patterns in the U.S.* (New York: Routledge, 2013).

6 For a thorough discussion of the G.O.P.'s rise in rural Wisconsin, with lessons that can be applied to neighboring states, I recommend Katherine J. Cramer, *The Politics of Resentment: Rural Consciousness in Wisconsin and the Rise of Scott Walker* (Chicago, IL: University of Chicago Press, 2016).

when it comes to vote choice.[7] The remaining rural, overwhelmingly white communities that do not give lopsided support to the Republican Party are predominantly found in New England.

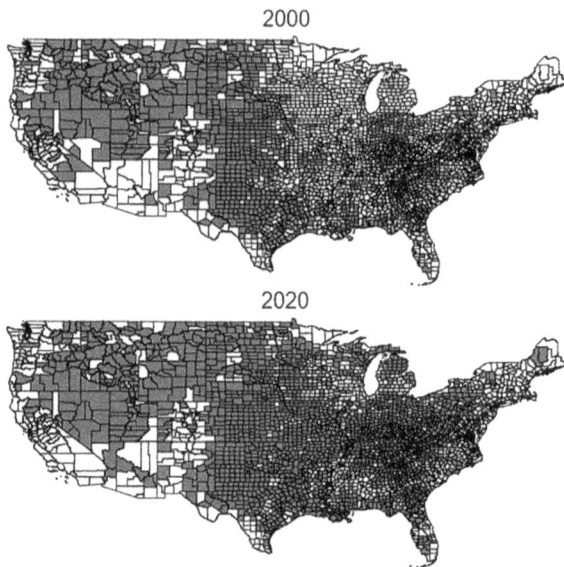

Figure 2.1: Landslide Republican Counties in 2000 and 2020.

The growing sea of red on the US map seems as though it must portend growing Republican strength overall. Again, these are not just Republican counties, they are landslide Republican counties. Unfortunately for the Republicans, people cast ballots, not land. Most of the places where Republicans win by landslide margins have small populations, and a huge percentage of these counties are shrinking. Although the population of the US continues to grow, largely because of immigration, that growth is not evenly distributed across the country. For the last several decades, growth has occurred predominantly in large metropolitan areas and their surrounding suburbs. The nation's rural communities, especially in the Midwest, with some exceptions, have been experiencing stagnant population growth or decline.

7 Suzanne Mettler and Trevor Brown, "The Growing Rural-Urban Political Divide and Democratic Vulnerability," The ANNALS of the American Academy of Political and Social Science, 699(2022): 130–142.

The unfortunate situation for the GOP is that it was becoming increasingly dominant over areas with fewer and fewer people, as population density has become increasingly correlated with support for Democrats.[8] The people leaving these areas furthermore tend to be the residents with the greatest human capital as measured by educational attainment. America's rural brain drain was well documented by Patrick J. Carr and Maria J. Kefalas in their book, *Hollowing Out the Middle.*[9] Whether for economic opportunities or cultural amenities, young people are leaving many of these communities in droves. Those that remain tend to be older, more Christian, and more conservative than the rest of the country.

The Republican advantage among rural whites is also evident when we look at individual-level data. The exit polls for the 2020 presidential election show that Trump won 57 percent of rural voters.[10] Among white rural voters, Trump won 65 percent of the vote. This is not a marked change from previous trends. In 2004, for example, exit polls showed that President George W. Bush won an identical 57 percent of the rural vote.[11] The difference, of course, is that Bush earned that impressive rural support in a year in which he won his reelection campaign with relative ease, whereas Trump earned that percentage of that rural vote but lost the election.

The more significant change between 2004 and 2020, according to exit polls, can be found in Republican performance in urban and suburban areas. Urban areas have long represented a challenge for Republicans. They have performed especially poorly in big cities in recent presidential elections. Like Trump, Bush also lost the urban vote in 2004, according to exit polls. However, he earned a respectable 45 percent of the urban vote, compared to Trump's 38 percent. Winning major urban areas is probably a pipe dream for Republicans, at least in the near future. The party's bigger problem is that it is also losing ground in the suburbs, which have traditionally been a major source of Republican votes. In 2004, Bush won 52 percent of the suburban vote; in 2020, President Biden narrowly won among suburban voters.

The declining Republican share of the suburban vote could potentially be disastrous for Republicans, while a political coalition of suburbs, small towns, and

8 Dante J. Scala and Kenneth M. Johnson, "Political Polarization along the Rural-Urban Continuum? The Geography of the Presidential Vote, 2000–2016," *The ANNALS of the American Academy of Political and Social Science*, 672(2017): 162–184.
9 Patrick J. Carr and Maria J. Kefalas, *Hollowing Out the Middle: The Rural Brain Drain and What it Means for America* (Boston, MA: Beacon Press, 2009).
10 "Exit Polls," *CNN*, https://www.cnn.com/election/2020/exit-polls/president/national-results/5
11 "U.S. President / National / Exit Poll," *CNN*, https://www.cnn.com/ELECTION/2004/pages/results/states/US/P/00/epolls.0.html .

rural areas could potentially maintain national dominance. Without the suburbs, the math becomes increasingly difficult for the party. The changing political profile of suburban communities can partly be explained by demographics. The old stereotype of suburbs as overwhelmingly white is becoming disconnected from reality, as an increasing number of racial and ethnic minorities have moved into these communities over the last several decades.[12] This trend can also be explained by surging Democratic strength among voters with a college degree, a group that is also found in great numbers in suburban communities.

Although Republicans cannot win with rural voters alone, having such a strong base of support among rural white voters offers several advantages. Many observers have pointed out that the nature of the Electoral College and the US Senate, both of which give rural voters disproportionate weight, provides the Republican Party a built-in advantage in national politics. Although true, this can also be overstated. Some Democrats are reasonably bitter that Wyoming, which has a small population and consistently votes Republican, has as much power in the Senate as massive California. They seem to forget that, for now, small rural states such as Vermont mostly continue to support Democrats.

Dominating rural America has other benefits, as well.[13] The House of Representatives, while coming closer to the spirit of "one person, one vote" than the Senate, often also seems to benefit Republicans – the GOP's share of House members is often higher than the party's share of the voters nationwide. This is often blamed on gerrymandering (the redrawing of district lines after the decennial census to give advantage to certain parties or incumbents), but that is not the entire story. The fact of the matter is that it is simply more difficult to create pro-Democrat gerrymandered districts because such districts are more challenging to create in urban environments.[14]

We should be careful to not overstate the homogeneity of rural communities. Although a greater percentage of rural America is non-Hispanic white than the nation overall, it is diversifying, and there have always been rural communities in the US that are majority non-white. At least implicitly, much of the discussion of the urban-rural political divide is focused on white rural residents. Again, given that they are a majority of rural residents, this is a defensible default position. However, it is worth asking whether Republican dominance of most rural areas

---

12 Matthew Hall and Barrett Lee, "How Diverse are U.S. Suburbs?" *Urban Studies*, 27(2010): 204–237.

13 Jonathan A. Rodden, *Why Cities Lose: The Deep Roots of the Urban-Rural Divide* (New York: Basic Books, 2019).

14 Nicholas Goedert, "Gerrymandering or Geography? How Democrats Won the Popular Vote but Lost Congress in 2012," *Research and Politics*, 1(2014): 1–8.

is because of the party's support from rural whites, or whether minority groups in rural areas are also more likely to support the party than those living in cities and suburbs. The 2022 CES indicates that this divide can be found in multiple groups. Unsurprising, the gap in party identification was massive among non-Hispanic whites (about 33 percent of urban whites identified as Republican, compared to 56 percent of rural whites). Among Hispanics, however, we also see a significant gap; about 22 percent of urban Hispanics identified as Republican, compared to about 30 percent of Hispanics in rural communities. We should not overstate the importance of living in rural communities *per se*, however. A lot of these effects diminish or vanish entirely after controlling for other individual-level variables.[15]

Although overwhelming Republican strength in rural areas and small towns is a boon to the party, it does not make up for the party's weakness in large, growing metropolitan areas. To begin with, American politics, culture, law, media, and growing sectors of the economy are dominated by people living in large cities. From this standpoint, being dominant in New York City or Los Angeles is more important than winning every vote in a hundred remote small towns.

It may be a mistake to assume that migration patterns of the last several decades will continue for the foreseeable future. Indeed, as I write this, migration patterns seem to be changing. During the years immediately preceding the completion of this book, long-term migration patterns reversed. For the first time in decades, more people were leaving the nation's large metros than entering them.[16] In fact, a majority of large urban counties lost population in 2021.[17] There are many different explanations for the recent exodus out of major cities. The COVID-19 pandemic massively increased the number of people working from home. Although some people have since returned to ordinary in-person work, many people appear to have made this a permanent transition, and this means that they no longer need to live within commuting-distance to their job.

Some of this migration may result from the explosive real-estate market, which has dramatically increased housing costs across the country, but especially in popular urban and suburban areas. Some people may badly want to live in one of the nation's largest cities, but they do not because it is prohibitively expensive, given their incomes. On the other hand, some people may be able to afford to live

15 Don E. Albrecht, "The Nonmetro Vote and the Election of Donald Trump," *Journal of Rural Social Sciences*, 34(2019): 1–32.
16 Grace O'Donnell and Adrian Belmonte, "Americans are Moving Out of Urban Counties Like Never Before," *Yahoo Finance*, April 28, 2022, https://finance.yahoo.com/news/americans-moving-urban-counties-141924038.html .
17 August Benzow, "Exodus from Urban Counties Hit a Record in 2021," Economic Innovation Group, March 31, 2022, https://eig.org/exodus-from-urban-counties-hit-a-record-in-2021/ .

these urban areas, but they find them increasingly less appealing due to issues such as rising crime and homelessness.

Some combination of all of these factors is probably responsible for recent migratory patterns. The question is whether this is an ephemeral trend, which will be followed by a return to the previous norm, or if major cities will now permanently struggle to attract new residents. One can envision a nightmare scenario for these municipalities: the work from home trend results in empty commercial real estate, the out-migration also results in declining home property values, these trends lead to declining tax revenues, leading to cuts in services or higher taxes – both of which may encourage additional out-migration.

On the other hand, perhaps we should not infer too much from trends that developed during an unusual period for the nation. The pandemic was an exceptional moment, and as it recedes further, we may simply return, more or less, to previous trends. In relatively recent history we experienced moments where the long-standing trend of migration from the countryside to the cities appeared to stall and even reverse. In the 1970s, for example, the nation seemed to be on the verge of a "rural renaissance," as large numbers of city and suburb dwellers decamped to small towns and rural communities.[18] It did not last, and by the mid-1980s the older pattern reasserted itself. It is possible that the current movement away from large cities proves similarly brief.

If the migration out of cities proves to be a long-term phenomenon, it will have many potential political consequences. Might we see an end to Republican dominance in 'flyover country'? Possibly, but that will partly depend on which urbanites are migrating outward. Are the most committed urban progressives likely to move to the exurbs or small towns, or will the leavers predominantly be moderates, Republicans, or apolitical people? Even if progressives are moving to rural areas, will they come to dominate politics as they typically do in urban communities? This may occur in some areas, but I suspect rural America is too spread out, and its political culture too well established, for these migrants to set the political tone for rural America in the near future. We can furthermore take it for granted that not all rural areas will benefit equally from these migratory patterns. The Texas panhandle and rural North Dakota are probably not going to experience a massive influx of moving vans, regardless of how frustrated many people may be with life in San Francisco or Minneapolis.

---

18 William H. Frey, "Migration and Depopulation of the Metropolis: Regional Restructuring or Rural Renaissance?" *American Sociological Review,* 52(1987): 240–257.

Young Americans' flight from Republican enclaves

It is correct to say that Republicans tend to perform very well in places that are losing population, but it is also important to note which people are leaving these areas. The exodus of people from more conservative small towns and rural areas into the big cities dominated by progressive politics is driven largely by the young.[19] There may be some political self-selection at work – young liberals in a conservative rural area may be especially prone to moving away. However, young people, across the political spectrum, are moving to these places for many reasons. This creates an additional potential problem for Republicans.

Figure 2.2 shows the migration patterns into overwhelmingly Republican counties (where Trump won 60 percent or more in 2020) versus those overwhelmingly non-Republican counties (where Trump earned less than 40 percent of the vote). The difference is remarkable. The migration data was compiled by using information from the US Census Bureau.[20] The population is divided by age into five-year increments. The most immediate and striking finding is the degree to which young people move, in massive numbers, into those overwhelmingly blue counties. While these data cannot tell us the reason for these moves, there are many plausible explanations. The big blue metropolises are where ambitious young people will find the most prestigious universities, as well as many of the best paying jobs. These are also the places where they can access a great number of cultural attractions. In contrast, we also see that young people flee those overwhelmingly Republican counties, which tend to lack those attributes.

These overwhelmingly Democratic communities that are such a draw for America's youth do not appeal to everyone, however. At around the age of 30, the trend reverses. Within the heavily blue counties, the net migration of older people is negative. The opposite is true in the heavily red counties, which begin to enjoy positive net migration among older Americans. Once again, we can easily imagine why this occurs. Although those metropolitan areas have many appealing characteristics, they tend to be extremely expensive. Unless one possesses extraordinary wealth, moving into one of these communities will entail living in a small

---

19 For a thorough discussion of these migration patterns, see George Hawley, *Voting and Migration Patterns in the U.S.* (New York: Routledge, 2013).

20 I should note that the migration data is a decade behind the electoral data. That is, the migration data covers 2000–2010. The data for 2010 to 2020 has not yet been compiled and posted at the Inter-university Consortium for Political and Social Research. Richelle Winkler, Kenneth Johnson, Cheng Cheng, Paul Voss, and Katherine J. Curtis, "County-Specific Net Migration by Five-Year Age Groups, Hispanic Origin, Race and Sex: 2000–2010," Inter-university Consortium for Political and Social Research [distributor], 2013–09–05. https://doi.org/10.3886/ICPSR34638.v1.

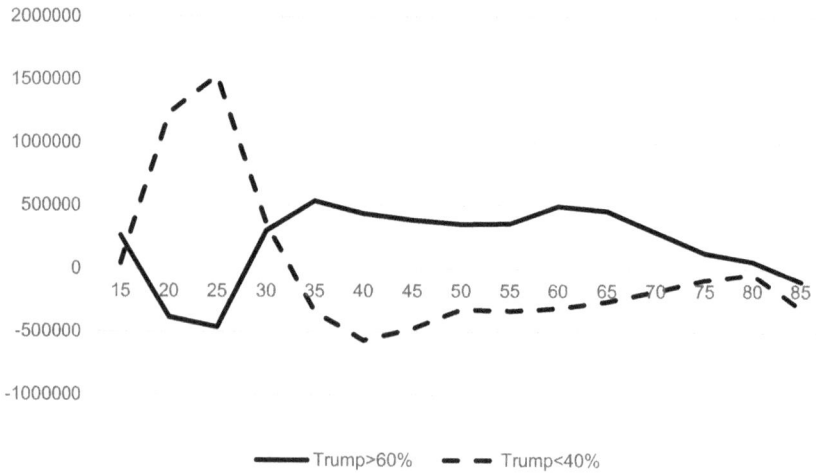

Figure 2.2: Net Migration into Strong Republican and Strong Democratic Counties by Age Cohort. Source: Richelle Winkler, Kenneth Johnson, Cheng Cheng, Paul Voss, and Katherine J. Curtis, "County-Specific Net Migration by Five-Year Age Groups, Hispanic Origin, Race and Sex: 2000–2010".

apartment, probably with roommates. People in their early 20s may not mind this situation, but many will not want to live this lifestyle in perpetuity. Most Americans eventually want to get married and start families, which is much easier to do in places with a lower cost of living. Even people who make a decent living and have little interest in family may wish to move to a place where their money goes a little farther, even if it means less access to high-quality restaurants, theaters, and other big-city amenities. The degree to which America is sorting and segregating by age cohort is an interesting and underexplored phenomenon.

Readers may object to my suggestion that Republicans tend to perform especially well in places that are losing population. After all, when talking about states, rather than counties, the trend looks markedly different. In recent years, some of the most strongly Democratic states experienced stagnating population growth or even population loss. Illinois, New York, and Hawaii experienced population loss in the early 2020s. In contrast, many states where the Republican Party currently has an advantage, such as Texas, Florida, Idaho, Utah, and Tennessee, experienced robust growth. Some conservatives have argued that this variation can at least be partially explained by differences in state income tax rates.[21]

---

21 Katherine Loughead, "Americans Moved to Low-Tax States in 2023," The Tax Foundation, January 9, 2024, https://taxfoundation.org/data/all/state/state-population-change-2023/ .

How can we explain this seeming incongruity? One thing to remember is that states are not uniformly Republican or Democratic. Lots of people are moving into Texas, but most of these new residents are moving into a relatively small number of counties that are already highly populated. The people moving into Texas are more likely to settle in or near cities like Houston, Dallas, San Antonio, and Austin (all of which have been strongly Democratic for many election cycles), rather than those smaller, intensely Republican communities that make up much of the rest of the state.

Republicans may take heart to know that, in the aggregate, hundreds of counties that strongly support them do continue to draw people; they just tend to attract older people. This difference may be consequential, however. Party identification is a powerful phenomenon, but it is not immutable, especially among young people who may not yet have firm partisan commitments. People who move into a new partisan context are likely to, over time, take on the partisan and ideological characteristics of their communities. Although a Republican that moves from a heavily Republican community into a strongly Democratic community is unlikely to make an immediate partisan change, her attachment to her party is likely to weaken.[22] In the past, this phenomenon had benefited the Republicans. In the mid-twentieth century, as there was massive migration from declining industrial cities in the Midwest into the Republican-dominated 'sun belt,' it bolstered Republican fortunes. More recent migration patterns, however, suggest that young adult movers are especially likely to settle, at least for a few years, in overwhelmingly Democratic communities.

Why are small towns and rural areas so politically different from places with higher population density? One answer may have nothing to do with community characteristics at all. As I noted earlier, rural people just tend to be older and white, and this captures much of the difference. This is not the entire story. Individual-level data continues to show an urban-rural gap, even after controlling for many of these differences.[23] One old argument suggests that urban voters are more likely to lean left because urban areas are more conducive to class consciousness.[24]

22 Thad Brown, *Migration and Politics: The Impact of Population Mobility on American Voting* (Chapel Hill, NC: University of North Carolina Press, 1988).

23 James G. Gimpel, Nathan Lovin, Bryant Moy, and Andrew Reeves, "The Urban-Rural Gulf in American Political Behavior," *Political Behavior*, 42(2020): 1334–1368.

24 Angus Campbell, Philip E. Converse, Warren E. Miller, and Donald E. Stokes, *The American Voter* (New York: John Wiley, 1960), 369.

Others have suggested urban voters lean left because their greater exposure to many kinds of diversity results in higher levels of tolerance.[25]

We should once again be careful that we are not overstating the geographic political differences in the US, however. The cultural, demographic, and political differences between these community types are real, but can be exaggerated. Not long ago, political discourse was dominated by misleading talk about "red states versus blue states," which suggested a massive ideological chasm between states based on their presidential vote tallies.[26] Trump's 2016 victory mostly ended these kinds of discussion. His surprise victories in many states long viewed as Democratic strongholds made talk about permanent red and blue states seem less plausible. We may eventually come to view current discussions of the urban-suburban-rural divide as similarly overblown.

The vanishing highly educated Republican

Declining support for Republicans in urban and suburban areas can partially be attributed to declining Republican support from voters with more education. President Trump declared in 2016, "I love the poorly educated."[27] A significant majority of white voters without college degrees apparently loved him back. Looking at exit polls, we see that Trump narrowly defeated Biden among voters without college degrees. Among white voters without college degrees, Trump won overwhelmingly, earning 67 percent of the vote from that demographic group. Unfortunately for Trump, he also performed unusually poorly among voters with higher levels of education. Among voters with a college degree, Biden won 55 percent of the vote. Even when limited to just white voters with a college degree, Biden defeated Trump with 51 percent of the vote.

The strong Democratic advantage among college educated voters is not a completely new phenomenon. Democrats often outperform Republicans among this group. The size of the gap seems to be increasing, however. Exit polls showed that George W. Bush tied with John Kerry among the college educated, each winning approximately 49 percent among that group (the rest going to a third-party candidate). We see similar growth in Democratic support from voters with the

---

25 Ronnie Janoff-Bulman, *The Two Moralities: Conservatives, Liberals, and the Roots of Our Political Divide* (New Haven, CT: Yale University Press, 2023).

26 Morris Fiorina, Samuel J. Abrams, and Jeremy C. Pope, *Culture War? The Myth of a Polarized America* (New York: Pearson Longman, 2005).

27 "Trump: I Love the Poorly Educated!" *The Daily Beast*, February 24, 2016, https://www.thedailybeast.com/cheats/2016/02/24/trump-i-love-the-poorly-educated.

highest levels of education, an advanced degree beyond a bachelor's degree. In 2004, Bush won 44 percent of these voters. Trump only earned 40 percent.

Beyond vote choice in presidential elections, we can also look at party identification among voters with higher levels of education over time. The GSS is a useful tool for examining this because it has asked similar questions over so many years. In Figure 2.3, I show the trends in party identification among respondents with at least a four-year college education. As I do throughout this book, I include self-described independents that admitted to leaning toward one party in the partisan camp; the political science literature has long demonstrated that these "partisan leaners" tend to be more politically similar to people who announce their partisan preference right away than to true independents that genuinely do not prefer one party over the other.[28]

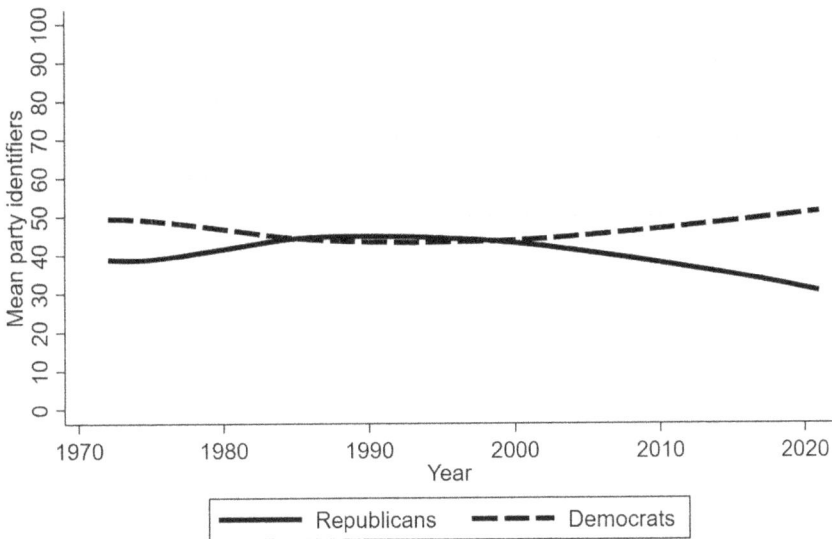

Figure 2.3: Mean Percent Republican and Democrat among College Grads. Source: Cumulative GSS. Note: Figure LOWESS smoothed.

As we saw in the presidential exit polls, the trend in party identification shows that the partisan gap among the college educated is not new. It has changed over time, however. Throughout much of the 1980s and early 1990s, GSS respond-

28 Bruce E. Keith, David B. Magleby, Candice J. Nelson, Elizabeth A. Orr, Mark C. Westlye, and Raymond E. Wolfinger, *The Myth of the Independent Voter* (Berkeley, CA: University of California Press, 1992).

ents without college degrees were slightly more likely to identify with the Republican Party than the Democratic Party. Since the middle of George W. Bush's presidency, however, Republican support among voters with more education has been steadily declining. As of 2021, the Democratic advantage was higher than at any time the GSS has been conducted. Although there are many possible explanations for this, it is quite likely that the GOP's turn toward right-wing populism, which arguably began in the 1990s during the years Newt Gingrich was Speaker of the House,[29] increased during the Tea Party era, and reached new heights during the Trump Administration, has turned more educated voters away.

Declining Republican fortunes among the well-educated represents two problems for the Republicans. First, the percentage of the electorate with college degrees is only increasing. Thus, losing among these voters was a bigger problem for the Republican Party in 2020 than it would have been in 1972. The other problem, which is harder to directly quantify, is that the Democratic Party has an increasing advantage in human capital. In a democracy, numbers are important, but they are not everything. Having a decided advantage among the nation's elite is extremely valuable for a party. Beyond the obvious role business and educational elites play in shaping the culture, they also play an indispensable role in day-to-day politics. Populist appeals may bring in a lot of votes, but someone is going to have to fill the bureaucracies and congressional staffs, and Republicans will be at a disadvantage if they have a harder time finding qualified, sympathetic people to fill these jobs.

The growing partisan marriage gap

It is not surprising that the party that presents itself as the defender of 'family values' tends to perform well among Americans with traditional families. The marriage gap is an important element of US politics, and represents another potential problem for the GOP, given that Americans are staying single for an increasing period of time, and a growing percentage are choosing not to get married at all.

Despite being a consistent finding over multiple decades, the marriage gap has received less scholarly attention than demographic gaps of comparable impor-

---

29 For a thorough explanation of this history, I recommend Nicole Hemmer, *Partisans: The Conservative Revolutionaries Who Remade American Politics in the 1990s* (New York: Basic Books, 2022).

tance.[30] This is probably because there were good reasons to think the relationship between marriage and vote choice was spurious. That is, marriage itself may not directly influence vote choice at all, but it is instead downstream from other variables that predict both marriage and voting. For example, African Americans are less likely than non-Hispanic whites to be married and less likely to vote Republican.[31] Highly religious Americans are both more likely to be married and to vote Republican.[32] Indeed, when the marriage gap first emerged in presidential election voting in the early 1970s, it was explained as predominantly a function of racial and income gaps in both marriage and voting.[33]

As time passed, however, the marriage gap persisted and grew. Using the GSS, I calculated the percentage of each party's supporters that had ever been married, from 1972 until 2021.[34] I show this relationship in Figure 2.4. We see that, although there was a difference between Republicans and Democrats when it came to marriage rates in the early 1970s, the gap was small, and the overwhelming majority of both parties' supporters had been married. Since that time, we have seen marriage rates decline for both parties, but the decline has been much steeper among Democrats. This is another case in which a major demographic change (in this case, the decline of marriage) is reflected in the Democratic Party in the electorate, whereas Republicans, in the aggregate, have changed relatively little over the last decades.

Exit polls also show that the marriage gap was sizable and important in the 2020 presidential election.[35] Among married voters, Trump garnered 53 percent of the vote. Among the unmarried, Biden carried 58 percent. The results become more interesting when we break them down by race and gender. Trump won among both married men and married women, but he did just slightly better

---

30 Amy R. Gershkoff, "The Marriage Gap," in *Beyond Red State, Blue State: Electoral Gaps in the Twenty-First Century American Electorate*, eds. Laura Olson and John C. Green (Upper Saddle River, NJ: Pearson Prentice Hall, 2009), 24–39.

31 Robert Schoen and James R. Kluegel, "The Widening Gap in Black and White Marriage Rates: The Impact of Population Composition and Differential Marriage Propensities," *American Sociological Review,* 53(1988): 895–907; Scott J. South, "Racial and Ethnic Differences in the Desire to Marry," *Journal of Marriage and the Family,* 55(1993): 357–370.

32 Joshua J. Rendon, Xiaohe Xu, Melinda Lundquist Denton, and John P. Bartkowski, "Religion and Marriage Timing: A Replication and Extension," *Religions,* 5(2014): 834–851; George Hawley, *Voting and Migration Patterns in the U.S.* (New York: Routledge, 2013).

33 Herbert F. Weisberg, "The Demographics of a New Voting Gap: Marital Differences in American Voting," *Public Opinion Quarterly,* 51(1987): 335–343.

34 That is, I include people who have been widowed, divorced, or are currently separated in the married category.

35 "Exit Polls," *CNN Politics,* https://www.cnn.com/election/2020/exit-polls/president/national-results/0.

among married men. Trump also narrowly lost among unmarried men to Biden, who won 52 percent of the vote from that demographic. Biden trounced Trump, however, among unmarried women. He won 63 percent of that group's vote.

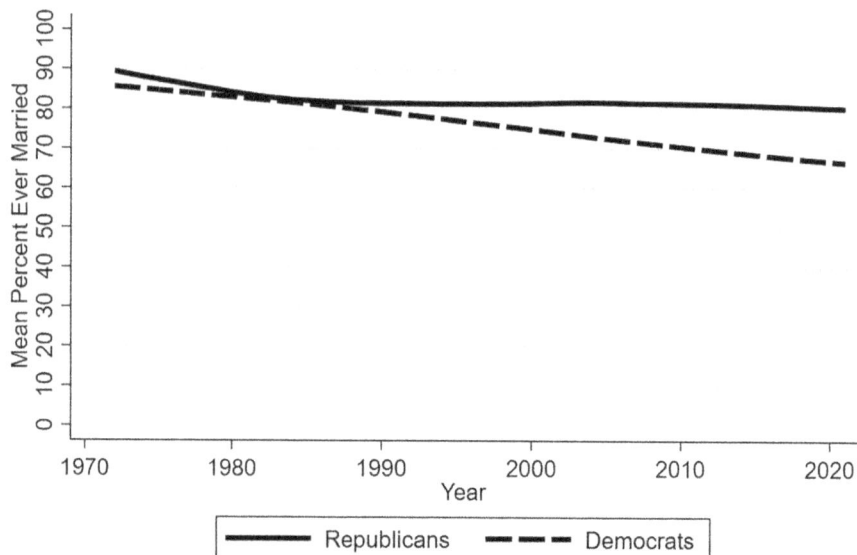

Figure 2.4: Mean Percent Married by Party. Source: Cumulative GSS. Note: Figure LOWESS smoothed.

The exit poll data suggesting a particularly large marriage gap among women do not, on their own, give any explanation for why that might be the case. It has not always been true that marriage had a seemingly different influence on men and women. Early scholarship on the phenomenon found that the effects of marriage did not differ according to gender.[36] More recent research, however, suggests that men and women do exhibit meaningful differences when it comes to the political effects of marriage. Economists Lena Edlund and Rohini Pande have suggested that the economics of marriage may explain both the marriage gap and the increasing tendency for women to support left-wing candidates and policies.[37] They argued that, traditionally, marriage has represented a kind of economic redistribution from men to women, because husbands, on average, tended to have higher

---

[36] Paul William Kingston and Steven E. Finkel, "Is there a Marriage Gap in Politics?" *Journal of Marriage and Family*, 49(1987): 57–64.

[37] Lena Edlund and Rohini Pande, "Why have Women Become Left Wing? The Political Gender Gap and the Decline of Marriage," *The Quarterly Journal of Economics*, 117(2002): 917–961.

incomes than their wives. By getting married, women are more likely to move into a wealthier class, and thus have less need for redistributive policies. At the same time, their higher household income as a result of marriage should make them more resistant to higher taxes. One potential problem with this conclusion, however, is that the marriage gap has remained consistent even as the economic gap between men and women in the US has gotten smaller over the last several decades, and, among younger people, the education gap now actually favors women.[38]

There are other possible explanations for these voting patterns. One plausible argument is that marriage changes the order of a person's preferences, and that this change tends to be more pronounced among women. Sociologist Kathleen Gerson, for instance, has argued that unmarried women tend to be more personally invested in questions about gender equality and policies that advance the specific economic interests of women. Married women, by contrast, tend to focus more on their domestic commitments and policy issues specifically related to the family.[39] She further argued that this is a major reason why women are unlikely to ever become a unified group of voters:

> As a result, despite feminist hopes and predictions, women are unlikely to emerge as a united voting block comparable to blacks or union members. Indeed, since the diversity in women's social positions is growing, their political views are likely to diverge further. A "family gap" between people living in traditional versus nontraditional households may well become as important or more important than the much-heralded gender gap between women and men. In the 1984 presidential election, for example, the difference between married and single voters was notably higher than the difference between male and female voters. Moreover, homemakers were almost as likely as married men and more likely than single men to choose Reagan/Bush over Mondale/Ferraro.[40]

Although the exact mechanism remains unclear, the marriage gap in politics is even more pronounced in the aggregate data than in individual-level data. In figure 2.5, I demonstrate the relationship between the median age at first marriage for women at the state level in 2020 and the state-level support for Trump that same year.[41]

---

38 Christine R. Schwartz and Hongyun Han, "The Reversal of the Gender Gap in Education and Trends in Marital Dissolution," *American Sociological Review,* 79(2014): 605–629.

39 Kathleen Gerson, "Emerging Social Divisions among Women: Implications for Welfare State Politics," *Politics and Society,* 15(1987): 213–221.

40 Ibid, 219.

41 I have previously conducted similar analysis for previous elections. George Hawley, "Home Affordability, Female Marriage Rates and Vote Choice in the 2000 Election: Evidence from U.S. Counties," *Party Politics,* 18(2012): 771–789; George Hawley, "How Marriages and Mortgages Influence

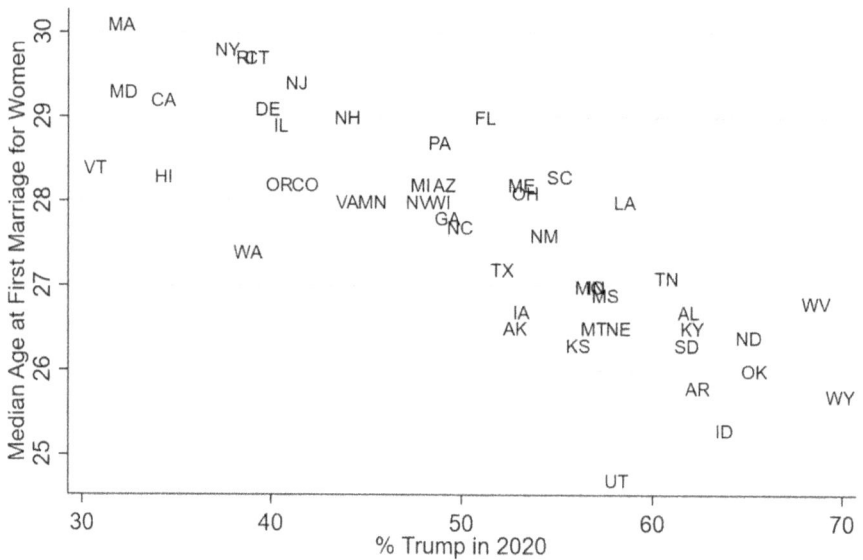

Figure 2.5: Median Age at Marriage and Support for Trump. Source: U.S. Census Bureau.

When examined as a simple least-squared regression model including no control variables, we found that each additional year added to the median age at first marriage led to more than a six-percentage point drop in support for Trump in 2020. The R-squared for this model is similarly impressive. R-squared is a statistical tool that tells us how much of the variance of the phenomenon you are examining is predicted by the other variables in a regression model. In other words, it shows how much variation of what you are studying is explained by the combined predictor variables. In the social sciences, it is not uncommon for even very complex models with a massive number of independent variables to predict a paltry amount of the dependent variable's variation. The median marriage age at the state level, however, even without including any other additional variables, explains a lot of the presidential vote. The R-squared in this simple model is 0.67. Put another way, more than two-thirds of the variance of state-level support for Trump can be explained by this variable alone.

To be clear, earlier marriages are not necessarily better marriages. Some social scientists have applauded the changing family norms increasingly prevalent in strongly Democratic states. Naomi Cahn and June Carbone, in their book, *Red Fam-*

Election Outcomes," The Institute for Family Studies, June 29, 2017, https://ifstudies.org/blog/how-marriages-and-mortgages-influence-election-outcomes.

ilies vs. Blue Families, argue that the trend among liberals to delay marriage and childbearing until they achieve a baseline of financial stability, and to embrace more egalitarian gender roles, tends to lead to better marital outcomes – notably, lower rates of divorce and teenage pregnancy.[42]

These different rates of marriage may have additional long-term consequences. Although it is now common for unmarried Americans to have children, it remains the case that, on average, married women have higher birthrates than unmarried women.[43] It is therefore not surprising that we see partisan differences in family size. According to the 2022 CES, about 46 percent of Democrats reported having no children, compared to about 29 percent of Republicans. Some of this may be explained by the partisan age gap; Democrats are younger than Republicans, on average, and many may not have started having children but will eventually. However, the gap remains even if we look at different age cohorts. Republicans have a significant fertility advantage across generations, which may grow even larger over time.[44] This is very important because of the consistent finding that partisanship tends to be transmitted from parents to their children.[45]

Religion and the GOP

The Republican Party has always presented itself, to at least some degree, as the party of pious Protestants, with some variation over time – in recent decades, as anti-Catholic bias has dissipated, the conservative Protestant identity has given way to a more ecumenical Christian identity. Voices in the early Republican Party maintained many social conservative elements of the Whig platform, such as enforcing the Sabbath by law. Republicans took a leading role in the passing of Prohibition.

The US has always had religious schisms. Back in the colonial era, different Protestant sects tended to dominate different regions, and hostility to minority re-

---

42 Naomi Cahn and June Carbone, *Red Families vs. Blue Families: Legal Polarization and the Creation of Culture* (New York: Oxford University Press, 2010).
43 Maddison Erbabian, Austin Herrick, and Victoria Osorio, "The Decline in Fertility: The Role of Marriage and Education," Budget Model, Penn Wharton, University of Pennsylvania, July 8, 2022, https://budgetmodel.wharton.upenn.edu/issues/2022/7/8/decline-in-fertility-the-role-of-marriage-and-education.
44 Lyman Stone, "The Conservative Fertility Advantage," Institute for Family Studies, November 18, 2020, https://ifstudies.org/blog/the-conservative-fertility-advantage.
45 M. Kent Jennings, Laura Stoker, and Jake Bowers, "Politics across Generations: Family Transmission Reexamined," *The Journal of Politics*, 71(2009): 782 – 799.

ligions – even different varieties of Protestantism – was the norm. Puritans domi-nated New England, and they had no patience for religious dissenters. Anglicans were the leading religious group in most of the Southern colonies, and they had no interest in extending religious tolerance to Puritans. The Quakers of the Dela-ware Valley were an unusual exception, embracing religious liberty out of princi-ple, but that courtesy was not extended to Quakers elsewhere.[46]

Although there was a Catholic presence in British North America from a very early date (Maryland was initially founded as a New World haven for English Cath-olics), it was overwhelmingly Protestant by the time of independence. It was not until large waves of migration from Ireland, Germany, and, later, Southern and Eastern Europe arrived on US shores that the nation's identity as a Protestant na-tion was threatened. Many conservative Protestants responded to this demograph-ic change by turning toward aggressive nativism and anti-Catholicism. Although neither the Whig nor the Republican Party ever made a major push toward serious immigration restriction throughout most of the nineteenth century, nativism was more common in these parties than in the Democratic Party's ranks. Most immi-grant groups responded by typically supporting the Democrats, though some groups, such as certain German immigrant communities, nonetheless generally supported the Republicans.[47]

Protestants were a key Republican constituency, but their influence changed over time, and the loyalties of different Protestant denominations were not set in stone. In the early twentieth century, Episcopalians were described as "the Re-publican Party at prayer." That denomination today, however, is now considered (at least at the leadership level) as quintessentially liberal. The South further compli-cates matters, as it was long both a Democratic stronghold and a major center of fundamentalist Christianity.

The politicization of different denominations has also varied over time. In the late nineteenth and early twentieth centuries, during the bitter disputes between Christian fundamentalists and Christian modernists, fundamentalist Christians fought an unsuccessful culture war over questions such as the teaching of evolu-tion in schools.[48] After being humiliated in the press during the so-called "Scopes

---

46 David Hackett Fischer, *Albion's Seed: Four British Folkways in America* (New York: Oxford Uni-versity Press, 1989).
47 Daniel Tichenor, *Dividing Lines: The Politics of Immigration Control in the United States* (Prince-ton, NJ: Princeton University Press, 2002).
48 The fundamentalist versus modernist divide was largely over how Christians should respond to the many challenges modernity posed for the religion. Should Christians continue to insist that the Bible, including the story of creation on the Book of Genesis, be treated as literally true, or should they argue that science and Christianity can be reconciled if they drop the insistence on biblical

Monkey Trial," fundamentalist Christians significantly pulled back from the national political arena.[49] We should not overstate this, of course. There was never a period in which fundamentalist Christians ever completely withdrew from politics, but they were nonetheless less organized and politically significant during the New Deal years.

Although the religious denominations that would later form the backbone of the Christian right were not especially influential in US politics during the Depression era and World War Two, they were undergoing many notable changes that would boost their later influence. Mostly jettisoning the term 'fundamentalist' as a self-description, theologically conservative Protestants founded the National Association of Evangelicals (NAE) in 1942. Although not yet exhibiting the loyalty to the Republican Party that would be a later hallmark of evangelicals, they were interested in returning to the political arena, where they focused especially on countering the influence of more liberal Christian groups that had long enjoyed influence in Washington, DC. Initially, they were particularly concerned about the Federal Communications Commission and broadcasting rights – they wanted to ensure that evangelical preachers had access to the nation's airwaves.[50]

Evangelicals were also galvanized by the Cold War. Because communism was inherently and openly anti-religion, and in practice Christians were brutalized on a massive scale in communist countries, vigorously promoting a hawkish stance against the Soviet Union and its allies was seen as a moral imperative for many evangelical leaders. Indeed, some evangelical leaders that tried to remain at least somewhat aloof from partisan politics – such as Billy Graham, for much of his career – felt no compunction condemning communism in the most vitriolic way, discussing the Cold War using apocalyptic rhetoric.

One might reasonably assume that the rising evangelical movement in the 1940s, and the modern American conservative intellectual movement, which started making waves in the 1950s, would be immediate allies. After all, 'tradition' was a key word associated with conservatives at *National Review* and related institutions. The two phenomena were not immediately connected, however. There was a significant demographic gap between the post-war conservatives and the new evangelical leaders. Within the early conservative movement, Catholics were mas-

---

literalism? Should Christians turn their attention to solving modern social problems, lobbying the state when necessary, or should they maintain their focus on bringing souls to Christ? See W.T. Connor, "Fundamentalism v. Modernism," *Social Science*, 2(1927): 101–106.

49 Daniel K. Williams, *God's Own Party: The Making of the Christian Right* (New York: Oxford University Press, 2010), 12–15.

50 Paul Matzko, *The Radio Right: How a Band of Broadcasters Took on the Federal Government and Built the Modern Conservative Movement* (New York: Oxford University Press, 2020).

sively overrepresented, at least in comparison to their share of the US population.[51] Evangelical Christians were not discussed as a powerful, organized constituency in the Republican Party until the late 1970s. It was during this period that prominent evangelical voices like Jerry Falwell joined up with effective political strategists and activists like Paul Weyrich, creating organizations like the Moral Majority, and playing important roles in Ronald Reagan's successful presidential campaigns.

In the last decades, disputes between different Christian denominations have dissipated. The Christian right may also be increasingly open to alliances across major religious groups, including Islam. During the height of the so-called 'War on Terror,' many conservatives spoke of a clash of civilizations between Islam and the West, with many believing they saw signs that biblical prophesies were being fulfilled. In the aftermath of disastrous American invasions of Iraq and Afghanistan, the weakening of militant Islamic terror groups, and the general decline in Islam-inspired terrorism in Western countries, talk of a globe-spanning religious clash have mostly disappeared. Indeed, over the last years, cultural conservatives in the US seem to be making tentative alliances with conservative Muslims over issues such as LGBT-related curriculum in public schools. It remains to be seen if this will lead to a broader alliance in the future.[52]

Instead of conflicts between religious groups, the major religious fault line is now between the conventionally religious, especially conventional Christians, and the growing population of secular Americans. For many years, especially during George W. Bush's presidency, many pundits continued to describe the US as though it was immune to the secularizing trends taking hold in most other Western countries. Progressives were sounding the alarm that the US was on the verge of a theocracy. The political success of same-sex marriage bans, as well as the election and reelection of President Bush, who was unusually outspoken about his sincere religious faith, seemed to confirm these fears.

The reality, however, was that religion was already on the decline by the early 2000s. After holding steady for over a decade, religious identity began to decline in the early 1990s, and this decline has since continued unabated. At first, this decline was primarily found in the more progressive 'mainline' denominations. This led some voices in the evangelical community to crow that progressivism was poison for religious communities, and those churches that maintained a more traditional approach to Christianity and culture remained strong and vibrant. Since that time,

51 George Hawley, *Conservatism in a Divided America: The Right and Identity Politics* (Notre Dame, IN: University of Notre Dame Press, 2022).
52 Niraj Warikoo, "LGBTQ and Faith Communities Struggle for Unity in Dearborn, Hamtramck," *Detroit Free Press*, October 12, 2022, https://www.freep.com/story/news/local/michigan/wayne/2022/10/10/lgbtq-faith-communities-dearborn-hamtramck-libraries-banned-books/10353638002/.

however, the largest evangelical denominations, including the Southern Baptist Convention, have also begun losing members.

Religious leaders and social scientists have been attempting to discern the causes of declining religiosity. For some observers, the real puzzle is not why religion is on the decline, but why it is still so robust. Many learned people predicted that conventional religion would be a thing of the past by now. Toward the end of his life, in the 1820s, Thomas Jefferson predicted the entire nation would soon be Unitarian. Nietzsche wrote of the death of God in the 1880s. In the 1960s, *Time* magazine asked, "Is God Dead?"

From the perspective of many secularists, the decline of religion is rather easy to understand: religious claims about the universe are simply not credible; we now have a better understanding of the origin of the universe, the emergence of life, and the source of human consciousness. As science advances, biblical claims become increasingly implausible, and rational people increasingly reject them. I have argued elsewhere that I find this explanation unpersuasive, in large part because it overstates the degree to which ordinary people, irreligious or otherwise, give much thought to the rationality of their beliefs.[53]

A thorough exploration of every possible explanation for growing secularism is beyond the scope of this book. However, it is worth considering the hypothesis that developments in partisan politics are at least part of the story. In 2002, Michael Hout and Claude Fischer wrote an influential article suggesting that the decline of Christianity in the US could be partially attributed to the rise of the Christian right.[54] They argued that, as Christianity in the US was increasingly associated with controversial figures such as Jerry Falwell, Pat Robertson, and Ralph Reed, Christians with more progressive beliefs, especially nominal Christians without strong attachment to their religion, abandoned religion entirely. Hout and Fischer's argument was not definitive. The data they presented could be explained in other ways. However, subsequent scholarship has suggested they had a point.[55]

The politicization of religion itself has had other consequences. Although the religious right may have accelerated the secularization trend among Democrats, it seems to have had the opposite effect on Republicans, who often seem to combine their partisan and religious affiliations into a single identity. This was a

---

53 George Hawley, *Demography, Culture, and the Decline of America's Christian Denominations*, (Lanham, MD: Lexington Books, 2017). 77–78

54 Michael Hout and Claude S. Fischer, "Why More Americans Have No Religious Preference: Politics and Generations," *American Sociological Review,* 67(2002): 165–190.

55 Paul A. Djupe, Jacob R. Neiheisel, and Anand E. Sokhey, "Reconsidering the Role of Politics in Leaving Religion: The Importance of Affiliation," *American Journal of Political Science,* 62(2018): 161–175.

key point in Michele Margolis's book, *From Politics to the Pews.*[56] Rather than a secularizing trend across all of the electorate, it is occurring at its most rapid pace among Democrats. This represents a major change. As of the 1970s, Democrats were, on average, slightly less Christian than Republicans, but the difference was not dramatic. In recent decades, the gap has grown quite large. This is partly due to growing numbers of religious minorities in the US (Muslims, Buddhists, Hindus, etc.) that tend to vote Democratic, but it is primarily driven by the growing number of people who say they have no religion when answering surveys.

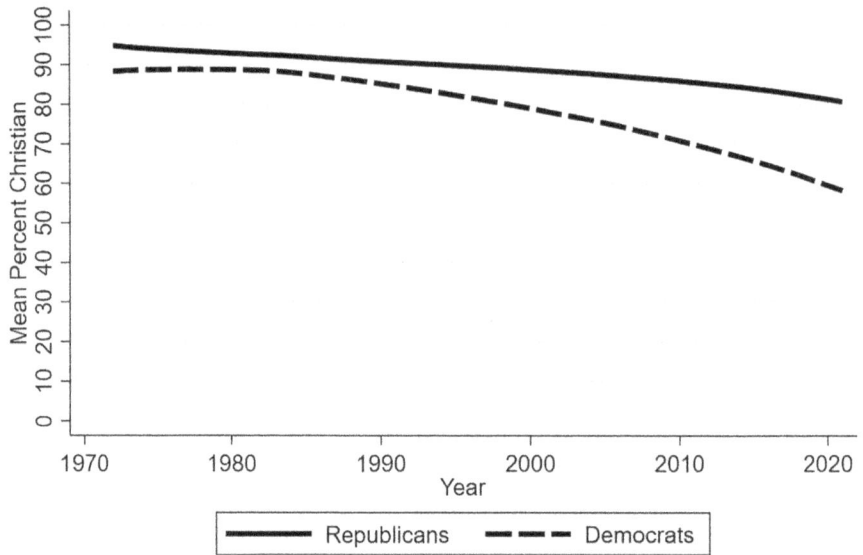

Figure 2.6: Mean Percent Christian by Party. Source: Cumulative GSS. Note: Figure LOWESS smoothed.

The 2022 CES, which includes a very large number of observations (61,000), also helpfully provides detailed information about the religious identities of its respondents. Beyond the older division (Protestant, Catholic, Jewish, other) which you often find in survey research, the CES tells you each respondent's specific religious denomination. This helps us see the degree to which different religious groups have, on average, different political commitments. In Table 1.1, I show the percentage of each religious category (including the major Protestant denomi-

---

56 Michele Margolis, *From Politics to the Pews: How Partisanship and the Political Landscape Shapes Religious Identity* (Chicago. IL: University of Chicago Press, 2018).

nations) that identify as Republicans. Keep in mind, once again, that Republican identification is not synonymous with vote choice in presidential elections. For example, a much greater share of evangelical Protestants voted for President Trump in 2020 than self-identify as Republican.

Unsurprisingly, evangelical denominations such as Assemblies of God, the Lutheran Church – Missouri Synod, and the Southern Baptist Convention (SBC) were the most heavily Republican. In many cases, we may question whether it is religion *per se* that is influencing political identity. The SBC, for example, is overwhelmingly white and Southern, both characteristics that are associated with Republican voting. That is not the entire story, however. Assemblies of God churches, for example, are comparatively diverse, yet also the most Republican religious group in this sample. According to Pew, about 20 percent of the denomination's members are immigrants and 25 percent are Latino.[57] That makes them less white, overall, than the Episcopal Church, which is majority Democrat.

We also see that some religious groups that are often considered part of the more 'liberal' mainline Christian family of denominations are nonetheless strongly Republicans when it comes to the ordinary members in the pews. A majority of the United Methodist Church's members identify as Republicans, for example. The same is true for the Presbyterian Church – USA. A near majority of the Evangelical Lutheran Church of America (which is considered a 'mainline' denomination, despite the name) identifies as Republican.

This survey is also helpful in that it disaggregates different varieties of irreligion. People who lack a religious identity are much less likely to identify as Republican than members of any Christian denomination. There is nonetheless a political distinction between those that do not belong to a particular religion and those that openly reject the most fundamental idea of religion. From the perspective of religious organizations, a religious "none" that does not ascribe to any particular religious doctrine and an atheist who is wholly opposed to a religious worldview may seem like a distinction without a difference. From a political science or sociological perspective, however, these are separate, though related, phenomena. Republicans will have a long way to go before they are appealing to a large percentage of atheists, but the unchurched who do not seem to think much about religion may be an easier group to reach.

---

57 "Members of Assemblies of God," Pew Research Center, https://www.pewresearch.org/religion/religious-landscape-study/religious-denomination/assemblies-of-god/.

Table 2.1: Religious identity and party identification.

Religious Group	% Republican	% Democrat
Assemblies of God	71	19
Lutheran Church – Missouri Synod	65	24
Southern Baptist	64	24
Presbyterian Church of America	59	25
Mormon	58	25
Non-Denominational Christian	58	25
United Methodist Church	55	34
Presbyterian Church – USA	51	40
Evangelical Lutheran Church of America	48	41
Jewish – Orthodox	47	35
Catholic	44	40
Orthodox Christian	40	40
United Church of Christ	36	56
Jewish – Conservative	34	54
Episcopal Church	33	56
Hindu	23	56
Nothing in particular	23	41
Jewish – Reformed	18	74
Agnostic	17	63
Muslim	16	52
Atheist	10	74

Source: 2022 CES

The impressive Republican strength within the Assemblies of God is an interesting development. This is the largest Pentecostal denomination in the US, and a variety of Protestantism that believes the miracles written about in the Book of Acts in the New Testament can still be performed by believers. They speak in tongues and attempt to miraculously heal the sick and injured. Pentecostal denominations are also some of the only Christian groups that continue to grow during this period of long-term secularization. The strong Republican identification within Assemblies of God is a relatively recent development. According to the 2012 CES, about 55 percent of the members of this denomination identified as Republican. That is still impressive, but considerably less than 71 percent. The fact that Republican identity has been declining among Mormons at a surprising rate (which I will note shortly) and rising in Assemblies of God is another sign of the party's changing demographic base. According to a 2016 Pew study, about 33 percent of all adult Mormons had a college degree (putting them above the national average of 27 percent). Among Assemblies of God identifiers, only about 15 percent had a college degree, making it, on average, one of the least educated religious groups in the US. The Republican domination of the largest Pentecostal denomination further shows how the GOP is increasingly becoming a party for people on the lower end of the socioeconomic spectrum.

Although Republican identification remains very strong among Mormons, it has declined over the last decade. According to the 2012 CES, when Mitt Romney (himself a Mormon) was the Republican presidential candidate, Republican identification was a remarkable 70 percent among Mormons. Republicans still have a sizable advantage among Mormons, but they are less monolithic, at least in terms of party identity, than they were several years ago. The change in the average level of Mormon commitment to the Republican Party was likely driven by changes in the party. It is not surprising that, compared to 2012 when Mitt Romney was the presidential nominee, the Republican Party inspired less fealty from Mormon voters when Donald Trump was its standard bearer.

Religious identity is not the only important measure of religiosity. Religion is a multifaceted social phenomenon, and from the perspective of social scientists it is helpful to disaggregate it into multiple parts. A person's religious beliefs include what someone thinks about the supernatural world. Is there a God or gods? What is God's nature? Is the Bible (or any other religious text) a literal description of God's actions in the world and a guide for human beings today? This can have important political implications. For example, certain religious doctrines contend that human life begins at the very moment of conception. This necessarily means that abortion is literally an act of murder. Certain interpretations of religious scripture may also make it difficult for some believers to tolerate homosexuality. Religious belonging is about group identity. Which religious group do you consider 'my people'? This is often connected to religious belief, but not necessarily so. One could not believe in any religious tenets, but still feel connected to Catholics, evangelicals, Jews, or Muslims, and feel personally affronted by attacks on those groups. Religious behaviors are those things you actually do as a result of your religion. Do you attend worship services? Go to Sunday School or Bible study? Do you pray? Do you tithe? These can have effects on political beliefs and activities, even when they do not seem to have a partisan component at all.

For all these reasons, it is worth examining the partisan divide on other questions of religion. Beyond religious identity, the importance of religion to a person's life has partisan consequences. The 2022 CES included a four-point scale to the question, "How important is religion to your life?" The possible answers ranged from "very important" to "not at all important." Among respondents that considered religion very important, about 52 percent identified as Republican. For those who did not think religion was important at all to their lives, only about 16 percent identified as Republican. The 2020 ANES asked a question with similar wording (that survey used a five-point scale). Among ANES respondents, about 58 percent of those that described religion as "extremely important," and 48 percent that described it as "very important" identified as Republican. Among ANES respondents that answered "not important at all," about 22 percent identified as Republican.

Biblical literalism is also an important predictor of party identification. The 2020 ANES showed that, among respondents that believed "The Bible is the actual word of God and is to be taken literally, word for word," about 59 percent identified as Republican. For those that believed that the Bible was the word of God, but not necessarily literal in every sense, this dropped to about 46 percent. Finally, for those that believe that "The Bible is a book written by men and is not the word of God," only about 20 percent identified as Republican. This question about the Bible remains useful and predictive, but as religious diversity increases in the U.S., it may eventually become an anachronism. Americans who follow religious texts other than the Bible (and treat those texts literally) are obviously not accurately captured by this question.

To see the influence of religious practices, we can look at the 2020 ANES question about worship attendance. Among respondents who ever attend worship services, about 51 percent identified as Republican, compared to about 32 percent of those that never attend services. The frequency with which they attend services also matters. Among respondents that said they went to services "every week," about 58 percent identified as Republican. We find a similar percentage among those that attend "almost every week." Among religious people that attend services "a few times a year," this drops to about 40 percent. Giving money to religious organizations is also correlated with party identification. About 57 percent of ANES respondents that gave money to a religious organization in the previous 12 months identified as Republican, compared to about 34 percent of those that did not.

We should keep in mind that some of these differences are driven by other demographic characteristics. Most notably, compared to young people, older people are much more likely to identify with a religion, to frequently attend worship services, and give to money to religious institutions, and they are more likely to identify as Republican. Nonetheless, these religion gaps are sizable, and further indicate that the country is increasingly politically polarized along religious lines.

Race, ethnicity, and the Republican vote

When Americans discuss demographic shifts, they could be referring to many possible things, such as a changing age distribution, shifts in family formation, religious decline, or even lifestyle choices. When the subject is brought up in the US, however, especially in the context of politics, shifts in the nation's racial and ethnic characteristics are the most common topic of discussion. The nation's transition from a country that was 90 percent non-Hispanic white in the mid-twentieth century to one that will soon have no single racial or ethnic majority is of course a major demographic development. This shift deserves serious study. We should not overestimate the political and partisan homogeneity of any group, of course, nor should we take it for granted that any group's voting patterns are permanently fixed. Nonetheless, the amount of change we typically see within any major racial or ethnic group over short periods of time is usually very small, and it is reasonable to expect that future changes will also occur at the margins. Given that neither party can usually anticipate a major windfall (or loss) due to a significant realignment within any large racial or ethnic group over a short period of time, it is worth considering their current patterns in detail.

Non-Hispanic whites

For much of US history, a discussion of "white voters" would have seemed redundant. Although the nation was multiracial from the beginning, non-whites for much of that history did not have political rights in most of the country, or those rights were severely curtailed. The constitutional amendments that followed the Civil War that were intended to bring racial equality into the realm of politics failed to achieve their goal, and racial discrimination in politics remained the norm. Southern states after Reconstruction quickly disenfranchised their African American populations, denying them rights until the 1960s, when the Civil Rights Movement successfully guaranteed the franchise for blacks. Even then, however, the nation remained about 90 percent non-Hispanic white.

Changes to immigration policy played a sizable role in the nation's changing demographics. After the quotas system that had been in place since the 1920s came to an end in 1965, the share of Americans with ancestry from Latin America, Asia, and Africa began to increase considerably. The current trajectory suggests non-Hispanic whites will cease to be an absolute majority in the US within two decades. The political consequences of this development have led to heated debate. White nationalists, as well as less extreme racists, have argued that this is part of a deliberate attempt to weaken the political clout of white people, and perhaps even expedite the 'genocide' of white people via political disenfranchisement and miscegenation. The left, as well as many moderates and conservatives, push back against this narrative, critiquing what is now called the "Great Replacement" conspiracy theory, noting that this theory has prompted violence from racist extremists.

Although we should not give weight to racist conspiracy theories, it is the case that white reactions to rapid demographic change will play a great role in the future politics of the US. Will the nation seamlessly transition into a place with no single racial majority, one where members of every group feel at home and welcome? Or will the process be very challenging, perhaps even leading to eruptions of violence? I think the more alarmist right-wing voices predicting mass violence and Balkanization will be proven mistaken. I similarly doubt that the progressives' worst fears about a white racial backlash will be realized. Low-level hostility and political polarization, however, are real possibilities.

One of the most important debates in social science is whether exposure to increased diversity results in greater tolerance or greater hostility toward outgroups. Group contact theory suggests more exposure to different social groups leads people to realize that their negative beliefs about those groups were mistaken and they subsequently become less prejudiced.[58] In contrast, group threat theory suggests that, as different social groups come into close contact, they view each other as competition for scarce resources.[59] Unfortunately for people looking for a nice, parsimonious explanation for important social phenomenon, these relationships are quite complicated. Sometimes greater contact between groups leads to more tolerance, sometimes we see the reverse. Some scholars have persuasively argued that rising levels of immigration have led to renewed white support for the Republican Party and conservative policies.[60]

To be clear, party identification is not a perfect proxy for tolerance toward minority groups, even if the Republican Party is viewed as the party that is reactionary on issues related to race and immigration. However, voting patterns at the state level provide little evidence that diversity on its own makes whites more Republican. California and Texas are both highly diverse states, yet white vote choice differs dramatically between them. Biden won a narrow majority of the white vote in California, according to exit polls.[61] Trump, in contrast, won two-thirds of the white vote in Texas.[62]

Looking nationwide at white party identification, one could make the case that growing diversity has been driving whites into the Republican Party. According to the ANES cumulative file, in 1972, about 37 percent of white respondents identified

---

58 The most influential early text from this genre is Gordon Allport, *The Nature of Prejudice* (New York: Addison-Wesley, 1954).

59 For political scientists, the most important early example of this argument was made in V.O. Key. *Southern Politics in State and Nation* (New York: Alfred A. Knopf, 1949).

60 Marisa Abrajano and Zoltan L. Hajnal, *White Backlash: Immigration, Race, and American Politics* (Princeton, NJ: Princeton University Press, 2017).

61 "Exit Polls, California," CNN Politics, https://www.cnn.com/election/2020/exit-polls/president/california.

62 "Exit Polls, Texas," CNN Politics, https://www.cnn.com/election/2020/exit-polls/president/texas.

as Republicans (compared to about 48 percent that identified as Democrats). In 2020, about 52 percent of whites identified as Republican – the Democratic share having dropped to about 38 percent. This does seem to indicate that Republicans have been able to remain competitive during a period of significant demographic change because of the party's growing strength among whites.

We should of course not immediately infer that the nation's changing demographic profile is the reason for this shift. Much of the Democratic Party's declining fortunes in the latter decades of the twentieth century can be attributed to the massive shift of white Southerners from the Democratic to the Republican Party. This was driven largely by racial concerns, especially the Democratic Party's embrace of civil rights legislation, but not necessarily by changes in the nation's aggregate racial composition. I will discuss racism in the Republican Party in the electorate in greater detail in Chapter 6.

We should again remember that changes in party identification do not automatically translate into changes in vote choice. Richard Nixon won reelection by a landslide, despite Democrats having a significant advantage in party identification in 1972. We must also keep in mind that, when thinking about party identification, there are not just two options – Republican or Democrat. Beyond third party supporters (who have never been more than a negligible percentage of the population), respondents to these surveys have the choice of identifying as independents. It is true that, as I mentioned earlier, political scientists tend to include "independent leaners" in the partisan camp, but there is always a contingent of voters that are true independents, feeling no closer to the Democratic or the Republican Parties. In the 1972 ANES, about 15 percent of respondents were true independents, compared to about 12 percent in 2020.

As we think about partisan shifts within racial groups, we should remember that geographic differences are important. According to exit polls, in the aggregate, Donald Trump did no better among white voters in 2016 than Mitt Romney in 2012. However, Trump gained white votes where it mattered, and lost them in places he had plenty of white voters to spare. Trump's huge wins among whites without a college education helped put several Rust Belt states back in play for Republicans. The fact that he lost ground in places like Utah turned out to matter very little in that election. This suggests that the question should not be how well the Republicans do among white voters overall, though more voters from any group anywhere is always good for any party, but which white voters, in which swing states, are persuadable. This, of course, applies to other groups, as well. Republicans continue to perform very poorly among Hispanic voters across most regions of the country, but if they can perform well among Hispanics in a couple of critical states, such as Florida and Texas, they can remain competitive into the foreseeable future, even with quickly changing national demographics.

African Americans

The relationship between the Republican Party and African Americans is complex and has taken many turns over the course of the last century. There are also many misconceptions about this history. How did the party of Lincoln, formed expressly to end slavery in the United States, come to be the party that earned only 12 percent of the African American vote in the 2020 presidential election?

Republican rhetoric and behavior during the Civil Rights era and its immediate aftermath are important explanations for African American voting patterns. Senator Barry Goldwater, who earned the Republican presidential nomination in 1964, was explicitly opposed to the Civil Rights Act. Goldwater was crushed in the general election by President Lyndon Johnson, but he did win the popular vote in several Deep South states. This was a critical moment in the realignment among Southern whites. President Nixon, with his "Southern Strategy" of appealing to these voters, continued this trend and used it to win the White House. African American voters saw that this was occurring and switched their party loyalties accordingly. This is not the entire story, however, and it downplays developments that were occurring before the 1960s.

Although Barry Goldwater certainly deserves some of the blame for the Republican Party's shedding of black voters, his importance in this regard should not be overemphasized. Goldwater was far from the most racist Republican leader of the twentieth century. In fact, Goldwater himself seemed not to be personally prejudiced against African Americans, and his opposition to civil rights legislation does appear to have been driven by sincere principles about the constitutional limits of federal power. This was not true of many other prominent Republicans. In the nineteenth and early parts of the twentieth centuries, there was a movement within the Republican Party that not only chose not to court black voters, but that actively sought to drive them away from the party.

After the Civil War, the Republican Party dominated American politics, and for a time sought to fundamentally transform the defeated South. After Reconstruction, however, white Southerners reasserted white supremacy, African Americans were systematically disenfranchised, and the Democratic Party asserted its control over the region. Because of the Democratic Party's lock on the "Solid South," close competition between the two parties for control of congress and the presidency at the national level resumed.

Republicans, however, were not willing to permanently concede the South, even after the 1896 election, in which they demonstrated they could win massive victories without Southern support. A problem for the Republicans in the South, however, was that there the party had a firm reputation as the party for African Americans and Northern "carpetbaggers." Supporting the Republicans was simply unthinkable for most white Southerners, even years after the Civil War and Reconstruction had ended.[63]

To solve the problem, throughout the South whites began taking control of the Republican Party at the state level, pushing blacks out of leadership positions. Starting in the 1870s, the "Lily-White Movement" to assert white control of the Southern GOP began in Texas and spread throughout the region. This was especially outrageous when one considers that these state parties had been largely built from the ground up by African Americans themselves.

The Lily-White Movement yielded few dividends in terms of electoral victories. The Democratic Party remained dominant in the South even when the Republican Party was at its peak of popularity nationwide. The movement did, however, signal at an early date that the Party of Lincoln was no longer primarily interested in questions of civil rights. The assertion of white control of the Southern GOP also meant that black delegates ceased to be a major presence at the national Republican convention. The Lily-White Movement continued, with various levels of intensity, throughout the early twentieth century. As late as the 1928 election, Herbert Hoover was investing heavily in these efforts.[64] It is important to note that, in many parts of the country, African Americans were not just lured away from the Republicans by the Democrats – they were often given a push.

As was the case with white Americans, African Americans swung heavily toward the Democrats in 1932 as a result of the Great Depression and President Hoover's ineffective response to the crisis. Although President Roosevelt was not a consistent advocate for civil rights, and many policies from his administration were highly discriminatory, his energetic approach to the economy earned him loyalty from black voters in his subsequent elections.

There were other developments throughout this period that further pushed African Americans toward the Democrats. As Christopher Baylor demonstrates in his book, *First to the Party*, new alliances between civil rights organizations and organized labor – especially between the National Association for the Advancement of Colored People and the Congress of Industrial Organizations – helped black advocates gain the attention of Democratic leaders in the 1930s and 1940s.[65] This was significant because organized labor had historically been hostile to black advocates, viewing African Americans as scabs who drove down the wages of white

---

63 Boris Heersink and Jeffery A. Jenkins, "Whiteness and the Emergence of the Republican Party in the Early Twentieth-Century South," *Studies in American Political Development*, 34(2020): 71–90.
64 Ibid.
65 Christopher Baylor, *First to the Party: The Group Origins of Political Transformation* (Philadelphia: University of Pennsylvania Press, 2018).

workers. Labor was furthermore one of the most important elements of the Democratic coalition.

Despite the movement of African Americans toward the Democratic Party, a significant contingent of African American voters and leaders remained committed to the GOP, and hoped they could revive its tradition of racial progressivism. In 1956, President Eisenhower earned an impressive 39 percent of the African American vote.[66] Richard Nixon ran on a comparatively progressive platform in his 1960 bid for the presidency. His supporters even believed he had a realistic chance of earning Martin Luther King's endorsement – the evangelist Billy Graham, for example, expressed confidence he could persuade King to give Nixon his support.[67] This possibility vanished after Kennedy's swift show of support for King and his movement after King's arrest in Atlanta.[68]

As Goldwater's campaign for the Republican nomination in 1964 gained momentum, many black Republicans were horrified, given Goldwater's opposition to civil rights legislation. Most black Republicans preferred the more progressive Nelson Rockefeller. This is not to say that there were no African Americans in the conservative wing of the Republican Party. J.A. Parker, for example, was a prominent black member of Young Americans for Freedom in the 1960s.[69] Such figures represented a tiny minority of black Republicans, who were themselves an increasingly small minority of African Americans.

Given the Republican Party's efforts to expand its support among pro-segregation whites in the South, and its increasing association with a conservative movement that was generally opposed to civil rights legislation and seemingly indifferent to black oppression, one may wonder why so many blacks remained part of the GOP by the late 1960s. There were many reasons for this continued loyalty. One explanation, of course, is that partisanship tends to persist over time, even if one strongly dislikes one candidate at the top of the ticket in one election cycle. It is additionally important to note that, although overwhelming majorities of African Americans supported new civil rights advances, they were not monolithic when it came to other policies. It is not the case that all African Americans were on board with every element of the Democratic Party's agenda.

---

66 Leah Wright Rigueur, *The Loneliness of the Black Republican* (Princeton, NJ: Princeton University Press, 2015), 31.
67 Daniel K. Williams, *God's Own Party: The Making of the Christian Right* (New York: Oxford University Press, 2012), 54.
68 Rigueur, *The Loneliness of the Black Republican*, 37.
69 David W. Tyson, *Courage to Put Country above Color: The J.A. Parker Story* (Washington, DC: Lincoln Institute for Research and Education, 2009).

Republicans have subsequently sought to win back lost ground among African Americans, with minimal success. In the latter decades of the twentieth century, some conservatives sought to use the immigration issue as a wedge between African American and Latino activists, arguing that large-scale immigration, particularly immigrants with fewer skills and less education, represented a particularly significant threat to black economic wellbeing.[70] These efforts have achieved negligible effects, at least when it comes to vote choice. Other Republicans have sought to revive much older history when making appeals to black voters, noting that, in the nineteenth century, the Republican Party was the party of emancipation, and the Democratic Party was the party of the Ku Klux Klan. This line of argumentation has also failed to persuade a significant percentage of African Americans to switch parties.

The Democratic Party's consistent impressive showing among black voters has been a source of frustration for many Republicans. Based on some measures, it seems as though a greater share of the black vote should be up for grabs. Of all the major racial groups in the US, blacks are the most Christian by a considerable margin.[71] There is furthermore a significant contingent of black voters that identify as ideological conservatives, yet nonetheless continue to support the Democratic Party. Political scientists Ismail K. White and Chryl N. Laird argue that this phenomenon can be largely explained by the black historical experience and trends in contemporary black communities.[72] They note that African Americans' history with slavery, discrimination, and white supremacy resulted in very strong group identities that persist to this day. They further argue that group solidarity, as expressed via strong support for the Democratic Party, is continuously reinforced by social pressures from their communities.

Regardless of the explanation, overwhelming black identification with the Democratic Party has been one consistent element of the electorate over many decades. According to the cumulative ANES, about 11 percent of black respondents identified as Republican in 1972, compared to about nine percent in 2020. There may be some positive signs for Republican in this regard. In the 2022 midterm elections, the GOP performed better among African Americans than in previous recent

---

70 Daniel Tichenor, *Dividing Lines: The Politics of Immigration Control in America* (Princeton, NJ: Princeton University Press, 2002).

71 "Christians by Race/Ethnicity," Pew Research Center Religious Study Landscape, https://www.pewresearch.org/religion/religious-landscape-study/compare/christians/by/racial-and-ethnic-composition/.

72 Ismail K. White and Chryl N. Laird, *Steadfast Democrats: How Social Forces Shape Black Political Behavior* (Princeton, NJ: Princeton University Press, 2020).

midterm elections.[73] It is nonetheless still a long way off from being competitive with this demographic.

Hispanics

When scholars and pundits discuss how immigration has and is changing the demographics and politics of the US, Hispanics are the group that justifiably receives the most attention, given their large numbers. This group is somewhat different from the racial categories typically used by the US Census Bureau. "Hispanic" or "Latino" (terms that are used interchangeably by most social scientists) are not races, according to current classification schemes. Instead, they are treated as an ethnic group. Indeed, and this is somewhat strange, the only two ethnic groups that are recognized by the Census Bureau and surveys that use similar classifications are "Hispanic" and "not Hispanic." This means, of course, that Hispanics can be of any race, yet they tend to be treated as a single racial group. As of 2020, the Hispanic population in the US was more than 62 million people, making them an extremely important category of voters.[74]

The notion that there is a single Hispanic/Latino identity in the US is questionable. To what extent does an immigrant from Argentina feel a sense of shared identity and linked fate with an immigrant from Guatemala, or with someone whose family has lived in the Southwest since before the Treaty of Guadalupe-Hidalgo, which ended the Mexican-American War? Do people with those backgrounds feel a shared sense of identity with a white American who speaks no Spanish but whose parents emmigrated to the US from Spain? According to George Isidore Sánchez, a leader in the fight for civil rights for Latinos:

> They are just too many different peoples to be adequately covered under one umbrella. While they could be called, loosely, "Americans who speak Spanish" they would have to be treated in separate categories – for, by way of illustration, though a Cuban in Florida and a Mexican in Laredo both speak Spanish, they really have little else in common (even though both may be aliens or citizens, or a combination).[75]

---

73 Patrick Ruffini, *Party of the People: Inside the Multiracial Populist Coalition Remaking the GOP* (New York: Simon and Schuster, 2023)

74 Cary Fund and Mark Hugo Lopez, "A Brief Statistical Portrait of U.S. Hispanics," Pew Research Center, June 14, 2022, https://www.pewresearch.org/science/2022/06/14/a-brief-statistical-portrait-of-u-s-hispanics/.

75 George I. Sánchez to Julian Samora, February 20, 1952. Quoted in Benjamin Francis-Fallon, *The Rise of the Latino Vote: A History* (Cambridge, MA: Harvard University Press, 2019), 15.

Nonetheless, from a social science perspective, we must draw boundaries some-where, and if we find that Hispanics, as a group, exhibit distinct political and socio-logical characteristics, we can justify our continued use of the category, as long as we acknowledge its potential problems.

For this book, I am especially interested in which attributes among the US Lat-ino population are associated with identifying with the Republican Party. The 2022 CES is a useful tool in this instance because of its large sample size, which includes more than 5,000 Hispanic respondents. Even more helpfully, it asks the following question of these respondents who describe themselves as having a Latino back-ground: "From which country or region do you trace your heritage or ancestry?" Respondents were encouraged to check all that apply, so they had the option of identifying with more than one country or region. From this, we can see how much variation exists among Latinos when it comes to party identification.

Table 1.2: Hispanic partisanship by heritage or ancestry.

Country/Region	% Republican	% Democrat
Cuba	42	41
Spain	27	45
Other Hispanic	30	40
US	25	44
Mexico	23	49
South America	27	50
Puerto Rico	26	43
Central America	26	43
Other Caribbean	18	49
Dominican Republic	18	48

Source: 2022 CES

From this table we see that Democrats have a decided advantage among Latinos. Cubans are the only group where Republicans appear to have an advantage – but the difference was less than one percentage point. This may be somewhat mislead-ing, however. Latinos are slightly more likely than other large groups to identify as true independents. According to the 2022 CES, about 23 percent of Hispanics iden-tify as genuine independents, compared to about 21 percent of African Americans and 16 percent of non-Hispanic whites. Hispanic respondents were also consider-ably less likely to strongly identify with either political party. Whereas about 42 percent of whites and blacks were "strong" partisans of either party, this was only true for about 32 percent of Hispanics.

Hispanic vote choice also seems to vary significantly by geographic region. Ac-cording to 2020 exit polls, 75 percent of Hispanic voters in California voted for Joe

Biden.[76] In Texas, Biden won a less impressive 58 percent of the Hispanic vote. In Florida, Biden only earned 53 percent of the Hispanic vote. The GOP's ability to keep earning a respectable share of the Hispanic vote in a few critical states will thus play a major role in determining the party's ability to remain competitive at the national level. Sensible Republicans will want to discern the reasons for Donald Trump's comparatively high level of support among Hispanic voters in Texas and Florida.

It is not surprising that Latinos in the US tend to have slightly weaker party attachments than other groups. Scholars have known for decades that early socialization is one important factor in determining partisan affiliation.[77] Compared to other large demographic groups in the US, a large percentage of Hispanic voters were not born and raised in the US, which means the process by which they became acclimated to the country's. politics was, on average, different from other groups. However, being an immigrant, or having immigrant parents, even after controlling for race and ethnicity, is associated with a greater likelihood of supporting the Democratic Party.[78]

Political scientists, as well as politicians and political activists, have taken a great interest in the origins of Latino partisanship.[79] For Republicans, the party's long-term prospects are strongly tied to its ability to make gains among Latino voters. This can be overstated, and the claim that "demographics is destiny," and various iterations of that claim, can lead to noxious, racist conclusions. It is nonetheless just simple political math that a group that is large and growing, and overwhelmingly favors a particular party, will change a nation's electoral landscape. What, then, might help the GOP achieve greater success among this group of voters?

The party's stance on immigration is the most common argument for the Republican Party's weak showing among Latino voters. By attacking immigration

---

76 "Exit Polls," CNN, https://www.cnn.com/election/2020/exit-polls/president/california.

77 Angus Campbell, Philip E. Converse, Warren E. Miller, and Donald E. Stokes, *The American Voter.* (New York: Wiley, 1960).

78 George Hawley, "Immigration Status, Immigrant Family Ties, and Support for the Democratic Party," *Social Science Quarterly* 100 (2019): 1171–1181.

79 R. Michael Alvarez and Lisa García Bedolla, "The Foundations of Latino Voter Partisanship: Evidence from the 2000 Election," *The Journal of Politics* 65 (2003): 31–49; Diana Evans, Ana Franco, J.L. Polinard, James P. Wenzel, and Robert D. Wrinkle, "Ethnic Concerns and Latino Party Identification," *The Social Science Journal* 49 (2012): 150–154; Kenneth E. Fernandez and Matthew C. Dempsey, "The Local Political Context of Latino Partisanship," *Journal of Race, Ethnicity, and Politics* 2 (2017): 201–232; Leonie Huddy, Lilliana Mason, and S. Nechama Horwitz, "Political Identity Convergence: On Being Latino, Becoming a Democrat, and Getting Active," *RSF: The Russell Sage Foundation Journal of the Social Sciences* 2 (2016): 205–228.

and, sometimes, immigrants themselves, the party alienates voters who are personally immigrants, as well as the children and grandchildren of immigrants. Political scientists have suggested that the party's weak support among Hispanic voters can be traced to the 1990s, when the Republican Party was peaking in its nativism. In California, especially, where Republican-endorsed anti-immigrant sentiment was expressed in the nativist Proposition 187 and Proposition 227, Latino voters were made painfully aware that the GOP was, on the whole, anti-immigrant, and by implication anti-Latino more generally. Many scholars have argued that this period solidified anti-Republican attitudes among Latino voters.[80] Other scholars have noted that majorities of Latinos oppose other efforts to crack down on undocumented immigration, such as workplace raids.[81] Pro-immigrant Republican strategists have long argued that anti-immigrant messages from Republican politicians and conservative leaders are wholly unproductive from a political standpoint. Grover Norquist, president of Americans for Tax Reform, put it this way after Republicans suffered terrible electoral losses in the 2006 midterm elections:

> The best lesson of the 2006 congressional election is that anti-immigrant rhetoric and votes in favor of walling off the southern border did not win votes for Republicans. What seemed so exciting when bandied about on right-wing talk radio was not a winner on Election Day. Not only was there no "upside" with the white or African American vote for focusing on immigration, there was a downside as the Republican vote among Hispanics fell to 30 percent.[82]

Republicans who want the party to shift toward a pro-immigration stance can also note that President George W. Bush, according to exit polls, won an unusually large percentage of the Latino vote for a Republican presidential candidate (44 percent), and this can be attributed to his pro-immigrant talking points and policy agenda – an agenda that was never implemented because of restrictionist Republicans in congress who blocked comprehensive immigration reform.

There are some problems with this argument, however. To begin with, Democrats had a large advantage over Republicans among Latino voters in the early 1980s, long before these anti-immigration measures were being seriously consid-

80 Shaun Bowler, Stephen P. Nicholson, and Gary Segura, "Earthquakes and Aftershocks: Race, Direct Democracy, and Partisan Change," *American Journal of Political Science* 50 (2006): 146–159.
81 Mark Hugo Lopez and Susan Minushkin, "Latinos and Immigration Enforcement," Pew Research Center, September 18, 2008, https://www.pewresearch.org/hispanic/2008/09/18/iii-latinos-and-immigration-enforcement/.
82 Grover Norquist, *Leave Us Alone: Getting the Government's Hands off Our Money, Our Guns, Our Lives* (New York: HarperCollins, 2008), 189.

ered.[83] Other research additionally shows that anti-Republican attitudes in California were already growing before the party began pushing new nativist policies,[84] and there was no dramatic change in Latino partisanship during the period the most draconian laws were under consideration.[85] The claim that George W. Bush experienced a huge windfall of Latino voters because of his pro-immigrant views and policies may also be challenged. Most importantly, it appears that the exit polls showing a very strong level of Latino support for Bush were exceptionally flawed; they apparently oversampled Latinos especially likely to vote Republican. The actual percentage was probably closer to 39 percent.[86]

If we are going to use exit polls to determine what kind of Republican candidate attracts Latino voters, Trump's relatively strong showing among Latinos in 2020 seems to undermine the case that nativism is the party's primary problem. Exit polls suggest Trump won 32 percent of the Latino vote.[87] That is not a great showing, but it is nonetheless an improvement over Mitt Romney's 27 percent in 2012.[88] None of this is to say that Republican nativism is not a cause for the party's poor performance among Hispanic voters. I am simply arguing that it is almost certainly not the entire explanation, and a Republican shift toward a pro-immigration position might help, but it would likely not be a panacea.

As is the case with African Americans, many Republicans have hoped that Latinos' purported social conservatism will ultimately bring them to the party. It has historically been true that, on many issues, Latinos have been at least as socially conservative, on average, as non-Hispanic whites. Some Republicans were hopeful that a focus on social issues such as abortion and same-sex marriage might draw new Latino voters into the party. These efforts have yielded minimal dividends. One explanation for this Republican failure is that, although many Latino voters express support for certain conservative social policies, it does not appear that

83 John L. Korey, Edward L. Lascher Jr., "Macropartisanship in California," *The Public Opinion Quarterly* 70 (2006): 48–65.

84 Joshua J. Dyck, Gregg B. Johnson, and Jesse T. Wasson, "A Blue Tide in the Golden State: Ballot Propositions, Population Change, and Party Identification in California," *American Politics Research* 40 (2011): 450–475.

85 Iris Hui and David O. Sears, "Reexamining the Effect of Racial Propositions on Latinos' Partisanship in California," *Political Behavior* 40 (2017): 149–174.

86 David L. Leal, Matt A. Barreto, Jonho Lee, and Rodolfo O. de la Garza, "The Latino Vote in the 2004 Election," *PS: Political Science and Politics* 38 (2005): 41–49.

87 "Exit Polls," CNN, https://www.cnn.com/election/2020/exit-polls/president/national-results.

88 "President Exit Polls," *The New York Times*, https://www.nytimes.com/elections/2012/results/president/exit-polls.html .

these policies are especially important for determining their party identification and vote choice.[89]

Asian Americans

Republicans were hopeful that Latinos could be persuaded to join the party because of their ostensible preferences for conservative social policies, even though, as a less affluent demographic compared to non-Hispanic whites (on average), it seemed understandable that Latinos would support the Democratic Party. In contrast, as one of the wealthier demographics in the US (again, on average), Republicans could be optimistic that Asian American voters would find the party appealing based on their economic interests. That has also not been the case in recent elections. Most recent surveys show that Asian Americans remain much more likely to identify as Democrats than Republicans (it was 26 percent Republican compared to 50 percent Democratic in the 2022 CES, and 26 percent compared to 56 percent in the 2022 Asian American Voter Survey).[90] Asian Americans have also had comparatively low rates of political participation, especially considering their relatively high average socioeconomic status.[91]

As is the case for Latinos, one can reasonably question the extent to which there is a widely shared Asian American identity. Do Americans who trace their ancestors back to India feel they have common interests and a sense of linked fate with Americans who trace their heritage to Japan? The recent trend to combine Asian Americans with Pacific Islanders (AAPI) strikes me as additionally questionable. Compared to Latinos, Asian Americans are more diverse when it comes to religion and the language. Of course, the development of a pan-ethnic identity is something that happens at an individual-level, and thus will vary. Some research indicates that rising feelings of pan-ethnic identity among Asian Americans has increased lately in large part because of anti-immigrant and anti-Asian rhetoric from certain Republican politicians.[92] Other scholarship indicates that pan-ethnic con-

89 Rodolfo O. de la Garza and Jeronimo Cortina, "Are Latinos Republicans but Just don't Know it?" *American Politics Research* 35 (2007): 202–223.
90 "2022 Asian American Voter Survey Tables," APIAVote, AAPI Data, and Asian Americans Advancing Justice, July 2022, https://aapidata.com/wp-content/uploads/2022/07/AAVS-Tables.html.
91 Janelle S. Wong, S. Karthick Ramakrishnan, Taeku Lee, and Jane Junn, *Asian American Political Participation: Emerging Constituents and their Political Identity* (New York: Russell Sage Foundation, 2011).
92 Danvy Le, Maneesh Arora, and Christopher Stout, "Are You Threatening Me? Asian-American Panethnicity in the Trump Era," *Social Science Quarterly* 101 (2020): 2183–2192.

sciousness varies by party (Democrats are more likely to have a strong Asian American identity than Republicans) and by experiences of discrimination.[93] As is the case with Latinos, Asian American rates of support for the two major parties varies by heritage. According to the 2022 Asian American Voter Survey, Asian Americans that identify as Vietnamese are the most Republican group (about 39 percent Republican), followed by Filipinos (32 percent), Koreans (31 percent), Japanese (25 percent), Indian (20 percent), and Chinese (18 percent).[94]

Asian American support for the Democratic Party may be partly explained by religious patterns. Of the major racial groups in the US, Asian Americans are, by a considerable margin, the least Christian – about 34 percent of Asian Americans identify as Christian, according to the Pew Religious Landscape Study.[95] The 2022 CES showed a similar percentage. As the parties become increasingly polarized by religion, and the Republican Party remains viewed as the party of Christians in particular, non-Christian groups may find the GOP alienating. Asian Americans are also more likely to live in metropolitan areas, which influences their political socialization.[96] Other scholarship indicates that Asian American support for the Democratic Party is driven heavily by their patterns of early socialization – both within their families and with peer groups that lean Democratic.[97] Feelings of social exclusion, which apparently increased during the COVID-19 pandemic, also seem to have played a role reinforcing Asian American loyalties to the Democratic Party.[98] Finally, despite relatively high average levels of economic wellbeing, Asian Americans, on average, tend to favor progressive economic policies.[99]

93 Natalie Masuoka, "Together They Become One: Examining the Predictors of Panethnic Group Consciousness Among Asian Americans and Latinos," *Social Science Quarterly* 87 (2006): 993–1011.
94 "2022 Asian American Voter Survey Tables," APIAVote, AAPI Data, and Asian Americans Advancing Justice | AAJC, July 2022, https://aapidata.com/wp-content/uploads/2022/07/AAVS-Tables.html#By_Ethnic_Group.
95 "Christians by Race/Ethnicity," Pew Research Center, https://www.pewresearch.org/religion/religious-landscape-study/compare/christians/by/racial-and-ethnic-composition/.
96 Tanika Raychaudhuri, "Socializing Democrats: Examining Asian American Vote Choice with Evidence from a National Survey," *Electoral Studies* 63 (2020): 102–114.
97 Tanika Raychaudhuri, "The Social Roots of Asian American Partisan Attitudes," *Politics, Groups, and Identities* 6 (2018): 389–410.
98 Nathan Kar Ming Chan, Jae Yeon Kim, and Vivien Leung, "COVID-19 and Asian Americans: How Elite Messaging and Social Exclusion Shape Partisan Attitudes," *Perspectives on Politics* 20 (2022): 618–634.
99 Janelle Wong and Sono Shah, "Convergence Across Difference: Understanding the Political Ties That Bind with the 2016 National Asian American Survey," *RSF: The Russell Sage Foundation Journal of the Social Sciences* 7 (2021): 70–92.

The partisan happiness gap

Certain progressive and even centrist pundits have promoted a narrative that Republicans are bitter reactionaries, seething with anger as they are increasingly left behind by a modern world that does not share their resentments.[100] As President Obama famously stated about the Republican base: "They get bitter, they cling to guns or religion or antipathy to people who aren't like them or anti-immigrant sentiment or anti-trade sentiment as a way to explain their frustrations."[101] Although not a demographic gap *per se* it is worth knowing if there is a partisan difference in subjective feelings of wellbeing.

The problem with the claim that Republicans are fearful and unhappy, whereas Democrats are optimistic and cheerful, is that empirical evidence seems to suggest otherwise. The GSS has long asked respondents about their own sense of happiness: "Taken all together, how would you say things are these days—would you say that you are very happy, pretty happy, or not too happy?" Looking at data from 2021, we find that about 25 percent of Republicans described themselves as "very happy," compared to about 16 percent of Democrats. Republicans were also slightly less likely than Democrats to describe themselves as "not too happy" – about 19 percent versus about 25 percent. I should additionally note that this poll was conducted during a time when Democrats controlled the White House and both chambers of the US Congress.

This gap in self-described happiness, while not large, has been curiously persistent. I created Figure 2.7 by finding the mean happiness value for both Republicans and Democrats for every year of the GSS. I altered the order of the variable so that higher scores indicate a greater level of happiness. Over more than four decades, there has never been a GSS where the mean happiness score for Democrats exceeded that of Republicans. It is true that Republican happiness has been decreasing in recent years, but this is also true of Democrats. For both parties, unfortunately, the mean happiness score reached an all-time low in 2021.

The partisan happiness gap is not a new finding, and scholars have sought to explain why it developed and has persisted. The consistency of the finding, despite

---

100 For examples of this kind of argument, see Randall J. Stevens, "How the Republican Party became a Haven of Resentment and Rage," *The Conversation*, September 17, 2015, https://theconversation.com/how-the-republican-party-became-a-haven-of-resentment-and-rage-47073; Rebecca Solnit, "Why are US Rightwingers so Angry? Because they Know Social Change is Coming," *The Guardian*, December 20, 2021, https://www.theguardian.com/commentisfree/2021/dec/20/right wingers-us-social-change-coming.

101 Ed Pilkington, "Obama Angers Midwest Voters with Guns and Religion Remark," *The Guardian*, April 14, 2008, https://www.theguardian.com/world/2008/apr/14/barackobama.uselections2008.

changes in both parties' demographic bases over the last 40-plus years is especially interesting. There are many possible reasons for this gap. As Paul Taylor of the Pew Research Center points out, Republicans, on average, have more money, are happier with their communities, and are more religious.[102] One might also reasonably speculate that racial differences between the parties might explain this. The Republican Party, having fewer non-whites, and thus fewer supporters subjected to racism, might be happier for that reason. However, according to the regression model Taylor created to determine the causes of subjective feelings of happiness, race was not significant.

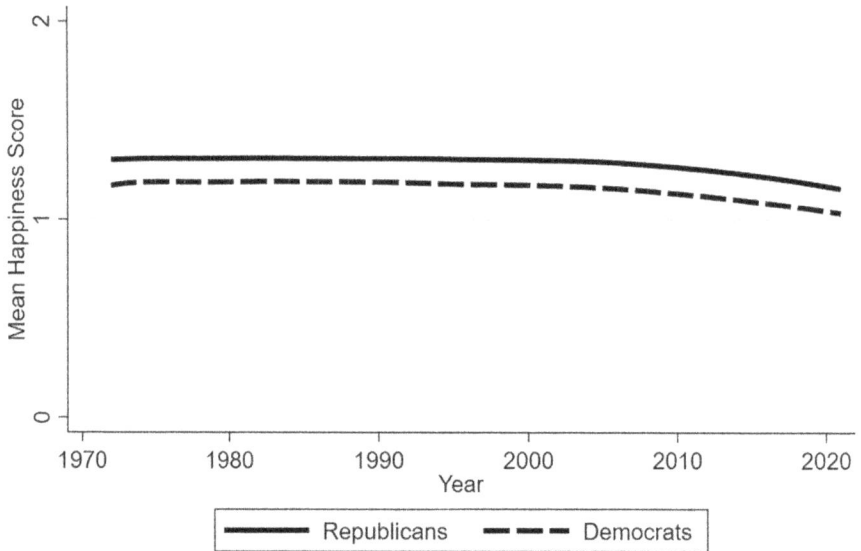

Figure 2.7: Mean Happiness Scory by Party. Source: Cumulative GSS. Note: Figure LOWESS smoothed.

Scholars have suggested several other reasons Republicans seem to have higher levels of subjective wellbeing. Examining a different survey that showed how happiness differed according to ideology, W. Bradford Wilcox of the Institute for Family Studies argued that different family formation patterns can explain this finding: "On the family front, conservative Americans (*not* politicians, admittedly) have a major advantage, in large part because they are more likely to embrace the family-first values and virtues that steer them towards wedlock and fulfilling family

---

102 Paul Taylor, "Republicans: Still Happy Campers," Pew Research Center, October 23, 2008, https://www.pewresearch.org/social-trends/2008/10/23/republicans-still-happy-campers/.

lives."[103] According to this theory, liberals are less happy because they are less likely to form nuclear families, instead pursuing other paths to happiness that are less likely to achieve that end.

Other studies have suggested a different mechanism to explain this apparent happiness gap. Psychologists Jaime L. Napier and John T. Jost argued that conservative happiness is partly explained by their nonchalance toward inequality.[104] In other words, growing levels of inequality decrease liberals' happiness, on average, but do not have a similar effect on conservatives. This work builds on "system justification theory," which suggests that people differ in their tendency to justify the existing social order.[105] On the other hand, conservatives are also more likely to display other traits associated with wellbeing, such as a belief in personal agency.[106] Other work indicates that conservatives are more likely to feel purpose and meaning in life.[107]

Perhaps we should be skeptical of self-reported claims about happiness. Scholars examining other measures of happiness have reached different conclusions. For example, a separate study found that, compared to conservatives, liberals were more likely to use positive emotional language. They were also found to smile more in photographs.[108] The authors of the study were careful not to say that their results were definitive, but they did think it was potentially important that self-reports were not consistent with behavioral indicators of happiness. The problem, for now, is that social scientists at this point have not established a reliable and universally agreed upon measure of happiness – self-reports may be misleading, but so too might smiles and positive language.

103 W. Bradford Wilcox, "Why are Liberals Less Happy than Conservatives?" The Institute for Family Studies, October 13, 2022, https://ifstudies.org/blog/why-are-liberals-less-happy-than-con servatives.

104 Jaime L. Napier and John T. Jost, "Why are Conservatives Happier than Liberals?" *Psychological Science* 19 (2008): 446–572.

105 John T. Jost, Mahzarin R. Banaji, and Brian A. Nosek, "A Decade of System Justification Theory: Accumulated Evidence of Conscious and Unconscious Bolstering of the Status Quo," *Political Psychology* 25 (2004): 881–919.

106 Barry R. Schlenker, John R. Chambers, and Bonnie M. Le, "Conservatives are Happier than Liberals, but Why? Political Ideology, Personality, and Life Satisfaction," *Journal or Research in Personality* 46 (2017): 127–146.

107 David B. Newman, Norbert Schwarz, Jesse Graham, and Arthur A. Stone, "Conservatives Report Greater Meaning in Life Than Liberals," *Social Psychology and Personality Science* 10 (2019): 494–503.

108 Sean P. Wojcik, Arpine Hovasapian, Jesse Graham, Matt Motyl, and Peter H. Ditto, "Conservatives Report, but Liberals Display, Greater Happiness," *Science* 347 (2015): 1243–1246.

Mental health is another area where we often find a difference between Republicans and Democrats. Studies have consistently found that, at least according to self-reports, Republicans suffer fewer mental health problems.[109] Looking at a more specific source of potential mental health problems, researchers found that Democrats were more likely to suffer from mental distress than Republicans as a result of the COVID-19 pandemic.[110]

Recent GSS surveys seem to validate these findings. Starting in 2018, the survey asked the following question: "In the past seven days, how often have you been bothered by emotional problems such as feeling anxious, depressed or irritable?" The possible responses were "never," "rarely," "sometimes," "often," and "always." In 2021, about 28 percent of Republicans responded, "never." For Democrats, it was only about 15 percent. Democrats were about twice as likely as Republicans to respond "often" or "always." The 2022 CES provided similar results. About 25 percent of Republicans and 15 percent of Democrats described their mental health as "excellent."

Some of this can be explained by different gender ratios in each party. Women are more likely to be Democrats than men, and, at least according to the GSS, women are more likely to report problems of mental health. Gender differences do not explain the entire phenomenon, however, as a greater percentage of both Republican men and Republican women reported "never" experiencing emotional problems than Democratic men. The 2022 CES found a similar gap. In that survey, about 29 percent of Republican men and 21 percent of Republican women reported that their mental health was "excellent." For Democratic men and women, it was 19 percent and 12 percent, respectively.

Although interesting, we should exercise caution before drawing strong inferences from these data. Self-reported descriptions of mental health given to a pollster are not objective measures. Rather than indicating a gap in mental illness between the parties, this may just indicate a gap in beliefs about mental illness and trust in psychiatry. One study showed that Democrats have become increasingly likely to report higher levels of stress, anxiety, and depression when Republicans win high-profile elections, but it could find no evidence that their behavior (as measured by their use of internet search engines) changed in any significant

---

109 Frank Newport, "Republicans Report Much Better Mental Health Than Others," Gallup, November 30, 2007, https://news.gallup.com/poll/102943/republicans-report-much-better-mental-health-than-others.aspx#1.

110 Soyoung Kwon, "The Interplay between Partisanship, Risk Perception, and Mental Distress During the Early Stages of the COVID-19 Pandemic in the United States," *Psychology, Health, and Medicine* 1(2023): 69–85.

way. According to the researchers: "Democrats were no more likely to search for stress relief, nor mental illness, nor treatment for mental illness before or after the election. This suggests that some Democrats reported mental health declines after Trump's election as a form of reverse cheerleading, where partisans report evaluations that are more negative than their true beliefs to reflect badly on a president of the opposing party."[111]

Conclusion

We must be cautious when interpreting these kinds of data. It is important that we not overstate the political or cultural homogeneity of any large group in the US. We should furthermore not take it for granted that current rates of Republican voting and party identification for different groups will remain indefinitely. Group identities and interests are not permanently fixed, and parties have historically been able to adapt to changing demographics by altering their platforms and types of appeals.

It is nonetheless the case that the Republican Party appears to be seriously disadvantaged going forward, assuming most of the present trends we see continue. This chapter did not provide an exhaustive list of the various demographic divisions in party identification and vote choice. One especially notable omission was age. I did not dive deeply into the generation gap in politics because it is partly explained by many other gaps. Once you account for race, education, community type, and other variables, age *per se* appears less statistically significant and substantively important – though its effects never disappear entirely.[112] Contrary to the common notion that people naturally become more conservative as they age, the evidence for this claim is weak – in the aggregate, we may see some movement to the right within a generation as it gets older, but the shift is small.[113] Regardless of its source, however, the age gap in partisan politics represents a massive looming threat to the Republican Party. The Baby Boom generation, as well as Generation X, which also gives the party a lot of support, will be around for many

---

111 Masha Krupenkin, David Rothschild, Shawndra Hill, and Elad Yom-Tov, "President Trump Stress Disorder: Partisanship, Ethnicity, and Expressive Reporting of Mental Distress After the 2016 Election," *SAGE Open* 9(2019): 1–14.

112 For a good recent review of the generation gap in US politics, I recommend Kevin Munger, *Generation Gap: Why the Baby Boomers Still Dominate American Politics and Culture* (New York: Columbia University Press, 2022).

113 Johnathan C. Peterson, Kevin B. Smith, and John R. Hibbing, "Do People Really Become More Conservative as They Age?" *The Journal of Politics* 82 (2020): 600–611.

years to come, but not forever. The GOP will at some point need to make successful appeals to a greater percentage of Millennials and Generation Z, or it will have a very difficult time remaining competitive into the future.

Indeed, Republicans should be very concerned by these data. Republicans are losing in most groups that are growing in the US – especially racial and ethnic minorities and secular people. The large groups that Republicans dominate are shrinking. Rural, evangelical, white Christians will almost certainly remain a critical base for the GOP for the foreseeable future, but the party has probably reached a ceiling on how much support they are going to gain from that group, a group whose influence is likely to wane further in the decades ahead. The marriage gap is also a problem for the party, given the declining rate of traditional family formation. To remedy the problem, Republicans will need to either make themselves more appealing to single voters or pursue policies that lead to higher rates of family formation – or both.

The party's declining fortunes among college educated Americans is unquestionably a major problem, though it is possible that this recent decline was more because of the party's change in style than in substance. Donald Trump ostentatiously embraced a comparatively low-brow rhetorical strategy, one that a huge majority of white Americans without a college education found highly appealing. That same rhetoric seems to have turned off a large number of more educated Americans that might otherwise find the Republican agenda attractive. A great challenge for the Republican Party going forward will be in regaining ground among highly educated Americans without losing the gains Trump made for the party among those with less education.

Chapter 3
Republican policy preferences

Political observers often take it for granted that Americans are fighting a "culture war," though the stakes and dividing lines of this conflict are too infrequently defined. I nonetheless concur that cultural antagonisms are at least as central to American political life as wonkish debates about economic policy. This does not mean that questions about policy are irrelevant. If they were, party politics in the US would be even more incoherent and dysfunctional than they are now. Political scientists continue to debate the degree to which issues matter when it comes to party identification, approval ratings for politicians, and vote choice.

In this chapter, I will note the debates within political science about public attitudes toward policy, noting that some scholars remain skeptical that significant portions of the electorate have meaningful and consistent opinions on most matters of public policy. Then, using multiple sources of data, supplemented by findings from my personal interviews, I will note what Republicans have to say about various policy issues in multiple issue domains (economic policy, social policy, foreign policy). I find little evidence that Republicans are moving substantially to the right on any significant issues. In fact, over the last several decades, they seem to have moved at least somewhat to the left or center.

Do voters have meaningful policy preferences?

Few would argue that policy concerns play no role in vote choice and party identification. We can also reasonably say that not all issues are weighted equally by voters. It is therefore useful to disaggregate issues according to the electorate's ability to understand and care about them. Perhaps unfortunately, there is not necessarily a linear relationship between how much an issue impacts people's material needs and the degree to which voters care about it. Some issues will have extremely important effects on people's wellbeing, but they are also extremely complex and not likely to stir great emotions. Many elements of economic policy would fall into this category. In contrast, some issues are intensely polarizing, but may only impact a small percentage of the population or be more symbolic than substantive. This is arguably the case for many of the ephemeral culture war disputes that briefly attract tremendous attention.

Some work by political scientists suggests policy plays a surprisingly small role in election outcomes. Based on some of this work, one could question whether voters follow policy debates and punish incumbents who support policies they op-

https://doi.org/10.1515/9783111469720-003

pose. Recent literature about the nature of partisanship, which suggests party identification is both durable and primarily driven by social identities, suggests policies are of secondary importance to voters.[1] The fact that some voters will change their policy preferences to be aligned with their party further suggests policy is not a dominant concern for the typical voter.[2] This poses something of a problem for certain theories of democracy, especially those contending that voting based on anything other than public policy concerns is inherently irrational.[3] Rational or not, we may have to accept that non-policy considerations are important to many voters – perhaps most of them.

Even if we accept that policy issues matter to voters, and they do not just become *post-hoc* rationalizations voters use to justify their choices, we can nonetheless expect that some issues are more likely to motivate voters than others. Edward Carmines and James Stimson created the helpful distinction between "easy issues" and "hard issues,"[4] whereby easy issues, according to this dichotomy, are issues that people can form opinions on, even if they are otherwise mostly ignorant about politics or policy. According to Carmines and Stimson, easy issues have three characteristics: "1. The issue would be symbolic, rather than technical. 2. It would more likely deal with policy ends than means. 3. It would be an issue long on the political agenda."[5] They argue that racial desegregation was a quintessential easy issue (their article was written in 1980). In contrast, the subject of US withdrawal from Vietnam had been a hard issue.

Just as we should distinguish easy issues from hard issues, we should disaggregate voters who make decisions based on easy issues from those that focus on hard issues. From a normative perspective, we tend to think highly of voters that make decisions based on issues rather than some other reason. Carmines and Stimson suggest this approach may be mistaken. A voter fired up about an easy issue may possess no more sophistication or knowledge than a voter who uses partisanship or candidate personality to make a decision. After all, "the distinguishing characteristic of the easy issue is that it requires almost nothing of the voter."[6]

---

1 Lilliana Mason and Julie Wronski, "One Tribe to Bind Them All: How Our Social Group Attachments Strengthen Partisanship," *Political Psychology* 39 (2018): 257–277.
2 Michael Barber and Jeremy C. Pope, "Does Party Trump Ideology? Disentangling Party and Ideology in America," *American Political Science Review* 114 (2019): 38–54.
3 For the most influential book taking this perspective, see Anthony Downs, *An Economic Theory of Democracy*, (New York: Harper, 1957).
4 Edward G. Carmines and James A. Stimson, "The Two Faces of Issue Voting," *American Political Science Review* 74 (1980): 78–91.
5 Ibid, 80.
6 Ibid, 85.

Other scholars have since noted that poorly informed voters have a difficult time applying their personal values to hard issues.[7]

More recent research has noted additional examples of easy and hard issues. Abortion has long been a clear example of an easy issue.[8] Even if the specifics of abortion policy can often be quite technical, most people can quickly form a strong opinion on the subject without conducting extensive research. Issues related to homosexuality, such as same-sex marriage, are also sometimes discussed as easy issues.[9]

What issues Republicans say they care about

National surveys asking multiple choice questions about public policy can be helpful tools for scholars. This is especially true of high-quality surveys that ask many of the same questions, year after year. Surveys must be designed and interpreted with great caution, however. Poorly worded questions (whether the result of an inexperienced researcher or an unscrupulous pollster trying to influence the results) can paint a misleading picture of where the public stands.

Multiple-choice surveys about questions of public policy have an additional problem: respondents may not actually have a meaningful opinion on some issues and give answers that are essentially arbitrary. One tool for resolving this problem is to give respondents the option of admitting they do not know the answer or that this is not something they have thought about. An additional problem, especially with online surveys, is that some respondents may simply check boxes without even reading the questions. There are ways to determine whether some interviewees are being careless and to then drop those respondents,[10] but you can never be sure you have resolved all these problems, and you must just hope that these kinds of responses will show up as random noise in the dataset, rather than cause misleading findings.

7 For example, see Lauren Elliott-Dorans, "The Influence of Values on Hard Issue Attitudes," *Journal of Elections, Public Opinion, and Parties* 32(2022): 377–395.
8 Alan I. Abramowitz, "It's Abortion, Stupid: Policy Voting in the 1992 Election," *The Journal of Politics* 57 (1995): 176–186.
9 Heysung Lee, ""Easy" and "Hard" Issues: Attitude Extremity and a Role of the need to Evaluate," *Social Science Quarterly* 102 (2021): 2930–2941.
10 Dominik Johannes Leiner, "Too Fast, too Straight, too Weird: Non-Reactive Indicators for Meaningless Data in Internet Surveys," *Survey Research Methods* 13 (2019): 229–248.

To supplement my examination of preexisting datasets with many questions, as well as my in-person interviews with individuals and small groups, I commissioned a survey of Republicans about their thoughts on policy. Specifically, after asking a small number of basic demographic questions, I asked subjects a simple question: "Politicians are responsible for considering a lot of different issues. In your view, what is the most important government policy issue facing America today?" This was an open-ended question, where they were given space to write an answer, whether brief or long. The survey deliberately did not first ask any other questions related to politics or policy, to avoid priming respondents to think about any particular subject ahead of time.[11]

Working with Qualtrics, I conducted this survey in the summer of 2022. In total, the survey included 1,030 subjects. From this, we can see which issues consistently ranked high among Republicans. The survey did not tell subjects that they were limited to one policy issue. Many subjects provided a long list of issues they considered most important.

Once I had the list of respondents, I categorized different answers. This was not always an easy task. I wanted to work with a reasonable number of possible categories, but fewer categories required lumping things together that may not be alike. Should every expression of concern about the economy (taxes, monetary policy, etc.) just be grouped together in the broader subject of "the economy"? If not, how many different categories of economic issues would be appropriate? It was also not immediately obvious how finely I should slice the subject of foreign policy. After carefully reading every answer, I decided to err on the side of a larger number of categories. Table 3.1 shows the top 20 most common issues mentioned by these Republican respondents.

Many respondents mentioned the economy, but they did not focus on policy specifics. The typical Republican wants a strong economy, with low unemployment and low inflation, but is not apparently concerned with how that goal is achieved. They are not wonks. This is a mistake that many of the more populist-oriented conservative policy advocates seem to make. The typical Republican may say that she opposes things like tax cuts that benefit the rich or that she wants more trade restrictions. That said, the average person, on any side of the political aisle, is mostly ignorant of the specifics of economic policy or how those policies impact the nation's economy. The GOP has not historically built its economic policy agenda based on what polls well. If it did, its platform would be considerably more left-

---

11 For a useful introduction to the concept of priming, see Jon A. Krosnick and Donald R. Kinder, "Altering Foundations of Support for the President through Priming," *The American Political Science Review*, 84 1990): 497–512.

wing. As I will demonstrate shortly, higher taxes on the rich are consistently popular, according to polls, but rarely pursued by Republican politicians. This has not apparently hindered the party's ability to please its voters, most of whom are not personally wealthy.

The survey's first notable result was the overwhelming concern Republicans in this period placed on inflation. Almost half of all respondents (476) listed inflation as one of their top concerns. I should note that, unsurprisingly, although the question specifically asked them about policy, few suggested any policy mechanisms to get it under control. They recognized inflation was happening, it was bad, and they wanted government to fix it, but they did not apparently have much interest in what policies would make that happen. Typical responses related to inflation included, "Inflation that is breaking people and causing a lot of problems in the United States"; "The high prices of food and gas it [sic] crazy ridiculous. We need the prices to be lower and more affordable"; and "The most important government policy issue facing America is inflation and gas and oil prices. We should be drilling our own oil not importing it."

The second most common issue brought up in the survey, mentioned by 160 respondents, was immigration. Views on this subject were not unanimous. Some respondents stated directly that they wanted the federal government to create a pathway to citizenship for undocumented immigrants. Comments expressing nativist views, however, were much more common. As one respondent put it, "Immigration is the most important issue facing America at this time. I think that we should stop making people Americans just because they were born here legally or illegally."

Although it was the second most common issue named as most important by Republicans, it still only represented about 10 percent of the issues mentioned. If we remove those Republicans that wanted a more progressive immigration policy from this category, it becomes an even smaller percentage. Nonetheless, ten percent represents a significant percentage when we compare it to other kinds of issues. Furthermore, many of the anti-immigration Republicans in this sample were caustic in their description of the problem. Republicans who are single-mindedly focused on the immigration issue are far from a majority, but they are a substantial minority, and potentially very significant in Republican primaries. Placating these voters without alienating voters of all races and ethnicities that do not share their nativist views will be a great challenge for the GOP in the years ahead. I will discuss attitudes toward immigration and immigrants in greater detail in Chapter 5.

The next most common issue, mentioned 155 times, was the economy as a broad issue. That is, these respondents wanted the government to do something to make the economy better, but they did not mention which element of the economy they found most troublesome. For example, one respondent just said, "The economy and how bad it is currently, it must get better than it is today."

One common response did not involve policy specifics at all. Seventy-two respondents used the survey as an excuse to criticize President Biden, the Democratic Party, or both, but did not declare what, specifically, they found objectionable. According to one respondent, the key issue to worry about was: "The Democrats and how they are destroying American values and lifestyle. Our country is losing ground with their weak agenda."

I was surprised by how little the Republican respondents seemed to care about certain issues that had been receiving extraordinary attention from the media in preceding months. For some time, the issue of transgender rights, and especially the question of what kind of health care and education policies should be put in place for children that identify as trans, has been one of the leading "culture war" issues in the US. Yet no Republicans in this survey indicated that they considered this one of the most important issues facing the nation. In more than a thousand responses from Republicans, not a single respondent mentioned transgender issues, aside from one oblique reference from someone insisting that economics is all that matters: "Economy is the only thing, not January 6th, not how people identify. Economy only."

The dearth of responses related to COVID-19 and the government's response to the pandemic was also surprising. It is true that, by the summer of 2022, most pandemic-related restrictions were lifted, and vaccines had already proven very effective at reducing hospitalization and death. Given the fact that the disease continued to have a high death toll (though mostly among older people and people with preexisting conditions), and conspiracy theories on the right about the disease, the lockdowns, and the vaccines remained rampant, I was surprised to find that it was not a subject at the forefront of most of these respondents' minds. Only 18 respondents listed COVID as their leading concern. Only three specifically mentioned vaccine mandates as their greatest concern. Once again, the issues that were getting so much attention from Fox News and right-wing voices on X did not correspond to the issues that animated the typical Republican.

The almost total lack of interest in foreign policy questions was also interesting, and likely a dramatic change from Republicans of previous generations – thought leaders on the right used to discuss Soviet aggression and, more recently, radical Islamic terrorism as imminent, existential threats. In my survey, more Republicans expressed concern about climate change than terrorism.

Table 3.1: Top Policy Concerns for Republicans

Issue	Percent
Inflation	31.1
Immigration	10.4
The Economy (General)	10.1
Abortion	5.5
Pres. Biden and/or Democrats	4.7
Crime	3.6
Gun Control	2.9
Government Spending	2.7
Healthcare	2.3
Jobs	2.3
Climate Change	1.6
Partisanship/Polarization	1.4
Taxes	1.4
Racism	1.4
Foreign Policy	1.4
Bad Politicians	1.4
Women's Rights	1.4
Social Security and/or Medicare	1.4
Russia	1.2
COVID-19	1.2

Source: Qualtrics Survey of Republican Voters, summer 2022
Note: Answers the result of open-ended question about issue concerns

The 2020 ANES included a similar question, asking: "What do you think are the most important problems facing this country?" This is obviously different from my own question, which specifically asked about public policy. It is nonetheless worth comparing those results, as they appear to prompt similar kinds of responses, and we can look for continuities and changes over that period. As was the case with my survey, the ANES allowed respondents to name more than one issue. In this analysis, I look only at the first issue ANES respondents listed. Unsurprisingly, in 2020, the year when the US was hit by the COVID-19 pandemic, answers related to health care were the most common answer – about 20 percent gave an answer in that category. About five percent of respondents provided an answer related to elections. This part of the survey was conducted at a time when Republican paranoia about Democrats "stealing" the election from Trump was ramping up. About four percent named "the media" as one of the biggest problems facing the country. I will discuss Republican hostility to mainstream sources of information in the next chapter.

Almost ten percent of Republicans gave an answer related to "unity" or "division" as one of the nation's biggest problems. An additional five percent expressed a concern related to "partisan politics." There is fortunately a contingent of Republicans that find this era of partisan division to be a major problem. About five percent listed a problem related to "race relations."

On this ANES survey, answers related to the economy were relatively uncommon. Well under one percent of Republican respondents listed "foreign trade" or "protection of US jobs" (some of President Trump's major campaign issues in 2016) as the first important problem they cited. About two percent gave an answer related to unemployment. The overall size of government, taxes, budget priorities, and poverty were each named by less than one percent of all Republican respondents. About three percent listed immigration.

Republicans and economic issues

On most economic issues, the Republican Party has focused on the same theme for decades: they are the party of low taxes and smaller government. Conservative elites today continue to praise President Reagan's policy of tax cuts and deregulation. President Trump discussed tax cuts as his signature policy achievement while in office. Although the Republican platform has remained focused on these big ideas, it is an agenda that has surprisingly little popular support, at least if we are looking at survey data. Voters in general, and even Republican voters specifically, are not particularly enthusiastic about tax cuts, at least if they believe they predominantly benefit the wealthy. The Republican electorate is surprisingly ambivalent about the GOP's historical economic agenda. This does not mean that Republican politicians are wrong to pursue these policies, perhaps they count on the economic growth they believe these policies deliver to overcome any misgivings the public may initially have toward them. In any case, it appears that the GOP succeeds in spite of its economic agenda, rather than because it enjoys widespread popular support, even among self-described conservative voters.

Taxes

The Republican Party in government has made many ambitious promises about shrinking the federal government over the last decades. Their list of long-term successes is relatively short. The US federal government has not shrunk, despite many extended periods in which Republicans controlled the White House, the US Congress, and, sometimes, both. The deficit continues to grow. Institutions such as the Department of Education continue to exist. When it comes to the size of government, conservative and libertarian cynics are not completely off base to use the analogy of a ratchet. It does seem to only turn in one direction. When Democrats are in power, it turns quite quickly. When Republicans are in control, the state may grow more slowly (though this is not guaranteed), but it rarely shrinks. When there is a major crisis of any sort, much of the electorate insists that leaders "do something." When the crisis passes, however, there is often little will to undo legislation or shrink government agencies.[12] Although the US has experienced periods in which the federal government pursued deregulation, the general trend has been toward a larger government.

There is one area where Republicans have consistently achieved substantive victories: taxation. To this day, conservatives treat the Reagan tax cuts as a pivotal movement in their party's history. President George H.W. Bush is largely remembered for his broken promise to never raise taxes. His son, President George W. Bush, learned from that history and pursued tax cuts of his own. President Trump did the same. Given that pursuit of lower taxes is now, apparently, an essential characteristic of any Republican with national ambitions, we might reasonably infer that Republican voters feel passionately about this issue.

This inference can be tested easily, as different data sets have asked multiple questions related to this issue. The GSS for example, has asked many different questions relating to taxation over the years. One common progressive critique of the Republican tax agenda is that they consistently pursue "tax cuts for the rich." Conservative economists will respond that this description is unfair. Even if it is technically true that higher earners are more likely to directly benefit from a cut to the income tax, or another source of wealth such as capital gains or dividends, other workers also directly benefit from lower taxes and enjoy indirect benefits from the increased economic activity that tax cuts generate. Whether this is an accurate description of how tax cuts influence the economy is beyond the scope of this book. However, we can determine whether Americans, Republican or otherwise, believe the tax burden on the wealthy is too high.

In four separate years (1987, 2000, 2008, and 2021), the GSS has asked respondents whether "people with high incomes should pay a larger share of their income in taxes than those with low incomes, the same share, or a smaller share." Every time the question was asked, large majorities responded that the rich should pay more taxes. In 2021, the percentage that wanted the rich to pay a "larger" or a "much larger" share was about 71 percent. Unsurprisingly, when we restrict the sample to Republicans, the percentage drops, but not as much as you would expect if you assumed Republican voters are obsessive tax cutters. About 51 percent of Re-

---

12 For a scholarly treatment of this phenomenon, see Robert Higgs, *Crisis and Leviathan: Critical Episodes in the Growth of American Government* (New York: Oxford University Press, 1987).

publican GSS respondents thought the rich should pay more taxes. In that year, only about five percent of Republicans believed the rich should pay a "smaller" or a "much smaller share." The Republican electorate, overall, supports a relatively progressive tax system.

Other surveys show similar findings for taxes. In the 2020 ANES, respondents were asked, "Do you favor, oppose, or neither favor nor oppose increasing income taxes on people making over one million dollars per year?" A plurality of Republican respondents (about 42 percent) favored raising taxes on people making at least this much money. About 29 percent opposed this policy and about 30 percent neither favored nor opposed it. Republicans are much more skeptical about tax increases than Democrats and independents, but they are not uniformly opposed to higher taxes, especially on people with high incomes.

This is not to say that Republican elected officials have a free hand to raise taxes without paying a political cost. Support for higher taxes, unsurprisingly, is lower among wealthier Republicans, a group that undoubtedly has a lot of influence within the party. Republican officials may furthermore be more concerned with aggregate economic growth, which they hope tax cuts will promote, rather than how well specific economic policies perform in polling before they are implemented. I spoke with some Republicans who still considered the tax issue as central to their understanding of the party's ideology. As one interviewee put it, "I think the tax cut passed under Trump was one of his accomplishments."

Spending

Given how difficult Republicans in Congress and the White House have found it to cut spending, we could reasonably infer that spending cuts are unpopular. However, it may be the case that the electorate is polarized on this issue, with Democrats (who historically have had an edge over Republicans when it comes to party identification) almost universally opposing any cuts, and Republicans in the electorate desperately wanting them, but never enjoying sufficient political power to do so. Polling data can once again give us some indication of Republican attitudes toward spending both in general and on specific programs.

Over its history, the ANES has asked many questions about spending. It will be useful to first see how different partisan groups feel about spending in a general sense. For many years, the survey has asked some variation of the question, "Some people think the government should provide fewer services, even in areas such as health and education, in order to reduce spending. Where would you place yourself on this scale, or haven't you thought much about this?" The scale ranges from one to seven, with a higher value associated with a greater preference for higher spending. This question has been asked consistently since 1992. In figure 3.1, we see the trend for supporters of both parties.

Unsurprisingly, we see that Democrats have consistently been more in favor of higher spending levels than Republicans, on average. We additionally see that Republicans in 2020 are very similar to Republicans in 1992. In between, there was some movement. The Republican preference for higher spending reached its peak in 2004. In 2020, the gap between the parties reached an all-time high, but this was mostly because Democrats' support for higher spending reached an all-time high. It is interesting, however, that the two parties seem to move together on this question. There is always a gap, but when Democrats increase their support for higher levels of government spending, Republicans seem to move in the same direction.

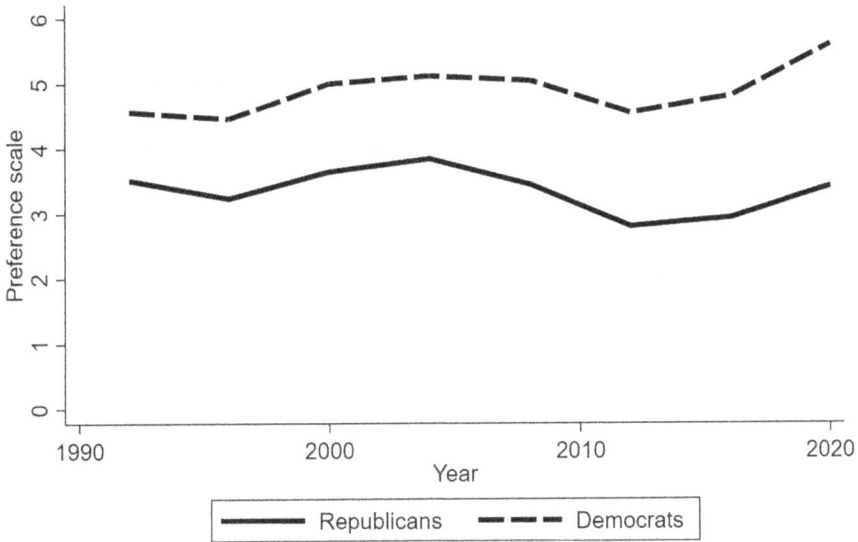

Figure 3.1: Support for Spending More on Gov. Services. Source: Cumulative ANES. Note: Higher values indicate support for more spending.

This question about greater spending is quite generic, however. It is easy to favor spending cuts when presented in an abstract manner. These Republicans may think they are only targeting "waste, fraud, and abuse." The 2020 ANES asked subjects questions about different programs and kinds of spending, asking whether the government should spend more money on them, less, or maintain current levels. When presented in this way, Republicans become much more ambivalent about spending cuts.

For spending on anything related to law and order, there was almost no desire among Republicans for cuts. Only about four percent of Republicans wanted to spend less money "dealing with crime." Keep in mind that this survey was conducted during 2020, a period when the "defund the police" movement experienced a surge of attention. If that movement was seeking to expand support for its agenda across the political spectrum, it was clearly not successful. Almost 70 percent of Republicans wanted to increase federal spending on crime prevention. The wording does not specify how that money would be spent, but I suspect most of these Republican respondents were thinking specifically about police, rather than other policies related to crime prevention – such as additional social workers and mental health counselors. A comparable percentage of Republicans supported spending less money on border security. Only about five percent of Republicans thought the government should spend less money on securing the nation's border. The overwhelming majority wanted to spend more.

Republicans were also very opposed to spending cuts on infrastructure. Only about three percent were in favor of reducing federal spending on "building and repairing highways." Almost 60 percent wanted the federal government to spend more on these projects. This kind of infrastructure spending has very large bipartisan support and may be an issue where the two parties could reach some kind of compromise in the future without seriously alienating either side's supporters.

Republicans in the electorate were even generally favorable toward federal spending on environmental protection. Only about 16 percent wanted to see less money spent on this issue. About twice as many wanted to spend more. The rest thought current spending levels were about right. Attacking the Environmental Protection Agency and other efforts to safeguard the environment may be common themes in conservative discourse, but among ordinary Republicans, it is clearly not a high priority. The same is true of education. Republican leaders have long excoriated the Department of Education. President Reagan famously promised to abolish it, only to back down.[13] According to the 2020 ANES, only about 12 percent of Republicans wanted to cut federal spending on public schools. I should note that this survey predates the most recent controversies about Critical Race Theory in public schools, as well as the recent heated debates about how (if at all) school children should be informed about issues relating to the LGBT communities. It is possible that there has been a subsequent rise in Republicans hostility toward public schools not captured by these data. Republicans are also, on average, very opposed

---

13 Dan Bauman and Brock Read, "A Brief History of GOP Attempts to Kill the Education Dept," *The Chronicle of Higher Education*, June 21, 2018, https://www.chronicle.com/article/a-brief-history-of-gop-attempts-to-kill-the-education-dept/.

to reduced spending on Social Security – a program that consumes a considerable percentage of the federal budget. Only about seven percent of Republicans supported cuts to Social Security, and about 47 percent wanted to see Social Security spending increased. This may be a function of Republicans being much more likely to be older.

Of the spending questions on the 2020 ANES, there was only one on which a majority of Republicans said the federal government should spend less, and that was on "welfare programs." Even here, it was only a very narrow majority that favored cuts. This may furthermore be an issue where question wording is extremely important. Although a little over 50 percent of Republicans said they wanted to see cuts in welfare, only about one in five Republicans wanted to reduce "aid to the poor." Granted, "aid to the poor" could mean many things beyond cash welfare payments. However, I take this as evidence that "welfare" as a concept has been very effectively demonized within conservative Republican discourse, to the point that attitudes toward government assistance will vary tremendously depending on whether or not that particular word is used to describe it.

We should keep in mind that the concept of welfare has also been heavily racialized, and this has helped turn public opinion against expanded welfare benefits. "Welfare" has come to be viewed as primarily benefiting racial minorities, especially African Americans. As such, it is often viewed less as a means of helping the unfortunate get through a difficult time than a stealthy form of racial wealth redistribution.[14] When Ronald Reagan lambasted "welfare queens" living the high life on taxpayer dollars, listeners understood that he was speaking specifically about African Americans in urban areas.[15]

Republican voters may also think of Social Security as distinct from welfare because they feel as though they spent their working life paying into Social Security, and that the checks they receive upon retirement is simply the government paying their own money back to them. This is not how Social Security actually works, of course. It is not the case that the Social Security benefits are simply your own dollars being paid back to you after a few decades in a vault somewhere, nor will the amount of Social Security you receive over your lifetime necessarily match what you paid into the system over your working career.[16]

---

14 Martin Gilens, *Why Americans Hate Welfare: Race, Media, and the Politics of Antipoverty Policy*, (Chicago, IL: University of Chicago Press, 1999).
15 Jill Quadagno, *The Color of Welfare: How Racism Undermined the War on Poverty*, (New York: Oxford University Press, 1996).
16 For an example of someone attempting to work out the numbers on this issue, see Patrick W. Watson, "You Haven't Earned Your Social Security – It's Welfare," *Forbes*, July 9, 2018, https://www.

Trade

Foreign trade was a key issue for the 2016 Trump campaign. This was also a case in which the Trump Administration made at least some effort to follow through on its promises, seeking to renegotiate trade deals, while also breaking with the pro-trade precedent set by previous Republican presidents. The economic results of these efforts are questionable, as is the premise that foreign trade harms the US interests. Trade is also the least controversial aspect of Trumpian right-wing populism. Economic protectionism has many critics that make important points worth considering, but nativist immigration policies prompt a furious backlash from progressives in a way that trade policy does not.

Before Trump, other major populists had made foreign trade a central element of their campaigns. Ross Perot ran for president on an anti-free-trade platform, with a special emphasis on opposing NAFTA. Pat Buchanan similarly campaigned on a promise to implement new trade restrictions and bring manufacturing back to America. This was also a central element to several of his books.[17]

In the decades preceding Trump's first presidential campaign, the Republican Party, at least compared to the Democratic Party, tended to be the party of free trade. Opposition to trade was more frequently associated with progressive politics, especially labor unions. This was not the case for the entirety of the Republican Party's history, however. In the nineteenth century, like the Whigs before them, the Republican Party believed in protectionism as a means of encouraging native industry. Perhaps that protectionism was a mistake, but it is certainly true that the US did become a global economic powerhouse while maintaining high tariffs – I leave it to more qualified scholars to debate whether that growth would have been even faster under a free-trade system.

Certain moderate populists would like to keep the attention on the supposedly deleterious effects of contemporary US trade policies,[18] and their case is strength-

---

forbes.com/sites/patrickwwatson/2018/07/09/you-havent-earned-your-social-security-its-welfare/?
sh=70d2fabb6fe6.

17 For example, See Patrick J. Buchanan, *Where the Right Went Wrong: How Neoconservatives Subverted the Reagan Revolution and Hijacked the Bush Presidency* (New York: St. Martin's Press, 2004); Patrick J. Buchanan, *The Great Betrayal: How American Sovereignty and Social Justice are Being Sacrificed to the Gods of the Global Economy* (Boston, MA: Little Brown, 1998).

18 Oren Cass of American Compass, for example, has been one voice making the case for a new conservative approach to trade questions. For an example of his argument, see Oren Cass, "Searching for Capitalism in the Wreckage of Globalization," *American Compass*, March 9, 2022, https://americancompass.org/essays/searching-for-capitalism-in-the-wreckage-of-globalization/.

ened by the fact that Trump won the presidency making strong claims about trade. It is not immediately obvious that trade is an issue that voters care very much about. It is true that economic and political elites tend to be more favorable toward free trade than the general public,[19] but the electorate does not appear to give the issue very much attention.

Trade may be one of those issues where public opinion matters very little because it is a quintessential "hard issue." People know that they do not like it when factories close, but discerning which trade policy (if any) was responsible for the closure of any specific plant may be difficult. Following the debates and negotiations that revolve around trade issues, and developing strong feelings about what represents the best possible policy, requires a higher level of political sophistication than, say, having an opinion on culture war issues such as "drag queen story hour" at libraries. There is some evidence that trade policy is at least partially sensitive to public opinion, but only in a very general sense – democracies where the public is strongly free-trade tend to have lower tariffs.[20] It may also be the case that support for free trade can be bolstered if the government takes steps to compensate people in industries that are harmed by new agreements.[21] Nonetheless, we should not overstate the general public's ability to understand trade policy or the ways trade policy could impact their own lives. Unlike other kinds of economic policies, people tend to have a harder time connecting changes to trade policies to their own economic prospects.[22]

The CES asks several questions about hypothetical tariffs. From this survey we immediately see that, at least in 2020, trade protectionism was extremely popular among ordinary Republican voters. On the question of whether the US should place "tariffs on $200 billion worth of goods imported from China," about 86 percent of Republicans supported the policy. Democrats were more split, with a slight majority opposing the idea. CES respondents were also asked about their feelings about "25 % tariffs on imported steel and 10 % on imported aluminum." The question was asked in two different ways, one specifying that the tariff would not apply to Canada and Mexico, and the other noting that it would apply to those countries. When told that the policy exempted other North American countries, about 72 percent of

---

19 Hong Min Park and George Hawley, "Determinants of the Opinion Gap between Elites and the Public in the United States," *The Social Science Journal* 57 (2020): 1–13.

20 Daniel Y. Kono, "Does Public Opinion Affect Trade Policy?" *Business and Politics* 10 (2008): 1–19.

21 Sean D. Ehrlich and Eddie Hearn, "Does Compensating the Losers Increase Support for Trade? An Experimental Test of the Embedded Liberalism Thesis," *Foreign Policy Analysis* 10 (2014): 149–164.

22 Sungmin Rho and Michael Tomz, "Why Don't Trade Preferences Reflect Economic Self-Interest?" *International Organization* 71 (2017): 86–108.

Republicans supported the policy. Without the exemption, however, Republican support dropped just below 50 percent. Finally, the CES asked respondents how they felt about increased "tariffs on European aircraft and agricultural products." We once again see a clear partisan divide, with about two-thirds of Republicans supporting the policy, and a comparable percentage of Democrats opposing it.

The trade questions in the CES are potentially problematic, however. Respondents were only given the option of supporting or opposing a policy. Having no opinion or admitting to having no knowledge of the subject were not options. This makes it very likely that a large percentage of respondents expressed a preference for something they had never thought about before. We can be confident that a large percentage of these respondents would have declined to offer an opinion, because that is what happened in the 2020 ANES, which also asked questions about trade, but gave respondents the opportunity to say they "neither favor nor oppose" the policy. On the question asking respondents whether they "favor or oppose free trade agreements with other countries," just under half of all respondents did not favor or oppose the policy. Once again, however, Democrats were more in favor of free trade agreements than Republicans in 2020.

Although we must include some strong caveats when commenting on these data, it is interesting to see that Republicans in 2020 were, on average, much more negative toward free trade than Democrats. Donald Trump is the most likely explanation for this partisan divide. By attacking the existing trade agreements, Trump sent a strong signal to the electorate on an issue many voters likely did not think or care about very much, and people subsequently determined their attitude toward trade largely based on their feelings toward Trump.

By looking at opinions on trade before Trump became a political figure, we can make some sense of how much he has influenced opinions on this issue. Although it unfortunately did not ask questions identical to what was included in the 2020 CES, the 2012 CES did ask respondents a question about trade. Specifically, it asked respondents if they favored or opposed a new free trade agreement with South Korea. In that year, when trade was not a high-profile partisan issue, Republicans and Democrats were almost identical. About 53 percent of Republicans supported the policy, versus about 51 percent of Democrats. Although not definitive, this suggests that Trump was personally responsible for the Republican electorate's turn toward protectionism. The next question is whether Republican voters' new opposition to free trade will remain intact after Trump exits the political stage. As far as I can tell, most Republican elites continue to hold the generally pro-trade positions they have held for decades. Without Trump pushing the issue, I would not be surprised to see trade once again become a low-salience issue not strongly connected to partisanship.

Environmental protection

As I previously noted, most Republicans in the electorate are at least theoretically open to the idea of using the federal government to safeguard the environment. At the very least, only a minority would favor cutting federal spending on the subject. This unfortunately tells us very little about the kinds of substantive policies that the average Republican voter would support. Being in favor of "protecting the environment" could mean nothing more than favoring the continued existence of national parks. It could also mean abolishing transportation via fossil fuels. Making sense of public opinion on environmental policy requires follow-up questions.

Environmental policy might be an issue where progressives can reasonably argue that experts, rather than public opinion, should be the main determinant of policy. After all, relatively few Americans understand the basic science of climate change, and they are certainly not qualified to interpret more sophisticated models. On the other hand, one could make the same argument about many kinds of policies. Voters having a say on issues they often do not really understand is apparently an unescapable element of democracy. The predictions of even honest, non-ideological, and careful scientists and other experts are often surprisingly wrong, suggesting that we should be careful before treating experts as infallible and deserving of a free hand to make whatever policies they think best.[23]

Environmental policy is unquestionably influenced by elections. Republicans in power are much less likely to support creating new environmental protections and often call for dismantling existing regulations. The two parties in congress furthermore seem to have moved farther apart on environmental issues over time.[24] The same is true for the parties in the electorate.[25]

One may question whether public opinion even matters when it comes to policy making about the environment, again because the topic can be quite complex. Furthermore, the number of people who determine their vote choice based on environmental concerns is probably small. People strongly invested in new environmental regulations are probably already strongly committed to the Democrats for many other reasons, and it will probably not change their vote even if their party

---

23 For a good explanation of the pros and cons of expert deference, see Ilya Somin, "When Should Voters Defer to the Views of Scientists?" *The Washington Post*, February 3, 2015, https://www.washingtonpost.com/news/volokh-conspiracy/wp/2015/02/03/when-should-voters-defer-to-the-views-of-scientists/.
24 Charles R. Shipan and William R. Lowry, "Environmental Policy and Policy Divergence in Congress," *Political Research Quarterly* 54 (2001): 245–263.
25 Riley E. Dunlap and Araon M. McCright, "A Widening Gap: Republican and Democratic Views on Climate Change," *Environment: Science and Policy for Sustainable Development* 50 (2008): 26–35.

fails to deliver substantive legislation. Several studies, however, have indicated that public attitudes can be an important predictor of policy outcomes related to the environment.[26]

Relying on public opinion to force politicians to pursue environmental legislation is potentially very difficult. The environmental movement suffers a collective action problem.[27] When discussed in generalities, legislation protecting the environment is very popular. Often new regulations place very high costs on narrow interests, however, and those businesses and property owners potentially affected by new policies will fight very hard to stop them or at least mitigate their disrupting effects. In contrast, a clean environment is a non-excludable public good. Although the environmental movement has a legion of dedicated activists, it is nonetheless at a disadvantage unless there is a critical mass of the population that truly does believe that climate change and other environmental issues represent an existential crisis. Given the degree to which American voters were apoplectic over high gas prices in 2022, it seems fair to infer that the typical American is not willing to pay substantially higher energy costs in the name of improving the environment.

We can probably take it for granted that, for the foreseeable future, the Democratic Party will take the lead on new environmental policies, though perhaps the Republicans will contribute some novel, market-based solutions to various problems. It is nonetheless worth investigating what the average Republican thinks about these issues, if only to get a sense of how hard they will push their party to stand against new progressive policies.

Although not directly related to policy, the 2020 ANES asked respondents how much climate change is affecting the weather in the US. A sizable minority of Republicans (a bit under 20 percent), believed climate change was not having any impact at all. However, all other Republicans seemed to believe climate change was at least a real phenomenon, and almost a quarter said climate change was affecting the temperature either "a lot" or "a great deal." These numbers suggest Republican resistance to efforts to combat climate change may be overstated, at least if we are thinking about ordinary Republican voters rather than elites. However, it is also undeniably the case that Republicans are less concerned about this issue than non-Republicans. Among non-Republican respondents to the 2020 ANES, only

---

26 Clara Vandeweerdt, Bart Kerremans, and Avery Cohn, "Climate Voting in the U.S. Congress: The Power of Public Concern," *Environmental Politics* 25 (2016): 268–288; Richard J. McAlexander, and Johannes Urpelainen, "Elections and Policy Responsiveness: Evidence from Environmental Voting in the U.S. Congress," *Review of Policy Research* 37 (2020): 39–63.
27 Mancur Olson, *The Logic of Collective Action: Public Goods and the Theory of Groups* (Cambridge, MA: Harvard University Press, 1965).

about three percent stated that climate change was having no impact on the US, and over 70 percent said its effect was "a lot" or a "great deal." Republicans also differ from other Americans in their level of concern about climate change. When asked how important they considered the issue, more than one quarter said climate change was "not at all important." About eight percent considered it "extremely important." By contrast, among non-Republicans, only about three percent thought it was not important at all, and almost 38 percent considered it "extremely important."

When thinking about environmental policy, it is of course important to consider trade-offs. One could conceivably reduce climate change drastically by immediately banning the use of all fossil fuels. The problem with such a plan is that it would instantly crash the global economy, and probably cause more human suffering than we could expect from even the most pessimistic climate change models. The ANES helpfully provides a question that asks subjects to think about the trade-off between environmental protection and economic growth and dynamism.[28] Subjects were asked to place themselves on a seven-point scale, with one representing the greatest concern for the environment and enthusiasm for being "tougher" on business, and seven being the position most concerned about the "burden on business." Among Republicans, the mean score on this scale was about 4.5, which indicates that they, on average, are more concerned about business. Among non-Republicans, the mean score was just about two. Republicans are also, on average, very skeptical about giving the government the authority to regulate carbon. According to the 2022 CES, only about 38 percent supported giving the "Environmental Protection Agency power to regulate carbon dioxide emissions." Among the population overall, more than two-thirds supported this policy. Among Democrats, about 92 percent supported giving the Environmental Protection Agency this authority.

In my survey asking Republicans which issues they cared about the most, respondents rarely mentioned environmental issues. Some of those who referred to this topic stated directly that they wanted to see fewer regulations, especially as it relates to energy. One respondent stated that he wanted the government to focus on "becoming energy independent instead of trying to go green." Another said, "Energy Independence. Our country has the capability to be independent we have the resources to not have to rely on any other country." For some of these

---

28 The question is worded as follows: "Some people think we need much tougher government regulations on business in order to protect the environment. Suppose these people are at one end of a scale, at point 1. Others think that current regulations to protect the environment are already too much of a burden on business. Suppose these people are at the other end, at point 7. And, of course, some other people have opinions somewhere in between, at points 2,3,4,5, or 6."

Republicans, energy policy was an important element of international relations, rather than an environmental issue.

Although Republicans, on average, are unquestionably less concerned about environmental issues, especially climate change, than Democrats, it is not the case that Republican voters in the electorate are united on this issue. Several survey respondents directly stated that the environment was their top concern. Sometimes their comments on the subject were vague ("Environment conservation for future generations to prosper and survive in a healthy manner.") Others were more specific ("The most important policy issue facing us today would have to be awareness of the environment. Take the Chinook Salmon population and the need to breach the Snake River Dams for example.")

Twenty-five respondents directly stated that climate change was one of their top concerns. Among Democrats, this percentage would surely have been higher, but it does indicate that Republican voters are not united in opposition to new environmental regulations. As one Republican put it, the greatest problem is "the environment generally, specifically climate change which I strongly believe is real and dangerous." A few others suggested that climate change represented a real existential threat to the world. For example, one respondent said, "There are too many storms, fires, flooding throughout USA due to climate change. We must address this." One respondent even stated that the Republican Party was directly to blame for the government's failure to act on this issue. According to this person, the most important issue is "climate problems due to pollution, which is causing forest fires, floods, and extreme weather conditions in this country, and the inability of Republican leaders to acknowledge these problems and work with Democrats to solve this important problem."

It was uncommon for Republicans in this survey to declare that they opposed environmental regulations as such. Although this is difficult to demonstrate empirically, Republican hostility toward environmentalists seems to have declined in recent decades – alternatively, environmental issues may be less salient for them than they once were, and they are less likely to bring them up unprompted. In my survey, some respondents did express skepticism about environmentalists' claims, however. As one Republican put it, we are "sacrificing all for environmental concerns."

Some social scientists concerned about climate change have sought to determine whether Republicans in the electorate can be persuaded that anthropogenic climate change is real and has significant negative consequences. This appears to be a difficult task, as partisan polarization on this issue seems to be increasing.[29]

---

29 Riley E. Dunlap, Aaron M. McCright, and Jerrod H. Yarosh, "The Political Divide on Climate

Some research indicates that educational campaigns can shift Republican opinions at least somewhat.[30] It does not appear, however, that personal experience with changing weather patterns (droughts, unusually warm winters, etc.) has much of an influence on individual views.[31] Cues from trusted elites, however, seem to have a much greater effect – far more than trying to promote scientific information among the public in a non-partisan manner.[32] Given the current trends among conservative opinion leaders and the most prominent Republicans, a major change within the Republican Party in the electorate seems unlikely, at least in the short term.

Given the minority of Republican respondents that were intensely concerned about climate change and the environment more broadly, we should not overstate Republican opposition to environmental regulations. Nonetheless, although there is not a specific cut-off delineating polarized from non-polarized opinion, the partisan differences when it comes to the environment are real and substantial, at both the elite level and in the broader electorate. For that reason, developing new environmental regulations that could enjoy widespread bipartisan support at present seems like a quixotic task. Truly sweeping and comprehensive policies at the federal level will probably only be likely during periods when the Democratic Party enjoys majorities in congress and controls the presidency.

Affirmative action and government efforts to assist minorities

I was ambivalent about where to include this section. Discussions of affirmative action are closely tied to questions about explicit racism, as well as racial resentment. One could also make the case that this subject is better characterized as a social issue rather than an economic one. Survey questions on this theme relate directly to the economic well-being of minority groups, however, and thus I feel

Change: Partisan Polarization Widens in the U.S." *Environment: Science and Policy for Sustainable Development* 58 (2016): 4–23.

30 Matthew H. Goldberg, Abel Gustafson, Seth A. Rosenthal, and Anthony Leiserowitz, "Shifting Republican Views on Climate Change through Targeted Advertising," *Nature Climate Change* 11 (2021): 573–577.

31 Risa Palm, Gregory B. Lewis, and Bo Feng, "What Causes People to Change their Opinion about Climate Change?" *Annals of the American Association of Geographers* 107 (2017): 883–896.

32 Robert J. Brulle, Jason Carmichael, and J. Craig Jenkins, "Shifting Public Opinion on Climate Change: An Empirical Assessment of Factors Influencing Concern over Climate Change in the U.S., 2002–2010," *Climate Change* 114 (2012): 169–188.

it is appropriate to discuss the issue here. I address other questions related to race in Chapter 6.

The ANES has consistently asked questions about how much assistance the government should provide to African Americans. Specifically, it has asked,

> Some people feel that the government in Washington should make every effort to improve the social and economic position of blacks. Suppose these people are at one end of a scale, at point 1). Others feel that the government should not make any special effort to help blacks because they should help themselves. Suppose these people are at the other end, at point 7. And, of course, some other people have opinions somewhere in between, at points 2,3,4,5 or 6). Where would you place yourself on this scale, or haven't you thought much about it?

On this question, we see very little change over time. White Republicans are overwhelmingly opposed to government efforts designed specifically to help blacks, and they have been for decades. The mean score for Republicans on this question was about 5.3 in 2000, and 5.1 in 2020 – recall that, on this scale, a higher score is associated with less support for greater aid to government assistance for African Americans. Once again, the real movement on this issue has occurred among Democrats. In 2000, the mean Democratic score on the variable was about 4.2. In 2020, it dropped to about 2.6, indicating that, over the last two decades, Democrats have become much more supportive of government efforts to uplift African Americans, whereas Republicans have stayed about the same.

Affirmative action is a more specific example of this kind of policy, made especially salient by the Supreme Court's recent decision to ban the use of affirmative action in university enrollment. Again, the ANES can give us an indication of change over time. For many years, the survey has asked, "Some people say that because of past discrimination blacks should be given preference in hiring and promotion. Others say that such preference in hiring and promotion of blacks is wrong because it gives blacks advantages they haven't earned. What about your opinion– are you for or against preferential hiring and promotion of blacks?" In 2000, almost 94 percent of Republicans opposed affirmative action, at least when framed in those words. This is about as close to a uniform opinion that we find in either party over a policy issue. By 2020, this percentage had barely moved at all – in that year, it was about 90 percent. Democrats, in contrast, have shifted a massive amount on this issue. As of 2000, only about 26 percent of Democrats expressed support for affirmative action. In 2020, this almost doubled, to just about 52 percent. It is notable that, despite this major shift among Democrats, in the aggregate, a large majority of the American electorate overall remains opposed to affirmative action.

Republicans and social issues

Social issues have long been a central element of the Republican Party's electoral strategy for decades. The fights over civil rights, especially desegregation, were pivotal to the realignment of Southern whites from the Democratic Party to the Republican Party. The rise of the Christian Right, which was itself a response to many secularizing trends in the US, further raised the salience of social issues. Supreme Court decisions ending prayer in schools, the gay liberation movement, increasing rates of divorce and out-of-wedlock births, and declining religiosity all attributed to the sense among cultural conservatives that the nation was being taken over by secular progressives. Republicans who emphasized these cultural anxieties often enjoyed considerable electoral dividends.

The shifting of politics toward cultural fights that Republicans tended to win, as opposed to bread-and-butter economic issues where Democrats had an advantage, frustrated some progressives. A new narrative formed among some progressive pundits, as they argued that Republicans were using cultural anxieties to convince people to vote against their economic interests. The public's attention turned toward largely symbolic fights over cultural issues that have little impact on their material well-being. The most significant work in this genre is Thomas Frank's bestselling book, *What's the Matter with Kansas?*[33] Frank's narrative suggests that poor, white, rural voters were consistently voting against the party that would pass legislation that would improve their lives in order to support the party that promised to punish their cultural enemies, but in practical terms just enriched the wealthy at their expense.

This description of US politics has been challenged by some social scientists, however. Andrew Gelman and his colleagues have suggested that Frank's description of US politics is incorrect, arguing that poor Americans in red states are not significantly different from poor Americans in blue states. Instead, their analysis of the relevant data indicates that the difference between these states is really found among economic elites. In strongly Republican states, the economic elites are overwhelmingly Republican, which is hardly surprising. The more interesting finding is that in the wealthier, more Democratic states, the elites lean toward the Democratic Party. Put another way, rather than focusing on why poor people in Kansas vote for Republicans (which they do not do in greater numbers than poor people else-

---

33 Thomas Frank, *What's the Matter with Kansas? How Conservatives Won the Heart of America* (New York: Henry Holt and Company, 2004).

where), it is more interesting to know why rich people in Connecticut vote against their own economic interests by voting for Democrats.[34]

Abortion

At present, evangelical Christians are, on average, one of the most consistently anti-abortion religious groups in America. This has not always been the case. The pro-life movement was once a predominantly Catholic phenomenon, as the theological position that life begins at the moment of conception has consistently been held by Roman Catholics. But Protestant thinking on the matter varies considerably by denomination, and the official stances of many denominations has changed over time. As recently as the early 1970s, the Southern Baptist Convention, the nation's largest Protestant denomination and considered by many to be the quintessential evangelical denomination in the US, was officially pro-choice.[35]

It was not really until the late 1970s, thanks in large part to Francis Schaefer and other pro-life evangelists, that a large percentage of Protestants became sufficiently outraged at the practice to politically mobilize over the issue. The movement of evangelical Protestants into the pro-life camp was also an important step toward the creation of an ecumenical religious right, one in which people from different faith traditions put aside their theological disagreements to focus on their shared political goals. For much of US history, theologically conservative Protestants were intensely hostile to Catholics, viewing them as a threat to republican values and the nation's Protestant identity. In recent decades, conservative Catholics and conservative Protestants have locked arms in pursuit of a common political agenda.

Abortion was not the entire reason for the religious right's creation. Opposition to racial integration in schools and the tax status of new private religious schools was initially a more important issue for the nascent religious right. It was also galvanized in the late 1970s by the issue of gay rights, with activists such as Anita Bryant leading the fight against the gay-rights movement. Renewed interest in "End Times" prophesies in the Bible also caused many Christians to take a new interest in foreign policy, especially events in the Middle East. Many Christians believed that the creation of Israel as in independent state following World

---

34 Andrew Gelman, David Park, Boris Shor, and Jeronimo Cortina, *Red State, Blue State, Rich State, Poor State: Why Americans Vote the Way they Do (Expanded Edition)* (Princeton, NJ: Princeton University Press, 2010).

35 Andrew R. Lewis, "Abortion Politics and the Decline of the Separation of Church and State: The Southern Baptist Case," *Politics and Religion* 7(2014): 521–549.

War Two was sign that Christ would soon return. None of these other issues, however, have led to the kind of sustained and energetic activism we have seen on the abortion issue.

As I was writing this book, the pro-life movement won a victory it had sought for more than 40 years. *Roe v. Wade*, the Supreme Court decision that guaranteed access to abortion nationwide, was overturned. This did not signal the end of the abortion fight, however; it simply moved the battle back to the states. This may result in abortion becoming even more contentious as a policy issue.

The ANES has consistently asked respondents their views on the abortion question, allowing us to discern the general trend on this issue for all partisan groups. Respondents have been asked to choose between four different options when it comes to abortion: "1. Abortion should never be permitted. 2. Abortion should be permitted only if the life and health of the woman is in danger. 3. Abortion should be permitted if, due to personal reasons, the woman would have difficulty in caring for the child. 4. Abortion should never be forbidden, since one should not require a woman to have a child she doesn't want." To simplify this analysis, I combined the two most restrictive options into a single category.

Here we see a case where there is a genuine trend toward polarization on a policy issue, with Republicans becoming more conservative and Democrats becoming more progressive. As of 1980, there was little difference between Republicans and Democrats on this issue. About 44 percent of Democrats supported one of these restrictive policies, compared to about 42 percent of Republican.

The gap grew in the 1990s, as Republicans became increasingly conservative, and by 2000, a slight majority of Republicans favored a drastically more restrictive approach to abortion policy. Over the last several election cycles, Democrats, in contrast, have increasingly rejected this approach. Pro-life Democrats, once a fairly common element of the electorate, are now an endangered species. In 2020, the two parties had become truly polarized along partisan lines on this issue. About 58 percent of Republicans supported strong restrictions on abortion, compared to about 17 percent of Democrats. This is one of those rare issues where we have seen a significant move in a more conservative direction within the Republican Party. Even here, however, we see much more movement among Democrats. This change in the electorate is driven, in part, by changes in elite discourse. As the leading figures of the two major parties became more consistently divided over this issue, leaving few prominent pro-life Democrats or pro-choice Republicans, voters slowly shifted their views in response.[36]

---

36 Greg D. Adams, "Abortion: Evidence of an Issue Evolution," *American Journal of Political Science* 41 (1997): 718–737; Edward G. Carmines, Jessica C. Gerrity, and Michael W. Wagner, "How Abor-

Anti-LGBT discrimination and same-sex marriage

Gay rights is another issue where specific policy positions and broader cultural attitudes are difficult to disentangle. I will discuss Republican feelings on the broader question of LGBT people in Chapter 5. On the question of policy, however, we have witnessed a sea change in public opinion when it comes to LGBT issues. Many people may not notice this, given that public discussions of this subject seem to be more heated than ever. However, tolerance toward gays and lesbians in America has increased dramatically over the last two decades, including among Republicans. Not long ago, same-sex marriage was a bitter, partisan issue. It was also strongly opposed by large majorities of the electorate. In 2004, Republicans were accused of cynically putting anti-same-sex marriage initiatives on the ballot in states across the country in the hope of maximizing voter turnout among Americans opposed to same-sex marriage. As recently as 2008, a ban on same-sex marriage passed in California, a quintessential blue state that President Obama easily carried that same year.

There can be no doubt that, between the two parties, Democrats in both leadership positions and in the electorate have been, on average, more enthusiastic about promoting LGBT rights than the Republicans. Though, within relatively recent memory, same-sex marriage was not a popular idea within either major party. The more interesting question is how Republicans' feelings have evolved over time. The ANES has asked a question over many election cycles that can help us make sense of this. It has asked respondents in many surveys: "Do you favor or oppose laws to protect gays and lesbians against job discrimination?" As far back as 2000, a majority of Republicans (about 57 percent), declared that they favored such laws. By 2020, that percentage had risen to more than 80 percent. Perhaps the results would have been different if the question was worded more specifically, and this tells us nothing about how they deal with individuals in their own lives, but this finding is nonetheless remarkable in that it seems so at odds with the notion that the typical Republican is intensely hostile to sexual minorities.

Feeling thermometer scores also show that Republicans have become more favorable to gay Americans. In 2000, the mean Republican feeling thermometer score was just about 42 – cool compared to most other social groups. By 2020, that mean score had risen to about 54. That is still not particularly warm, but the direction has been moving toward higher levels of tolerance.

---

tion Became a Partisan Issue: Media Coverage of the Interest Group-Political Party Connection," *P&P: Politics and Policy* 38 (2010): 1135–1158.

What about the more specific question of same-sex marriage? In 2004, the ANES asked respondents the following question: "Should same-sex couples be allowed to marry, or do you think they should not be allowed to marry?"[37] Respondents could choose between allowing them to marry, allow them to form civil unions but not marriages, neither, or some other option. In that year, more than three quarters of Republicans stated that they did not support same-sex marriage or a system of civil unions.

By 2020, attitudes among Republicans had shifted a great deal. In the more recent survey, just under 50 percent of Republicans favored full marriage equality for same-sex couples. Approximately 28 percent of Republicans in the survey favored some form of civil union that was called something other than a marriage. Barely one-in-five Republicans continued to oppose any kind of legal recognition for same-sex unions. For a policy question that, for many election cycles, was one of the most divisive and high-profile issues in the country, this transition is truly remarkable yet rarely remarked upon.

The popularity of same-sex marriage within the electorate appears to be a mostly irrelevant issue now, given that the Supreme Court decision, *Obergefell v. Hodges*, made same-sex marriage legal across the country. It is notable just how little pushback this decision has received from conservatives. Whereas *Roe v. Wade* resulted in almost four decades of sustained activism, Republicans, with a few notable exceptions, seem to have mostly acquiesced on this issue. Subsequent Republican presidential candidates have not campaigned on the promise to appoint Supreme Court justices who will overturn *Obergefell*, nor have I noticed any significant efforts by activists to force them to take such a position. Acceptance of same-sex marriage as a *fait accompli* seems to be the norm. As one interview subject put it, "I'm not pro the illegalization of gay marriage, but I wouldn't have voted for it to be legalized."

One subject I interviewed, a political consultant, noted this dramatic shift, and said that he was working to encourage older Republican legislators to accept the new reality. During a discussion of a Republican platform at the state level, he made the case that leaders needed to remove any language about defining marriage as between a man and a woman. I do not know his private opinions on the issue, but he recognized that this is now a political loser, even in one of the more conservative states.

---

37 I would have preferred to use the 2000 ANES for this section, for the sake of consistency. The 2000 ANES did not even ask a question about same-sex marriage, which itself demonstrates about how little salience the issue had at the time.

None of this explains why attitudes towards homosexuality shifted so swiftly in the US, including among Republicans. Part of the answer may be that opposition to gay rights was inconsistent with the way the religious right had begun framing its arguments. Political scientist Andrew Lewis has documented that the religious right has been slowly shifting its approach to fighting the culture war.[38] Over the last decades, the religious right mostly stopped describing itself as a moral majority or promising that they would revive republican virtues or communitarian values. Instead, religious right leaders have largely started using the language of liberalism, with a special focus on rights.

This shift in rhetorical strategies, Lewis argues, can largely be explained by the religious right's approach to the abortion issue. In an increasingly secular progressive society, the pro-life movement needed to develop an argument that could extend beyond narrow religious boundaries. The approach that had the most success emphasized a "right to life." The unborn, according to this argument, despite being totally dependent on their mothers, are nonetheless human beings, and as such they possess the same natural rights as anyone else. Although this did not fully resolve the question of when human life begins, and that question is still usually divided along religious lines, it is nonetheless an argument that does not depend on having a very specific biblical view on life. An emphasis on rights furthermore fit well with an American political culture that is permeated with talk about rights.

The religious right's approach to the abortion question spilled over into other policy areas. In particular, religious conservatives have embraced claims about their own religious liberty. This is significant because it indicates a defensive rather than an offensive rhetorical approach to the culture wars. Far from demanding America return to Christ, or even the more nebulous "Judeo-Christian values," those calling just for religious liberty say they will be satisfied if they are simply left alone – they want to be allowed to home-school their children and do not want Christian florists to be forced to work at gay weddings, for example.

Whether the religious right's turn toward religious liberty is sincere or a rational response to a secularizing society is not a question I can answer. A consequence of this shift, however, is that it is difficult to oppose same-sex marriage using this framework. That is, it is hard to argue that same-sex marriage somehow violates anyone else's religious liberty, provided people with religious objections to such marriages are not personally forced to play any role in them. This is likely one

---

38 Andrew Lewis, *The Rights Turn in Conservative Christian Politics: How Abortion Transformed the Culture War* (New York: Cambridge University Press, 2017)

reason why the religious right retreated on this issue with such remarkable speed, while maintaining such a strong stance on the abortion question.

This still does not answer the question of why public opinion shifted so quickly on same-sex marriage. Political scientist Darel Paul's book, *From Tolerance to Equality*, provides one of the more compelling explanations for how this change occurred.[39] Paul argues that support for same-sex marriage, and LGBT rights more broadly, was a top-down phenomenon, first popular among elites and subsequently embraced by most non-elite Americans. In his view, same-sex marriage and related policies have long been supported by leading figures in the news media, in entertainment, in academia, in psychology, and even in big business. College-educated Americans that were not necessarily elite followed, and eventually a large majority of Americans came to support these policies. The earlier quest for tolerance for sexual minorities was largely achieved, and many Americans moved far beyond that, celebrating the LGBT population as a welcome source of diversity, which in certain elite discourse is treated as an unquestionable blessing – we are now at the point where major corporations are expected to at least make a perfunctory acknowledgment of Pride Month.

Whether or not Paul's thesis is correct, public opinion on same-sex marriage has unquestionably changed over a relatively short period of time. It is now at the point that opposing same-sex marriage would likely cost most candidates more votes than they gain. Should *Obergefell* be struck down by future decisions, same-sex marriage would likely remain in place in the overwhelming majority of US states – though I would not be surprised if it was abolished in a few states such as Alabama. In a sense, the Supreme Court may have inadvertently done the Republican Party a favor when it took same-sex marriage off the political table. Had the struggle continued via the ordinary democratic process, the Republicans would have been caught between the remaining die-hard opponents of this policy who would insist that the party maintain consistency on the issue, and the rest of the public that long ago became comfortable with same-sex marriage. Because of *Obergefell*, the issue simply went away without elected Republicans needing to change any of their positions. Most prominent Republicans simply dropped the issue, and the culture war moved on to other subjects.

For the last few years, the subject of transgender people has garnered more public attention than the subject of homosexuality. The salience of this subject is relatively new, and most older surveys of public opinion do not address the subject at all. However, on this topic, Republicans do, for the most part, maintain a conser-

---

39 Darel E. Paul, *From Tolerance to Equality: How Elites Brought America to Same-Sex Marriage* (Waco, TX: Baylor University Press, 2019)

vative position, especially as it relates to gender-affirming care for children. Over the last years, many state legislatures with Republican majorities have passed laws restricting access to certain kinds of gender-related care for minors.

In my interviews, the issue of transgender people inspired some of the strongest emotions. Despite being a relatively trivial matter for most Republican voters, in terms of what it means for their lives, the contemporary debates about the issue have clearly touched a nerve. Purely from the perspective of keeping the base fired up (whether it is a sound perspective on any other grounds is a separate question), focusing heavily on transgender-related policies appears to be an effective tool for mobilizing parts of the Republican grassroots – though some Republican leaders seem to overestimate this, as very few Republicans think it is one of the most important issues facing the country and many say they would prefer to keep focused on the economy.

I did meet one person who thought the conservative handwringing on the issue was a strategic mistake. He thought the anti-trans views promoted by conservative media were wrong-headed, at least in the long term. He suggested that current negative attitudes toward this group would dissipate as more people met transgender people in their personal lives, and greater tolerance in the US public is probably inevitable. Before long, he suggested, being opposed to transgender rights will be a minority opinion, just as being opposed to same-sex marriage is now a decidedly minority opinion. He did hedge this opinion a little bit. He thought the question of transgender women in sports might remain an animating issue, and perhaps even grow if trans women and girls come to dominate an increasing number of sports, especially in high school. He specifically mentioned the case of Lia Thomas, the transgender woman who was performing well in collegiate swimming around the time of the interview.[40]

One person I interviewed suggested that the subject of transgenderism should be siloed off from the broader question of LGBT rights. He argued that revisiting the issue of gay marriage would be a mistake, and the GOP should just forget about it. However, he thought the questions about transgender people were fundamentally different, as, on this issue, the left was overreaching and alienating people who might otherwise be persuaded to ally themselves with a progressive cultural agenda.

---

40 Amanda Musa, "Transgender swimmer Lia Thomas nominated for NCAA 2022 Woman of the Year Award," CNN, July 15, 2022, https://www.cnn.com/2022/07/15/sport/lia-thomas-ncaa-woman-of-the-year-nomination/index.html.

Gun control

Gun control is another issue that attracts a lot of dedicated activists on all sides, and over time has become a bitterly partisan issue. Its salience is usually contingent on current events, however. Specifically, calls for gun control are loudest right after a mass shooting, when public opinion is most galvanized around the issue. Typically, opponents of new gun control legislation are able to effectively stymie efforts to pass meaningful new laws, and the window in which new gun control regulations were on the top of voters' minds passes, leaving the status quo (or something close to it) in place.[41]

Many commentators have noted that the gun control issue plays out very differently in the US compared to other advanced democracies. Other countries implemented sweeping gun control legislation that would be considered unthinkable in the US with relative ease. For example, following a mass shooting in the 1990s, Australia implemented comprehensive gun control legislation that made private ownership of firearms extraordinarily difficult, and resulted in more than a third of all civilian guns in the country being surrendered and destroyed.[42] Some of this difference can be explained by the Second Amendment to the US Constitution, which states: "A well regulated Militia, being necessary to the security of a free State, the right of the people to keep and bear Arms, shall not be infringed." The language is unfortunately clunky and ambiguous. However, most gun-rights advocates insist that the Constitution protects the rights of US citizens to personally own firearms. Gun control proponents tend to prefer a different interpretation, arguing that the emphasis should be placed on the phrase, "well regulated Militia," which could be satisfied by National Guard troops under the strict control and supervision of state governments. At present, the Supreme Court holds that the Second Amendment protects the rights of individuals to own firearms.

The gun-rights movement is well-funded and highly motivated, but absolutist positions on the Second Amendment, such as insisting that there should be no (or almost no) regulations on the private use of firearms is uncommon, even among Republican voters. The 2020 ANES asked several questions relating to firearms. For example, it asked, "Do you think the federal government should make it

---

41 Although control advocates tend to use mass shootings to attempt to rally people to their cause, the evidence that people really change their views in response to such shootings, even temporarily, is weak. Benjamin R. Kantack and Collin E. Paschall, "Does 'Politicizing' Gun Violence Increase Support for Gun Control? Experimental Evidence from the Las Vegas Shooting," *Social Science Quarterly* 101 (2020): 893–908.

42 Simon Chapman and Philip Alpers, "Gun-Related Deaths: How Australia Stepped Off the 'American Path,'" *Annals of Internal Medicine*, 158(2013): 770–771.

more difficult for people to buy a gun than it is now, make it easier for people to buy a gun, or keep these rules about the same as they are now?" Just about half of all respondents believed it should be more difficult to purchase guns. Well under 10 percent wanted it to be easier to do so. If we restrict the sample to only include Republicans, however, we continue to see that people who want very few limits on gun ownership are clearly in the minority. A large majority of Republicans (about two-thirds) said they were satisfied with gun laws that are currently on the books. Even among Republicans, the share of the vote that wanted less restrictive gun laws was only about 11 percent. Republicans, on average, may not want to enact sweeping new gun restrictions, but they are not keen on rescinding those already in effect.

When it comes to more specific policies, we continue to find that certain gun control measures are extraordinarily popular. For example, almost 95 percent of ANES respondents favored requiring background checks for potential gun purchasers. The numbers are very similar even when the sample is restricted to Republicans alone. Fewer than 10 percent of Republicans opposed background checks.

For other forms of gun control, however, we do see a greater level of partisan polarization. The 2022 CES had a somewhat different set of questions about guns. The CES asked respondents whether they want to "ban assault rifles." An overwhelming majority of Democrats (about 87 percent) said that they supported such a policy. In contrast, about two-thirds of Republicans opposed this idea. This is another issue where we can find clear evidence of partisan polarization. Questions about "assault rifles," however, can be a bit confusing, as most people with little personal experience with firearms do not understand the distinctions between different kinds of weapon. Some people conflate "assault rifles" with "machine guns" – the latter being a kind of automatic weapon that is already heavily regulated.

There are a number of possible explanations for American exceptionalism when it comes to the politics of gun control. Part of the issue is that gun ownership is now so clearly divided along partisan lines. About 71 percent of Democrats surveyed in the CES stated that no one in their household owns a gun. Among Republicans, however, it was just about 44 percent, indicating that a majority of Republicans have a gun in their home. The ANES recorded similar percentages. This finding is aligned with other research showing that gun ownership is an increasingly partisan phenomenon, and it is now a powerful predictor of vote choice.[43] In

---

43 Mark R. Joslyn, Donald P. Haider-Markel, Michael Baggs, and Andrew Bilbo, "Emerging Political Identities? Gun Ownership and Voting in Presidential Election," *Social Science Quarterly* 98 (2017): 383–396.

an era of polarization, issues so divided along partisan lines are likely to spur intense disagreements.

Just as party identification is strongly predictive of gun ownership, the two parties are polarized in their attitudes toward the most important pro-gun lobbying organization: the National Rifle Association (NRA). According to the ANES, the mean feeling thermometer score for the NRA is relatively neutral – just above 50. This masks the huge partisan gap on this issue. Among Republicans, the mean score was quite warm (about 74). Among non-Republicans, however, it was very cold (about 29), making it one of the more disliked organizations among Democrats.

Beyond the contentious nature of US partisan politics, which makes compromise difficult for many kinds of policies, and the current Supreme Court's interpretation of the Second Amendment, there are reasons the gun-control debate can be particularly challenging. Guns fit well in a certain interpretation of US political culture, one that celebrates the rugged individualism of the frontier. Guns remain an important element of rural American culture, which is also increasingly associated with the Republican Party. Individual gun ownership is also associated with resistance to tyranny, a common theme on the political right.

Many contemporary gun control opponents insist that the ability to violently resist government overreach is the primary reason the Second Amendment exists. According to this argument, it is important for US citizens to have the theoretical ability to overthrow the government. From this perspective, gun ownership is not just a right; owning, maintaining, and training in the use of firearms is an important civic responsibility.

Political scientists Alexandra Filindra, and Noah Kaplan have argued that there is now a racial element to the gun control debate, arguing that racial resentment is an important predictor of gun control attitudes.[44] They argue that gun ownership is increasingly becoming an implicit element of white identity. In a separate study, they examined whether sexism was also associated with pro-gun attitudes and NRA membership, but they found that the relationship between gender attitudes and gun ownership was small and inconsistent.[45]

---

44 Alexandra Filindra and Noah Kaplan, "Racial Resentment and Whites' Gun Policy Preferences in Contemporary America," *Political Behavior* 38 (2016): 255–275.
45 Alexandra Filindra, Noah J. Kaplan, and Beyza E. Buyuker, "Racial Resentment or Sexism? White Americans' Outgroup Attitudes as Predictors of Gun Ownership and NRA Membership," *Sociological Inquiry* 91 (2021): 253–286.

Republicans and foreign policy

In my survey of Republicans about top policy concerns, the near total absence of foreign policy was notable. The few responses related to foreign policy were not even consistent. This represents a major change in the Republican Party in the electorate, and it implies a major change in the discourse coming from elites in the party as well as conservative media. Twenty-years ago, around the time of the invasion of Iraq launched by President George W. Bush, foreign policy was one area where Republicans seemed to march in lockstep. The Global War on Terror was treated as an existential crisis, one that required bold leadership. Critics of Bush's wars on the left were treated as "useful idiots" for Muslim theocrats at best, fifth columnists attempting to subvert their own country at worst. Anti-war conservatives were extremely rare, and few had any positions of influence.

Something strange has occurred in the right's approach to foreign policy since then, however. As the wars in Iraq and Afghanistan dragged on, with death tolls that began exceeding optimistic early expectations, and the financial costs spiraled out of control, many conservatives, and some elected Republicans,[46] began to change their views on this subject. By the time President Bush left office, the tremendous optimism about the future of liberal democracy in the Middle East – which war proponents suggested would follow the toppling of autocratic governments – had clearly waned. Some conservatives protested when President Obama ended US combat operations in Iraq, but few remained enthusiastic promoters of President Bush's approach to foreign policy.

It is notable how little serious soul searching the mainstream right engaged in as the Global War on Terror diminished as a concern for most people. Although few significant Republicans today vociferously defend the Bush Administration's reaction to the 9 – 11 terror attacks, most have not directly attacked it, or offered a new alternative that is clearly distinct from that of the Bush era. Donald Trump, especially when he was campaigning for president in 2015 and 2016, was a partial exception to this, though a very notable one. Trump clearly stated, as the Republican presidential primaries were still ongoing, that he believed the invasion of Iraq had been a terrible mistake. Other Republican presidential hopefuls had criticized that war in the past – both Rep. Ron Paul and Sen. Rand Paul did so during their presidential primary campaigns. Trump was the first front-runner to make this argument. However, whereas Ron Paul offered a coherent foreign policy

---

46 For example, US Senator Gordon Smith, a Republican from Oregon, began to speak out against the war in Iraq, which he had initially supported, in 2006. Matthew Daly, "Smith Says Iraq War may be 'Criminal,'" *The Seattle Times*, December 8, 2006, https://www.seattletimes.com/seattle-news/smith-says-iraq-war-may-be-criminal/.

vision of his own (non-interventionism), it was not entirely clear what a "Trump Doctrine," if such as thing ever came into existence, would entail.

As president, Trump was arguably more dovish than other Republicans might have been, though we cannot know for sure how a different Republican president would have reacted to similar circumstances. It is true that President Trump did not begin any major new combat operations. On the other hand, he did pursue certain provocative policies, such as the decision to move the US embassy in Israel to Jerusalem, and assassinating Qasem Soleimani, an Iranian military officer. In the end, the Trump Administration's approach to foreign policy was never fully coherent. Trump's supporters can reasonably argue that his actions fit within an "America First" mindset, but the substantive guiding principles of Trump's decisions in office remain murky.

During my personal interviews, foreign policy was the area in which there was the least consistency across subjects. It was also an issue in which many subjects were willing to acknowledge their ignorance of the subject. "To be honest, I don't really know much about that" was a common, though not universal, sentiment throughout these conversations. This, I suspect, is also different from what one would have heard from Republican voters 20 years ago, when Manichean thinking about America's relationships with its adversaries was the norm.

Some people I spoke with thought about the issue in very practical terms. One woman, a stay-at-home mother, explained her thinking as follows: "I have a very maternal answer to that question. I've got an 18-year-old son, a 14-year old son, and girls are enlisting now, too, and possibly even being drafted. But I do not want them going and fighting ideological wars that have virtually nothing to do with the wellbeing of our own country." When I asked her for an example of an ideological war, she immediately named Afghanistan.

Although ambivalence was common, I did sometimes encounter the kind of foreign policy alarmism that was once very common among Republicans, both during the Cold War and during the War on Terror. In fact, one of my subjects, a retiree who otherwise seemed to have a strong grasp of politics and policy, nonetheless gave a response to a question about foreign policy that indicated he did not realize the Cold War was over, and that he believed communism was still on the march:

> Russia and China, who years ago used to get in battles over their common border, they were fighting each other all the time. That was the best situation in the world for the United States and Europe. Let them fight with each other. They're unifying. They're coming together. China is an economic power, beyond all reasonable limitations. And Russia isn't an economic power, but they have all kinds of soldiers that are ready to go to war and they don't care if they lose a couple hundred thousand if they can take another country and make it theirs. They are going to do that. I see the unification of those communist countries, where either our socialist lean-

ings in our country, and Europe already being socialist, I see our whole world going to become communist. It's either going to happen because of the Bidens and the Democrats – the Republicans I think represent the delay of that, perhaps – but ultimately, we're either going to be in a world war again, or we're all going to be communist. That's what I see.

In the electorate, there is little consistency when it comes to foreign policy attitudes. This perhaps should not be surprising. Foreign policy is incredibly complex, and given how little ordinary Americans know about the world beyond their nation's borders, we should not expect them to have a coherent set of beliefs about how their government should interact with the rest of the world. This is especially true in an era without clear ideological dividing lines across the globe, as was the case during the Cold War and, to a lesser extent, during the War on Terror. Foreign policy hawks can no longer plausibly argue that we are engaged in an apocalyptic struggle against an implacable, powerful, and united set of enemies.

Creating additional problems for ordinary voters trying to make sense of foreign policy, elites on the American right no longer speak with one voice on these issues. This is decidedly different from the mainstream right's foreign policy discourse during the Cold War or the early years of the War on Terror, where foreign policy was treated as the single most important issue, where a single misstep or moment of weakness could fatally weaken the country. Right-wing alarmism about foreign policy from conservative political and media elites has clearly declined, for good reason, and Republicans in the electorate have responded by becoming more divided and ambivalent about these issues.

The 2020 ANES shows that terrorism is no longer one of Americans' top concerns, on average. The survey asked respondents, "How worried are you that the United States will experience a terrorist attack in the near future?" Respondents were then asked to place themselves on a scale ranging from "extremely worried" to "not at all worried." Among all respondents, only about seven percent described themselves as "extremely worried." The results were very similar when the sample is limited to Republicans. In fact, this is one of the issues on which there was almost no discernible difference between Republicans and non-Republicans.

In my open-ended survey of Republicans, very few mentioned terrorism. Some only did so in connection to the related issue of control over the border, rather than use of American force abroad. As one subject put it, "I think the biggest policy issue facing America today and for a while now, is border security. There's no telling how many terrorists have just walked on into the country."

The data also show an interesting change in the electorate's attitudes toward one country in particular: Russia. Throughout the Cold War, Russia (more specifically, the Soviet Union) was viewed by conservative Republicans as the antithesis of everything they held dear.[47] As the interviewee I quoted above demonstrated, some older Republicans remain stuck in that Cold War mindset. On the other hand, there are now many Republicans who are neutral in their attitudes toward Russia and its authoritarian leader, Vladimir Putin. Some are even positively disposed toward Russia, viewing it as a bastion of tradition, serving as a counter to the decadent, feminized, and progressive West.

The 2020 ANES asked a general question about Russia: "How much is Russia a threat to the United States?" Respondents were then asked to place themselves on a five-point scale, from "not at all" to "a great deal." On this question, we see a much larger partisan gap. In particular, Democrats were much more likely than Republicans to believe Russia represented a significant threat to the US. A little under one-third of Democrats gave the most alarmist response to the question about Russia, compared to just under one-in-five Republicans who held this position. This is obviously a very different pattern than one would have seen during the peak of the Cold War, when anti-Russian attitudes were a hallmark of the right.

Partisan considerations are a major reason for the evolving attitudes toward Russia. Throughout the Trump Administration, the president was hounded by accusations that he had colluded with Russians during the 2016 election campaign to ensure his victory. The evidence for this was weak, and the investigations into the issue failed to deliver the smoking gun that many of Trump's opponents hoped would end his presidency. Unsurprisingly, as of 2020, there was a massive partisan difference on the question of Russian interference in the 2016 election. The 2020 ANES asked respondents whether Russia interfered in that election. Democrats overwhelmingly believed Russia tried to interfere in 2016 – about 88 percent held this position. Republicans, in contrast, were almost evenly split between those who thought Russia tried to interfere and those who rejected this idea. Republicans and Democrats were similarly split on whether Russia would seek to interfere with the 2020 election. About 68 percent of Democrats thought Russian interference in 2020 was either "extremely likely" or "very likely." Among Republicans, this was only about 12 percent. Paranoia about Russia, justified or not, has now shifted from a predominantly right-wing phenomena to a defining characteristic of the US left.

Beyond Russia, Iran is another country that has been a perennial source of concern for conservative pundits and foreign policy experts. Since the Islamic revolution in that country in the late 1970s, Iran has been viewed as a major threat to

---

47 For a thorough discussion of the outsized role the Cold War played in the development of modern conservative thought, see George Nash, *The Conservative Intellectual Movement in America Since 1946* (New York: Basic Books, 1976).

both its region and the United States. Iranians have funded terrorist groups outside their border for decades, most notably Hezbollah. On the other hand, Iran may not be as dangerous as hawks in the US suggest. The Iranians have not directly instigated hostilities with their neighbors, and from their perspective, the US (which supported Iraq during the brutal Iran-Iraq War in the 1980s and invaded two neighboring countries, Iraq and Afghanistan, during the Global War on Terror) is the real aggressor in the region.

Republican voters, for their part, remain skeptical of Iran, viewing it as a threat to American interests. The 2020 ANES asked subjects, "How much is Iran a threat to the United States?" Only about three percent of Republicans answered "not at all." Non-Republicans were only slightly more likely to take this position (about 8 percent). A plurality of Republicans (30 percent) took the most alarmist position on Iran, stating that Iran represented "a great deal" of a threat to the US. The 2020 CES asked a question about President Trump's decision to withdraw the US from the Iran Nuclear Accord. This was an area where responses were clearly divided by partisanship. About 87 percent of Republicans agreed with this decision, compared to about 24 percent of Democrats.

The 2020 CES also sheds insight into Republican broader views on foreign policy, especially as it relates to the use of force. That survey asked respondents about scenarios in which the military might be deployed. When asked whether they would support using the US military to "ensure the supply of oil," about 31 percent of Republicans supported this policy, compared to about 13 percent of non-Republicans. An overwhelming majority of Republicans (about 76 percent) supported using the military to destroy a terrorist training camp, whereas non-Republicans were more split on this question (about 54 percent were in favor of military action in this scenario). We see a smaller partisan difference when military action is not directly connected to national security concerns. For example, on the question of whether we should use the military to "intervene in a region where there is genocide or civil war," only about 41 percent of Republicans agreed, compared to about 49 percent of non-Republicans.

Particularly interesting, in my view, was a question about using the military to promote democracy. This was a major project of George W. Bush's presidency, which emphasized democracy promotion as the way to achieve ultimate victory in the Global War on Terror.[48] The 2020 CES makes it clear that the public, across

---

48 Bush's views on this were explained more clearly and forcefully during his second inaugural address: "So it is the policy of the United States to seek and support the growth of democratic movements and institutions in every nation and culture, with the ultimate goal of ending tyranny in our world," ("President Bush's Second Inaugural Address," National Public Radio, January 20, 2005, https://www.npr.org/templates/story/story.php?storyId=4460172).

the political spectrum, overwhelmingly rejects this idea. Only about 21 percent of the Republican respondents supported using the military in this way, compared to about 20 percent of non-Republicans. This is another rare question on which there is not any kind of substantive partisan difference in opinion.

On the other hand, although military force in the name of democracy promotion has fallen out of favor among voters across the political spectrum, there is still a general consensus that the US has a responsibility to "protect American allies under attack by foreign nations." About 80 percent of Republicans agreed, as did about 73 percent of non-Republicans.

There is one scenario in which Republicans are considerably less hawkish than non-Republicans. They are much less likely to support using the military to "help the United Nations uphold international law." Only about 31 percent of Republicans supported this policy, compared to about 57 percent of non-Republicans. This is also consistent with historical patterns, as conservatives have always been more skeptical of multinational organizations that threaten America's sovereignty, or at least its ability to engage in unilateral military engagements. Dislike of the United Nations, in particular, has a very long history on the right.

The main takeaway from the CES battery of questions on military force is that Republicans have not repudiated the party's hawkishness, which has been one of the party's consistent attributes since the Cold War. However, they lack the idealism and faith in democracy that inspired President George W. Bush, and they reject the commitment to multilateralism and international organizations we tend to see among Democrats.

Many anti-war conservatives and libertarians were optimistic that Trump would fundamentally alter the Republican Party's approach to issues of war and peace. That is not what happened, though it is true that Donald Trump did not launch any new major wars. His non-ideological hawkishness – his willingness to launch limited military strikes when he believed it was in the nation's interest – frustrated both neoconservatives who still supported George W. Bush's approach to foreign affairs, and voices on the right who would have preferred a more consistent non-interventionist approach. His dealings with the world do appear largely aligned with what ordinary Republican voters wanted to see. They do not have much interest in wars for the promotion of democracy, but they like it when the president attacks the nation's real and perceived enemies in limited operations.

The conflict between Russia and Ukraine has been the dominant international news since Russia invaded that country in February of 2022. As of this writing, that conflict is still ongoing. The 2022 CES helpfully asked a question about how the US should respond to that war. Respondents were given many possible ways the US might respond to that conflict and were asked which they supported (they could choose more than one). About 30 percent of Republicans agreed that the US "should not be involved"; about 42 percent agreed the US should "Send food, medicine and other aid to countries affected"; about 30 percent supported the argument that the US should "Provide arms to Ukraine"; about 11 percent believed the US should "Enforce a no fly zone"; about seven percent agreed that the US should "Use drones and air craft to bomb Russian troops"; about 14 percent wanted the US to "Send military support staff (non-combat)"; and only about six percent believed the US should "Send significant force to fight Russia."

It is notable that, when it comes the Ukraine-Russia conflict, Republicans tended to be somewhat less hawkish than Democrats. Only about 11 percent of Democrats believed that the US should not be involved at all and about 19 percent of Democrats supported creating a no-fly zone. Just over 50 percent of Democrats supported providing arms to the Ukrainians. Democrats were, however, almost as opposed as Republicans on the question of whether the US should fight Russia directly with a significant force.

Making sense of these gaps can be tricky. On the one hand, it might signal that we really are seeing a partisan realignment on the question of foreign policy. Perhaps Republicans really are transitioning into the party of non-intervention, and the Democrats are now the more hawkish party. A more concerning explanation, however, is that Republicans just became increasingly pro-Russia over the course of the Trump Administration. There certainly is an element of the American right, especially the far right, that has long admired Vladimir Putin's regime, looking to the Russian model as an example of authoritarian conservatism that they would like to follow. Another possibility is that American voters are simply taking positions on the Russia-Ukraine conflict based on their attitudes toward domestic partisan disputes: Democrats despise Russia because of their suspicion that Donald Trump colluded with Russia in the 2016 election, and they wish to see that country harmed; Republicans are pro-Russia for the same reason.

Does public opinion about policy really matter?

Theoretically, in a democracy, there should be a direct connection between what the public desires and what policies are implemented. The public rarely has the opportunity to directly weigh-in on questions of policy. They can make their views heard in states where important questions can be determined via direct democracy – in states where initiatives and referenda allow for policies to be directly presented to voters. Otherwise, voter input is only indirect: voters choose representatives, and representatives make policy.

The next question is whether elected representatives give much weight to public opinion when making policy. This can be a tricky question to answer. Even if a party's voters say their preferred policies align with the party leadership's agenda, we are left with a chicken-egg problem. Does the party create an agenda to maximize voter support, or do party elites create their own agenda, confident that their voters will eventually adopt the party's agenda as their own? On this question, the political science literature provides mixed results.

From a theoretical perspective, there is a political science tradition that states political parties and politicians exist for a single purpose: to win elections.[49] They will thus be flexible in their policy agenda, choosing popular positions that give them an advantage over their opponents. They face some constraints, of course. Political parties need to maintain some consistency over time in order to maintain voter trust, but in the long run, it seems obvious that parties that relentlessly pursue the median voter when it comes to policy will outperform parties that prefer ideological purity to popularity.

We can probably take it for granted that politicians have at least some interest in public opinion. If they really do not care about what the public desires at all, the fact that they also have extraordinarily high reelection rates would suggest something is wrong with our representative democracy. Fortunately, there is evidence that there is a causal connection between public opinion and public policy at the national level,[50] including evidence that voters sometimes hold representatives accountable when they vote for unpopular legislation.[51] There has never been a perfect relationship between changes in opinion and changes in policy, but more often than not they tend to move in the same direction.[52]

The greater concern for most scholars is that politicians care more about some voters than others. There is strong evidence that the nation's economic elites enjoy a disproportionate influence on public policy. The American Political Science Asso-

---

49 David R. Mayhew, *Congress: The Electoral Connection* (New Haven, CT: Yale University Press, 1974).
50 Benjamin I. Page and Robert Y. Shapiro, "Effects of Public Opinion on Policy," *The American Political Science Review* 77 (1983): 175–190; Paul Burstein, "The Impact of Public Opinion on Public Policy: A Review and an Agenda," *Political Research Quarterly* 56 (2003): 29–40.
51 Stephen Ansolabehere and Philip Edward Jones, "Constituents' Responses to Congressional Roll-Call Voting," *American Journal of Political Science* 54 (2010): 583–597.
52 Alan D. Monroe, "Public Opinion and Public Policy, 1980–1993," *Public Opinion Quarterly* 62 (1998): 6–28; Robert Y. Shapiro, "Public Opinion and American Democracy," *Public Opinion Quarterly* 75 (2011): 982–1017.

ciation's Task Force on Inequality and American Democracy put it this way in 2004:

> Generations of Americans have worked to equalize citizen voice across lines of income, race, and gender. Today, however, the voices of American citizens are raised and heard unequally. The privileged participate more than others and are increasingly well organized to press their demands on government. Public officials, in turn, are much more responsive to the privileged than to average citizens and the least affluent. Citizens with lower or moderate incomes speak with a whisper that is lost on the ears of inattentive government officials, while the advantaged roar with a clarity and consistency that policy-makers readily hear and routinely follow.[53]

Concerns about power inequalities are certainly not new. In 1956, C. Wright Mills famously argued that elites wield overwhelming influence in the US.[54] Some of the more interesting and concerning research on the connection between public opinion and policy outcomes suggests that wealthy Americans are far more likely to see their preferences translated into policy than other voters.[55]

Conclusion

Republicans in the electorate are, on average, more conservative (as the term is generally understood) than Democrats on policy. Conservatism is a relative term, however, and it would be an exaggeration to say that they are consistently conservative across multiple issues. Especially when it comes to economics, Republican voters have been consistently more 'populist' than most conservative opinion leaders and Republican politicians. Most of them could not be described as economic libertarians in any meaningful sense.

Republicans are also, compared to Democrats, quite conservative on the major social issues, but the contemporary gap needs to be looked at in historical context. Except for abortion (a major exception, mind you), Republicans have not been moving in a right-wing or reactionary direction on any major social policy issue. Although many of them seem animated by issues related to transgender people at the moment, this also needs to be put in historical context: until relatively recently, this was a very low salience issue. Twenty or more years ago, I think it is

---

53 Task Force on Inequality and American Democracy. "American Democracy in an Age of Rising Inequality," *Perspectives on Politics* 2 (2004): 651–666.
54 C. Wright Mills, *The Power Elite* (New York: Oxford University Press, 1956).
55 Martin Gilens and Benjamin I. Page, "Testing Theories of American Politics: Elites, Interest Groups, and Average Citizens," *Perspectives on Politics* 12 (2014): 564–581;

safe to say that most Republicans did not think about this issue at all. The fact that it is difficult to find polling on the question more than just a few years old is evidence of this. How those attitudes will evolve in the coming years remains to be seen.

Foreign policy attitudes among contemporary Republicans are all over the place. In practice, foreign policy is unquestionably a "hard question." The public's knowledge of the world beyond the US borders is low. This seems to be an issue where Republican leaders would have a lot of leeway to make decisions, confident that Republican voters will trust their judgment and rally around the flag – until, that is, one or more of those decisions has undeniably disastrous consequences. Republicans' typically low levels of interest in foreign policy questions might be viewed, in a way, as a positive development. It means they are not presently living in fear (justified or not) of a major act of terrorism or aggression from a foreign power.

What one thinks of these results will of course depend on one's perspective. Conservative pundits and activists can be justifiably frustrated that their arguments in favor of free-market economics have not really been embraced by the typical Republican voter. Progressives can be alarmed that, in comparison to themselves, Republicans remain opposed to much of their agenda, and lament that such a large part of the electorate remains opposed to reforms they consider obviously salutary. That being said, these data should remind them that the typical Republican is more centrist than one would infer from the loudest conservative commentators and the angriest elements of right-wing social media.

Chapter 4
How Republicans think about ideology

Ideology is a concept most people with any political awareness will intuitively grasp, but may not be able to define. In the US, we take it for granted that the Republicans are "conservative," and the Democrats are "liberal" or "progressive." These terms do not necessarily have a fixed meaning in the public mind. Among conservative media figures and intellectuals, questions of whether or not particular Republican leaders are sufficiently conservative have been a significant preoccupation. The general consensus among conservative thinkers is that they should strive to support the Republican primary candidates that are most aligned with conservative principles that have a shot at winning. During the 2016 Republican primaries, conservatives in the media repeatedly expressed concern that Donald Trump was insufficiently committed to conservative ideals – if he even knew what those ideals were. Republican voters, in contrast, remained just as likely as ever to describe themselves as conservative, yet they also enthusiastically supported Trump.

In this chapter, I examine Republicans' descriptions of the two major competing ideologies in the US, attempting to discern the degree to which they even have a meaningful understanding of terms like conservative or liberal. Do these concepts have any substantive meaning to voters, or are they simply markers of identity? Does being a "strong conservative" imply that a person is committed to a set of principles about domestic and foreign policy, or is the term just a way to indicate one's deep attachment to the Republican Party? If the latter, does this indicate that "conservative" simply refers to whatever the Republican leadership is currently promoting?

Scholarly definitions of ideology

Ordinary voters are not the only people confused about ideology. Different scholars have offered competing definitions of terms like liberal, progressive, conservative, reactionary, left-wing, right-wing, and even ideology itself. Ideology may be thought of as simply the label we attach to bundles of public policies, bundles that political parties create in order to maximize their votes – this definition assumes that policy preferences are cardinal to vote choice.[1] Some conservatives

---

1 Anthony Down, *An Economic Theory of Democracy* (New York: Harper, 1957).

https://doi.org/10.1515/9783111469720-004

have argued that ideology necessarily entails political fanaticism, and thus needs to be distinguished from other political principles[2] – such a definition makes the term largely useless for scholars of American political behavior, and thus has not been accepted by most political scientists.

Among scholars of ideology, the claim that the left-right division in modern politics is ultimately about the question of equality is dominant. From this perspective, the left represents the side that fights for equality and the expansion of rights.[3] The right, in contrast, defends existing privileges.[4] A related perspective contends that, even if the right does not fight for inequality *per se*, it does not place universal equality at the top of the hierarchy of values.[5]

Another view contends that ideologies are ultimately about fundamental beliefs about reality. For example, the division may be between those that believe that values have a real existence outside of specific cultural contexts, versus those who believe that values are entirely human creations, and thus subject to change as cultures evolve.[6] The side insisting on the existence of permanent values that are not human inventions tends to rely on an orthodox religious view of the world, but religion is not essential to this argument; one may, for example, be an avowed atheist and simultaneously affirm the existence of natural rights, applicable to all people at all times.[7]

A related argument holds that where we stand on the political spectrum is at least partly dependent upon our views about human nature: conservatism tends to be associated with the claim that human nature is mostly fixed, whereas progressivism is associated with a more optimistic view of human potential.[8] The former view of a fixed human nature can either be dependent on a biblical view of human beings (the doctrine of Original Sin), or a secular view suggesting that certain human failings are built into human nature because of evolution via natural selec-

---

2 Russell Kirk, *The American Cause* (Wilmington, DE: ISI Press, 2002), 2

3 Norberto Bobbio, *Left and Right: The Significance of a Political Distinction* (Chicago, IL: University of Chicago Press, 1997).

4 Corey Robin, *The Reactionary Mind: From Edmund Burke to Sarah Palin* (Oxford: Oxford University Press, 2013); Edmund Fawcett, *Conservatism: The Fight for a Tradition* (Princeton, NJ: Princeton University Press, 2020): Patrick J. Deneen, *Why Liberalism Failed* (New Haven, CT: Yale University Press, 2018).

5 George Hawley, *Right-Wing Critics of American Conservatism* (Lawrence, KS: University Press of Kansas, 2016).

6 James Davison Hunter, *Culture Wars: The Struggle to Define America* (New York: Basic Books, 1991).

7 George Will, *The Conservative Sensibility* (New York: Hachette Books, 2019).

8 Thomas Sowell, *A Conflict of Visions: Ideological Origins of Political Struggles* (New York: Basic Books, 2007).

tion, a perspective that suggests limits to social engineering. The progressive perspective suggests that human nature is malleable, and better social institutions could bring an end to most inequalities and anti-social behaviors. All these approaches to the ideological spectrum presuppose a relatively high level of political sophistication. They all assume that people possess a coherent view of the world and human beings, and they are able to translate that worldview into political commitments.

Another perspective suggests that people are drawn to certain political belief systems based on their personality types. Those advocating this perspective sometimes take an uncharitable approach, seeking to pathologize people who self-identify with the "incorrect" political category.[9] A more evenhanded approach suggests that different people possess different moral foundations, which inform their political ideologies.[10]

In the US context, the primary ideological divide is between liberals (or progressives) and conservatives. This can sometimes be confusing as many progressives declare that "neo-liberals" are their primary opponents. One can also find many other ideologies in the US, such as libertarianism. Nonetheless, among most Americans, to the extent that they use ideological labels, liberalism and conservatism remain the most common terms.[11]

Conservative as a self-description

If the US has really undergone a period of ideological polarization, at the very least we should see that Republicans have become more likely to describe themselves as conservative and Democrats have increasingly described themselves as liberal. The GSS gives us a way to test this, as it has asked respondents about their ideological leanings since the early 1970s. Specifically, it asked people where they would place themselves on a seven-point ideological spectrum, ranging from "extremely liber-

---

9 The quintessential example of this from the left is Theodor W. Adorno, Else Frenkel-Brunswik, Daniel Levinson, and Nevitt Sanford, *The Authoritarian Personality* (New York: Harper, 1950); there are fewer scholarly arguments from the right taking this approach, but they can be found from more popular polemicists. For example, see Michael Savage, *Liberalism is a Mental Disorder* (Nashville, TN: Nelson Current, 2005).
10 Jonathan Haidt, *The Righteous Mind: Why Good People are Divided by Politics and Religion* (New York: Pantheon, 2012): Arnold Kling, *The Three Languages of Politics: Talking Across the Political Divides* (Washington, DC: The Cato Institute, 2017).
11 The fact that, in the survey I commissioned for this chapter, only 18 respondents described themselves as "other" suggests that most Americans identify themselves on the common conservative-liberal scale.

al" (0) to "extremely conservative" (7). The mid-point on the scale is "moderate" or "middle of the road" (3). In Figure 4.1, we see how the mean score for supporters of both parties has changed since the question was first asked in 1974.

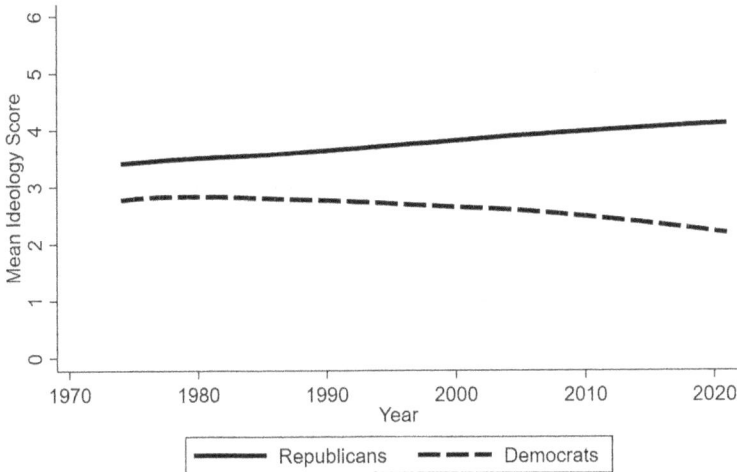

Figure 4.1: Mean Ideology by Party. Source: Cumulative GSS. Note: Figure LOWESS smoothed. Higher score indicates greater conservatism.

The figure demonstrates that supporters of the two parties have become, on average, more ideologically distant. We further see that there has been slightly more movement among Republicans than among Democrats. In 1974, both Republicans and Democrats averaged very close to the center. As of 2021, the mean score for Republicans was just above 4, which represents "slightly conservative." This suggests a more ideologically polarized electorate. Viewed in isolation, we may consider this clear, alarming evidence of ideological polarization.

The previous chapter demonstrates the problem with drawing such an inference, however. Across most issues, we find little evidence that Republicans have moved to the right, on either social or economic issues. Republicans, on average, are very similar to where they were decades ago when it comes to policy. This is especially interesting because, when it comes to self-described ideology, they claim to be more conservative than ever. In other words, the connection between self-described ideology and policy positions is weaker than we might expect.

A growing percentage of Republicans identifying as conservative and Democrats identifying as liberals does not necessarily indicate the nation's overall ideological distribution has changed. Political scientist Matthew Levendusky has convincingly demonstrated that the greater ideological consistency of both parties is due to a "sorting" of the population along ideological lines.[12] In the 1970s, there was still a great deal of ideological diversity in both major political parties. There were, for example, still conservative Democrats in the South and liberal Republicans in the Northeast. Since that time, this has become less common. As a result of this change, ordinary voters began receiving more consistent cues from political elites, helping them to better understand which political party was more aligned with their own ideological dispositions. Both parties, at both the elite and the mass level, are now more internally homogeneous.[13]

We must, however, not take it for granted that most Americans possess anything resembling coherent ideologies. In 1964, Philip Converse published his influential argument that very few Americans possess anything resembling a coherent, consistent set of political principles connected abstract ideals.[14] Although Converse may have overstated his case, subsequent scholars have found his analysis continues to hold up well.[15]

Some political scientists argue that ideology, however defined and from whatever its source, is upstream from party identification and policy preferences. That is, we choose the political party and set of policies most congruent with our ideology. Other scholarly literature suggests that social identity is paramount.[16] According to this view, the social characteristics that are critical to our sense of self determine which political party we align with, and we choose our ideologies to align with our political parties. This claim is congruent with the extensive literature in political science suggesting that ideological sophistication in the electorate is exceedingly rare. It also can explain why political anger can easily coexist with almost complete political ignorance – if partisan battles are more about identity than policy, then people can become emotionally invested in political outcomes even if the real-world stakes are low and they have little knowledge of or interest in government and policy.[17]

---

12 Matthew Levendusky, *The Partisan Sort: How Liberals Became Democrats and Conservatives Became Republicans* (Chicago, IL: University of Chicago Press, 2009)
13 Nolan McCarty, Howard Rosenthal, and Keith T. Poole, *Polarized America* (Cambridge, MA: MIT Press, 2006).
14 Philip Converse, "The Nature of Belief Systems in Mass Publics." In *Ideology and Discontent.* ed. David Apter. (New York: The Free Press, 1964).
15 Donald R. Kinder and Nathan P. Kalmoe, *Neither Liberal Nor Conservative: Ideological Innocence in the American Public* (Chicago, IL: University of Chicago Press, 2017).
16 Donald Green, Bradley Palmquist, and Eric Schickley, *Partisan Hearts and Minds: Political Parties and the Social Identities of Voters* (New Haven, CT: Yale University Press).
17 Lilliana Mason, *Uncivil Agreement: How Politics Became Our Identity* (Chicago, IL: University of Chicago Press, 2018).

The trend of Republicans becoming more likely to describe themselves as conservatives than Democrats to describe themselves as liberals may seem puzzling. There are a few possible explanations for this. It may be that conservatives have done a better job of marketing their ideology than liberals. One narrative suggests that politicians such as Ronald Reagan and media personalities like Rush Limbaugh very successfully demonized liberals and liberalism. Leading Democrats, for their part, failed to push back against these efforts, choosing instead to run from the liberal label. President Bill Clinton, who made every effort to present himself as a centrist who rejected "big government," is the quintessential example of this. According to this argument, asymmetric ideological demonization explains conservatism's growing popularity compared to liberalism. It is not explained by any element of the electorate actually becoming more aligned with the policy prescriptions associated with modern American conservatism.

This theory, while common and seemingly aligned with trends in political rhetoric over the last 40 years, has yet to be demonstrated empirically. In part, this is because it is a difficult theory to test. Political scientist Jacob R. Neiheisel examined this issue, attempting to discern whether anti-liberal rhetoric resulted in negative attitudes toward Democrats or caused people to be less likely to self-identify as liberals.[18] He found some evidence for the former, but none for the latter, which seems to undermine the idea that anti-liberal messaging from conservatives is to blame for the term's comparatively low level of popularity.

How do ordinary Republicans describe conservatism and liberalism?

There are many possible ways to consider whether Americans possess meaningful ideologies. The most common and obvious method is to simply ask subjects to place themselves somewhere on a one-dimensional ideological spectrum. Another method is to ask them their opinions about specific policies, and then draw inferences about their ideological orientation from their responses. As we have seen, these methods lead to inconsistent results.

Both approaches have a problem. They are not helpful for showing which respondents really understand the major ideological categories, even when they readily give a label to themselves. To gain a better understanding of this question, I commissioned a survey of 830 Americans, one that sought to accurately represent

---

18 Jacob R. Neiheisel, "The 'L' Word: Anti-Liberal Campaign Rhetoric, Symbolic Ideology, and the Electoral Fortunes of Democratic Candidates," *Political Research Quarterly* 69 (2016): 418–429.

US demographics, in the fall of 2020.[19] In this survey, I asked respondents some basic demographic questions (race/ethnicity, age, gender, region, religion, educational attainment), as well as basic political information (party identification, and ideology on the liberal-conservative scale). In this survey, 276 respondents identified as Republicans. These subjects are my focus here. When quoting these results, I corrected minor spelling and punctuation errors.

To better understand how Americans think about the two dominant ideologies of US politics, the survey provided an opportunity for respondents to explain how they define "liberal" and "conservative" in an open-ended manner.[20] Before asking this question, the survey did not ask respondents anything about specific policies or politicians, this was to avoid priming them about the subject. Responses were then coded according to whether they included a reference to policy (and which policies, if so), if they defined these ideological categories based on a particular worldview or set of values, whether the response expressed positive, negative, or neutral emotions toward the category, and whether the respondent's definition could be unquestionably described as "wrong" – that is, it had no resemblance to any common understanding of the terms. A minority of respondents provided responses that were nonsensical or failed to exhibit a good faith effort to answer the questions. They were dropped from the subsequent analysis.

Some respondents seemed to not understand the question. A few seemed to mistake conservatism with conservationism. According to one of their definitions: "Try to meet most needs of everyone, not just a certain group. Recycle, reduce, reuse." Another Republican, when asked to describe conservatism, stated, "[c]ommon sense and respect the way plants and animals are raised for consumption. GMOs are a part of everything." One person seemed to think that conservatives are defined by their reticence: "Someone who follows politics but doesn't talk about what's going on with politics or the government."

Several respondents were quite open about their lack of ideological sophistication, even if they did give themselves ideological labels. One acknowledged that she was "not sure, I don't know enough about politics and don't have an interest in it." A young Republican who described herself as "very conservative" sub-

---

19 The survey was conducted online via the respected survey company Qualtrics.
20 Specifically, the question asked: "We hear a lot about conservatives and liberals these days, but the meaning of these terms is not always clear. To you, what does it mean to say that someone is a 'conservative'? Please describe this term in one to five sentences. Note that any response you provide may be quoted in research resulting from this survey." The survey then asked the same question for the definition of liberal. The survey asked no questions about policy or politicians prior to these questions, to ensure that respondents were not primed to focus on any particular person, concept, or policy before giving their answer.

sequently admitted, "I am not sure what a conservative is. Honestly I just know that I am based off of family." Although this subject was notable for her honesty, she is not alone when it comes to the source of her ideological commitments. A long tradition in political science emphasizes the importance of family and early socialization to political identities.[21]

About half of all Republicans gave an answer that described conservatism in religious terms, or as a more traditional worldview. As one Republican put it, "I believe conservative typically comes from southern beliefs. Yet, it also comes from a lot of things which stem from a Christian and or church background." One stated that conservatism means "believing in God and living according to His Word."

They often discussed liberalism in religious terms, as well, usually emphasizing liberals' lack of moral bearings. About 23 percent of Republican respondents used the language or religion or worldview when describing liberals. According to one Republican, "liberals tell people that is alright to do the things that are against God." The subject of abortion was especially likely to inspire strong wording, such as the respondent who claimed that liberals "are okay with killing babies."

Some gave a similar definition, but used less negative language, for example, "to me [liberals are] those who wish to tear down tradition and change lifestyle. To discard the Bible"; "[t]o say that someone is liberal to me means that they look towards the future and trying to change the way things are, being different"; "[o]pen minded. Wanting the best for society at large. Frivolous, to some degree. Willing to at least listen to another viewpoint."

A few even described liberalism in a way that seemed almost positive. To take a few examples: liberals "are more open to things, they are modern"; "[t]o be liberal means that you're not so stuck to beliefs and convictions, they believe more in the free will of the people'"; and liberals are "open to changes. Not keeping things the same. These type of people are open minded and can see that the past is not always the right way to go." Overall, about 13 percent of Republicans used primarily positive language when describing liberalism.

In contrast, when describing liberals, some Republicans just listed a series of negative traits: "Evil. Wrong. Nazi liars. Out to get people. Hitler. Socialist. Doesn't have the best in mind for us." According to another Republican, liberals are defined by their "Marxist, communist views. Anti-American, full of hatred, racism. Willing to do whatever it takes to get what they want by stealing, killing or

---

21 Angus Campbell, Philip E. Converse, Warren E. Miller, and Donald Stokes, *The American Voter* (New York: John Wiley and Sons, 1960)

other means. No morals." Many Republicans defined liberals by their lack of work ethic. Some of these answers included: "They want free hand outs. They are lazy. They want universal healthcare. They are usually younger. They protest too much"; "[p]rogressive to change or communist and believe in changing the American way to people who live off the government and take drugs and burn cities"; and "liberals believe in free stuff for everyone motto is I want it and I want it now."

A majority of Republicans did not name any policies when describing either conservatism or liberalism – about 73 and 72 percent, respectively. It is worth noting which policies they mentioned when describing these ideologies. The number of mentions of different issues related to policy (some respondents listed more than one) can be found in Table 4.1.

Table 4.1: Policies Republicans named in their definitions of liberalism and conservatism

Policies associated with conservatism		Policies associated with liberalism	
abortion	23	abortion	26
limited government	21	big government	14
The US Constitution	12	welfare	12
taxes	12	socialism	11
spending	9	taxes	11
guns	7	same-sex marriage	10
same-sex marriage	5	spending	7
welfare	3	guns	6
immigration	3	health care	6
free speech	2	immigration	5
foreign policy	1	foreign policy	4
free trade	1	The US Constitution	3
law and order	1	criminal justice	3
private ownership	1	education	3
services	1	affirmative action	1
prayer in school	1	civil liberties	1
		civil rights	1
		regulation	1
		the environment	1

Source: Qualtrics survey conducted fall 2020

The frequency with which abortion was named as a defining issue for both liberalism and conservatism among Republicans immediately stands out. Although we saw in Chapter 3 that only a minority of Republicans maintain a doctrinaire pro-life stance, a significant contingent of Republicans care about this issue with great intensity. We additionally saw in Chapter 3 that this is one of the very few issues where Republicans, on average, have been moving in a more conservative direction for several decades. From the standpoint of partisan politics, this may potentially create problems for the GOP. It is quite likely that the Supreme Court decision that overturned *Roe v. Wade* in 2022 was a major reason for the Republican Party's poor performance in that year's midterm election.[22] Yes, pro-life advocates are a large and vocal element of the Republican coalition. However, among voters that say the abortion issue plays a major role in their vote choice, a significant majority hold pro-choice views. From a purely political standpoint, the abortion issue probably hurts the GOP far more than it helps. Unlike what we saw with same-sex marriage, however, at present it seems very unlikely that the Republican Party will soon embrace a more liberal position on the issue, at least officially. It is conceivable, however, that a growing number of Republican politicians will quietly back down from pro-life absolutism when it becomes clear that they must do so to win elections.

The size and scope of government, broadly understood, was also a common theme among Republicans when describing both ideologies. Some described this as the very essence of conservatism: "Conservative to me means to me someone who wants a more limited government"; "[c]onservatives believe in personal responsibilities and limited government"; and "conservatives are people that favor individual decision making, they do not favor large involvement of the federal government. Large government programs, intervention into everyday life is not what they want. They favor smaller government, less day to day government interaction in their personal lives."

Support for the US Constitution was another common theme in these answers. For these Republicans, conservatism meant defending the Constitution from liberals who reject and want to replace it. As one Republican put it, "[a] conservative is someone who believes in the constitution." Several gave answers indicating that support for the Constitution was almost interchangeable with other kinds of traditionalism: "Politically someone is conservative if they believe in upholding the Constitution and upholding traditional societal values"; "[a] conservative is someone who believes in the Constitution of the United States with strong moral and religious beliefs"; and "[w]hen you define your values based on tradition and how things were. How we stand by the Constitution."

Although most of these descriptions did not indicate a high level of political knowledge and sophistication, many did show at least a basic understanding of the ideological spectrum as it is commonly discussed in the US. They did, for example, grasp that American conservatism is an amalgamation of cultural traditional-

22 "Analysis Reveals How Abortion Boosted Democratic Candidates in Tuesday's Midterm Election," Kaiser Family Foundation, December 8, 2022, https://jamanetwork.com/journals/jama-health-forum/fullarticle/2800735.

ism and free-market capitalism. As one Republican put it, conservatism means "favoring free enterprise, private ownership, and socially traditional ideas. [It] is opposition to rapid changes, and supports keeping traditions in society. [It means] following the US Constitution to the letter."

Republican descriptions of ideologies from longer interviews

During my interviews, most participants were able to provide a definition of conservatism that, broadly speaking, aligned with how the conservative movement has traditionally described its values. According to one subject, the essence of conservatism was "personal responsibility. That's a big one. They all kind of come off of that." This same subject further argued that the Republican Party was not very good at promoting that value: "They're not really trying to go in a different direction they're just kind of trying to go, like, a decade in the past and try to get it to that point [...]. I feel like we should be going in a different direction, not just on the same path but back a decade." Another Republican similarly argued that individual responsibility and the rejection of collective thinking are key elements of conservatism:

> For what it's worth, I think that the Democratic Party, while they say they want to help people, in a certain sense they're passing that off. I think it could be paraphrased that "other people should help people." From my perspective, we have an individual responsibility to help others, and not to collectively pass that off to the collective. I think that's a big difference in how Democrats and myself and some Republicans view the role of government [...]. I think that individuals need to try to help the world around them individually.

Another interviewee similarly argued that, to him, conservatism was more important than the Republican Party: "Given the option between the term Republican and the term conservative, I would lean more towards conservative than Republican. I agree mostly with the Republican Party platform, however, certain elements of party members and their actions I disagree with." When asked about those disagreements, he said, "[s]pecifically, I disagree with some of the policy of members in the Senate who [...] lean more towards liberal or progressive in their votes than true conservative senators do. Them associating with the Republican Party makes me less willing to fully associate with the Republican Party."

One Republican who described himself as very conservative listed names associated with the conservative movement and the Republican Party from the mid-twentieth century as his ideological role models, stating that, "we need to get back to the conservatism of Buckley and Goldwater, free markets and traditional values." Two other people mentioned Reagan as a model for conservatism. Most, however, used more general language when talking about what conservatism means to them.

Conclusion

In terms of self-description, Republicans are becoming more conservative. They also, on average, tend to have very negative opinions of liberals and liberalism – though this is not universal. Answering the question of whether Republicans, or Americans more broadly, really possess coherent ideologies depends on how high one sets the bar.

From the open-ended survey question and my discussions with Republicans, I conclude that it would be a mistake to say the average Republican has no coherent understanding of the major ideologies in the US. Although they do not spend time reading books that attempt to work through the meaning and philosophical under-pinnings of ideological categories, most do have at least a general understanding of these terms, even if they are unable to directly connect them to specific policy pro-posals.

In the previous chapter, we saw that consistent conservatism (at least as the organized conservative movement understands the term) is relatively uncommon among Republicans. Majorities of Republicans take a moderate or even liberal po-sition on many questions of policy, and we find few areas where they have been moving further to the right. They nonetheless are increasingly likely to describe themselves as conservatives. This suggests that, for the electorate, the meaning of terms like conservative and liberal are moving targets. The typical Republican voter is not particularly concerned with ideological purity, and many do not appa-rently see a contradiction between flexibility on policy and viewing themselves in strongly ideological terms.

Policy is not the only source of political conflict. Cultural antagonisms, which are often, but not necessarily, connected to public policy, are also important. Even if Republicans and Democrats are not moving apart from each other on major is-sues of public policy, perhaps their attitudes toward cultural trends are large and growing. The next chapter considers this question in detail.

Chapter 5
Republican cultural attitudes

Positions on public policy may not be the best way to measure partisan polarization. Cultural differences, and resentments, may be even more important to understand if we wish to make sense of overheated rhetoric in US politics. Questions related to race, sex, and gender, questions that sometimes are only indirectly related to public policy, generate some of the nation's most heated disagreements. As I am writing this, conservative media seems more focused on whether Bud Light should have partnered with the trans Tik Tok personality Dylan Mulvaney than any question of substantive policy.

Pundits, scholars, and watchdog groups have recently shown particular concern about American attitudes toward demographic change, particularly non-Hispanic white attitudes about the forthcoming loss of their absolute majority status in the country. The notion that the population is being deliberately changed via policy, sometimes called the "Great Replacement" conspiracy theory, has been tied to a number of acts of terrorism.[1] Donald Trump's success in the Republican primaries and 2016 general election for president seemed to indicate rising animus toward immigrants and a turn toward nativism. Fear of religious decline, and the decline of Christianity in particular, has spurred a new field of study among academics fearful of an ascendant "Christian nationalism" on the right. These are all serious issues worthy of study.

We should nonetheless not overstate the degree to which Republicans and Democrats fundamentally differ on key cultural attitudes, nor should we overstate the degree to which either side has shifted on key questions. One older Republican I interviewed stated directly that he has been mostly unchanged in his views since his youth. He was nonetheless more strongly Republican now because he could no longer relate to the Democratic Party at all; he considered it too culturally alien.

I was not surprised that few people who agreed to be recorded by a political scientist for my research were willing to express crude bigotry, even with the knowledge that the conversation would be completely confidential and they would never see me again. The people I spoke with for this project knew I was writing about Republicans, and they reasonably wanted to present themselves as the best possible representatives of their fellow partisans. For this reason, it

---

1 Dustin Jones, "What is the 'Great Replacement' and How is it Tied to the Buffalo Shooting Suspect?" National Public Radio, May 16, 2022, https://www.npr.org/2022/05/16/1099034094/what-is-the-great-replacement-theory.

https://doi.org/10.1515/9783111469720-005

may be prudent to view their comments with a skeptical eye. Nonetheless, the cultural complaints I heard were generally not linked to issues related to the nation's changing demographic makeup. One person complained about the new pervasiveness of Spanish, but this was dwarfed by complaints about cultural trends that are disconnected from race and ethnicity (such as young people with weird piercings and hair dye). In many ways, these conversations would have probably been very similar if I had conducted these interviews in the 1960s – what's with all these young people with crazy hair and wild ideas? This may be a perennial sentiment among conservatives. Nonetheless, most of the Republicans I spoke with, especially older Republicans, seem alienated from young people right now. They are particularly baffled, and angered, by what they view as madness when it comes to issues of gender and sexuality. Some of this is probably just due to misconceptions about how radical the younger generation actually is on these matters. To hear some older Republicans talk about the subject, one might infer that a majority of Generation Z identifies as LGBT. Many Republicans also apparently take it for granted that there is currently a major push by the left to normalize and legalize pedophilia. Some of these misconceptions are undoubtedly due to conservative media, which has perfected the art of finding the most extreme sentiments expressed on social media platforms and treating them as common.

Not all Republicans are cultural reactionaries, however, and some of my interviewees were nonchalant about cultural changes. According to one Republican, "I feel like in regard to people saying the country's changing, I mean, I'm sure their grandparents felt the same way. It's always been changing." Another person part of the same group responded, "I would agree with that. It seems like conservatives are always against new social changes. But then you look at it later on down the line, they eventually don't necessarily support them but they say, 'it is what it is,' on issues like race or gay marriage. It's kind of like a pattern [...]. I don't think that's necessarily bad, because I think that as a society we should progress, and maybe conservatives should really just be there to kind of slow it down and say, 'Hey, let's think about this first before we have this sweeping societal change.'"

When thinking about demographic or cultural change, we are of course talking about many different kinds of change, some of which conservatives may consider benign. We therefore must disaggregate different kinds of changes and the policies they are associated with.

Republican views on immigration

I had difficulty deciding where to include immigration as a subject in this text. It is of course a policy issue, but it is also a major source of cultural change, and the policies surrounding immigration are complicated and not well understood by most voters. The political science literature furthermore indicates that cultural concerns play a greater role in determining immigration attitudes than economic concerns. There is also a strong and unsurprising correlation between racist attitudes and immigration restrictionist sentiments, and immigration restrictionism is one of the main issues white nationalist ideologues focus on.[2] This seems to indicate that this discussion would also fit in the chapter on racism among Republicans. On the other hand, it is not my position that skepticism toward large-scale immigration can only be rooted in crude prejudice. If that were the case, policy changes that lead to decreased immigration should perhaps be viewed with inherent suspicion. My decision to focus on this issue in this chapter was my attempt to split the difference, understanding that readers may think it fits better elsewhere.

Immigration was Donald Trump's signature issue in the run-up to the 2016 presidential election. During the speech that launched his campaign, he infamously decried immigration from Mexico, implying that undocumented immigrants were disproportionately drug dealers and rapists. One of his first acts in office was a ham-fisted attempt to implement an immigration "Muslim ban," which after an extended court battle was partially implemented, though indirectly. From this, one might infer that Republicans in the electorate are overwhelmingly anti-immigrant and their nativism is more pronounced than ever. The public opinion data, however, do not suggest a major surge in anti-immigrant animus, even from Republicans.

There is also scholarship suggesting that high immigration rates can cause a shift in attitudes among native-born Americans, especially native-born whites. In the most thorough investigation of this phenomenon to date, *White Backlash* by Marisa Abrajano and Zoltan L. Hajnal, the authors find that increasing rates of immigration cause many non-Hispanic whites to become more conservative in their policy preferences and more likely to vote Republican.[3] A meta-analysis of the relevant research has demonstrated that there is a connection between growing diversity and feelings of threat among white people.[4] More recent research indicates that feelings about immigration were a key explanation for why elements of the

---

2 George Hawley, *Right-Wing Critics of American Conservatism* (Lawrence, KS: University Press of Kansas, 2016).
3 Marisa Abrajano and Zoltan L. Hajnal, *White Backlash: Immigration, Race, and American Politics* (Princeton, NJ: Princeton University Press, 2015).
4 Eric Kaufmann and Matthew J. Goodwin, "The Diversity Wave: A Meta-Analyis of the Native-Born White Response to Ethnic Diversity," *Social Science Research* 76 (2018): 120–131.

white working class shifted from Democrat to Republican in the 2016 presidential election.[5]

Republicans are unsurprisingly more skeptical of immigration than Democrats. It is also clear that anti-immigrant attitudes were a powerful predictor of support for President Trump. But just how nativist is the Republican Party in the electorate? Fortunately, several public-opinion surveys ask many questions about immigration. This is a tricky issue to make sense of from surveys, as I have found that it is very sensitive to question wording. By looking at lots of different questions from many different polls, however, we can get a sense of where the typical Republican voter really stands on the issue.

The GSS can give us a sense of the trajectory of Republican opinion on this issue in recent years. From 2004 until 2021, the survey has been asking respondents their views on the proper number of immigrants to the country. Specifically, it asked them where they would place themselves on a five-point scale about immigration rates, with higher numbers indicating a preference for fewer immigrants.[6] Figure 5.1 shows this trend over time. For the sake of comparison, I also showed the trend for Democratic GSS respondents. For the purposes of creating a more intuitive figure, I recoded these data so that higher values indicate supporting a greater number of immigrants.

Note that, over the course of the period for which we have GSS data, the mean for Republicans scarcely changed at all. Every year, the mean fell between immigration should "remain the same as it is" and immigration should "decrease a little." To the extent that we see movement, it is in the direction of greater openness to higher immigration rates, but the difference between Republicans in 2004 and Republicans in 2021 was negligible. Looking at these data, one could say that, from one perspective, the parties in the electorate are "polarizing" on immigrant numbers. The mean score for the two parties are, after all, getting farther apart. It is once again asymmetric polarization, however. Both Republicans and Democrats appear to be moving in a more progressive direction when it comes to immigration numbers, but the Democrats are moving much more quickly. The notion that the typical Republican in the electorate is radicalizing on the immigration issue is simply not consistent with what these data show.[7]

---

5 Tyler T. Reny, Loren Collingwood, and Ali A. Valenzuela, "Vote Switching in the 2016 Election: How Racial and Immigration Attitudes, Not Economics, Explain Shifts in White Voting," *Public Opinion Quarterly* 83 (2019): 91–113.

6 Specifically, respondents were asked whether immigration should be "increased a lot," "increased a little," "remain the same as it is," "reduced a little," "reduced a lot."

7 Other researchers examining this subject have reached similar conclusions: Michael Hout and Christopher Maggio, "Immigration, Race, and Political Polarization," *Daedalus* 150 (2021): 40–55.

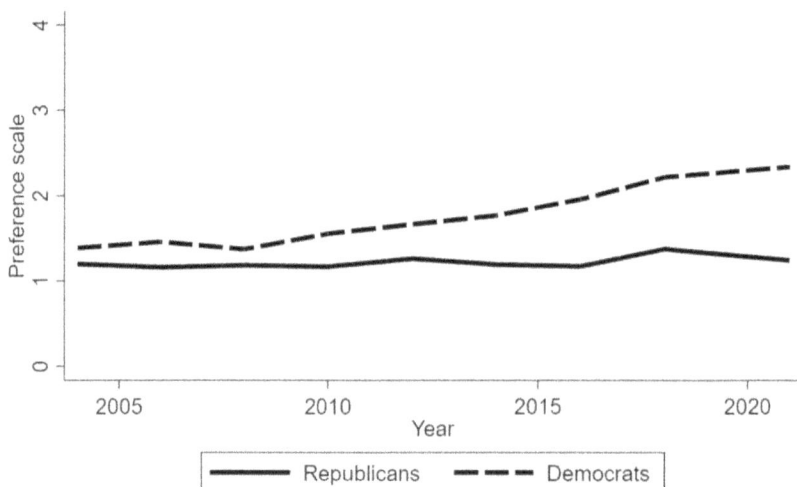

Source: GSS. Note: Higher values indicate support for more immigration.

Figure 5.1: Support for Immigration. Source: Cumulative GSS. Higher values indicate support for more immigration.

The 2020 ANES also provided a helpful battery of questions about immigration. Like the GSS, it asked about the total number of immigrants the country should allow. It also provided a five-point scale, ranging from "increased a lot" to "decreased a lot." This survey shows that Republicans have little desire to increase immigration. Only about 12 percent of Republicans wanted immigration increased, whether a little or a lot. However, drastic immigration cuts were also relatively unpopular. About 21 percent wanted immigration "decreased a lot" and about 22 percent wanted it "decreased a little." The most common response (at about 44 percent) was that immigration should be "left the same as it is now." At least in these data, a majority of Republicans are either satisfied with current immigration numbers (which remained high even during the Trump Administration) or wanted to see them increased even further.

Perhaps different survey questions will tell different stories. In 2021, the GSS asked subjects the degree to which they agreed with the statement, "America should limit immigration in order to protect our national way of life." On this question, we see a much starker partisan divide. When framed in this language, more than 63 percent of Republicans either agreed or agreed strongly that immigration should be limited. In contrast, only about 16 percent of Democrats agreed with this statement.

Another question on that survey seems to provide a very different picture. It asked about the level of conflict between "People born in America and people from other countries who have come to live in America." Their options were "very strong conflicts," "strong conflicts," "not strong conflicts," and "there are no conflicts." Because other questions indicated that Republicans are more skeptical about immigration, it seems intuitive that they would be more inclined to believe conflicts between immigrants and the native-born are inevitable. That is not what we see, however. Among Republicans, about 12 percent predicted "very strong conflicts"; among Democrats, it was about 16 percent. About 44 percent of Republicans said "strong conflicts," compared to 53 percent of Democrats.

How can we account for this? This may be a case of vague question wording causing people from different partisan camps to envision different kinds of "conflict." Although we cannot demonstrate this with the existing GSS questions, it is probable that Republicans and Democrats had different things in mind when they were considering hostilities between immigrants and the native-born. Rather than an indication that Democrats are more anti-immigrant than Republicans, these data probably indicate Democrats believe native-born Americans (especially white Republicans) are likely to create conflicts because of their nativism and xenophobia. Regardless of why we see this divide, it is interesting and potentially important that Republicans are actually not more pessimistic than Democrats when it comes to the future of relations between immigrants and the native born.

There is one class of immigrants that Republicans, on average, have no problem opposing, and they are willing to say they want them removed from the country: undocumented immigrants. This issue has been politically contentious for decades, and every effort to come up with a permanent way to end illegal border crossings has thus far failed. In the 2020 ANES, respondents were asked whether they favor or oppose "returning all unauthorized immigrants to their native countries." A plurality of Republicans (about 32 percent) said that they favor this "a great deal." When added to those who favor it "a moderate amount" and favor it "a little," a slight majority of Republicans (about 55%) said they favored deporting all of these immigrants.

This suggests that Republicans in the electorate tend to be major border hawks when it comes to illegal immigration. Making sense of their feelings becomes a bit more difficult, however, when we consider another 2020 ANES question about undocumented immigrants. The survey also asked these subjects, "Do you favor, oppose, or neither favor nor oppose providing a path to citizenship for unauthorized immigrants who obey the law, pay a fine, and pass security checks?" When the issue is framed this way, Republicans, the same Republicans that in a different question said they wanted all illegal immigrants deported, suddenly were mostly okay with these immigrants remaining in the country. A majority (about 56 percent) said they would favor this pathway to citizenship. An additional 20 percent said that they "neither favor nor oppose" such a policy. A little less than one quarter of Republicans opposed providing undocumented immigrants with a pathway to citizenship. These seemingly contradictory results within the same survey again demonstrate that public opinion surveys on immigration are extremely sensitive to question wording.

Although Republicans are not as uniformly anti-immigration as many of their opponents seem to believe, they are unquestionably more anti-immigrant than Democrats, on average. The question then becomes why Republicans tend to be more opposed to immigration, which is part of the broader question of why people in general develop anti-immigration attitudes.

For pro-immigrant activists, anti-immigration attitudes may represent nothing more than irrational bigotry. In their view, the benefits of immigration, for both the immigrants themselves, and society more broadly, are so obvious that there could be no other explanation for the phenomenon. From this perspective, anti-immigrant white Americans fear the "browning" of America, and that is the entire story. That being the case, nativist policy should be taken off the political table as a legitimate option.

Immigration skeptics on the right, especially those who want to maintain some distance from the intensely xenophobic extreme right, will typically lean on arguments disconnected from any kind of racist or anti-foreigner argument. They can argue, for example, that immigration has played a large role in exploding inequality in recent decades.[8] They sometimes point out that the steady stream of less-skilled and less-educated workers have consistently driven down the wages of native-born workers with fewer skills and credentials.[9] There is also a reasonable, non-racist cultural argument one can make about immigration. If Americans have a shared political culture, one that they wish to maintain into the future, it makes sense to prefer immigrants from countries that have similar political cultures. We certainly should not, according to this argument, accept unlimited immigration from countries with totally different political cultures, especially if we are not willing to engage in an aggressive program of assimilation. The late political scientist Samuel Huntington, for example, made this argument in his final book, *Who Are We?*[10]

---

8 F.H. Buckley, *Progressive Conservatism: How Republicans will Become America's Natural Governing Party* (New York: Encounter Books, 2022).

9 George J. Borjas, *Heaven's Door: Immigration Policy and the American Economy* (Princeton, NJ: Princeton University Press, 1999).

10 Samuel Huntington, *Who Are We? The Challenges to America's National Identity* (New York: Simon and Schuster, 2005).

Somewhat related to political culture, immigration's impact on partisan politics may also play a role in determining attitudes. That is, because immigrants and their descendants, on average, tend to be more supportive of the Democratic Party than the Republican Party,[11] it makes intuitive sense that Republicans would be more skeptical of immigration, and that skepticism would only increase as immigrants become an increasingly important part of the Democratic coalition.[12] This view also suggests that pro-immigrant attitudes among Democrats are also driven, in part, by partisan considerations. If more immigrant groups were to become reliably Republican, it is possible that they would be less enthusiastic about immigration.

Of these arguments, which best explains opposition to higher levels of immigration? There is evidence suggesting that economic considerations do play a role in immigration attitudes. Anti-immigrant attitudes tend to increase during periods of economic stagnation or contraction, for example.[13] A larger low-skilled white population at the state level is associated with more restrictionist policies, suggesting that people with more uncertain economic prospects are more likely to want less immigration.[14] There is another element of economics-based nativism. Beyond fear that immigrants will take jobs or at least drive down wages, some people are concerned that immigrants receive welfare benefits that should only go to citizens – a concept sometimes called welfare chauvinism.[15]

Although economic concerns can increase nativist sentiments, they are far from the entire story.[16] They may not be the primary arguments coming out of conservative think tanks, or the way Republican politicians prefer to frame the question, but cultural concerns and racial bias are unquestionably the most important

---

11 George Hawley, "Immigration Status, Immigrant Family Ties, and Support for the Democratic Party," *Social Science Quarterly* 100 (2019): 1171–1181.

12 George Hawley, "Political Threat and Immigration: Party Identification, Demographic Context, and Immigration Policy Preference," *Social Science Quarterly* 92 (2011): 404–422.

13 Vickie D. Ybarra, Lisa M. Sanchez, and Gabriel R. Sanchez, "Anti-Immigrant Anxieties in State Policy: The Great Recession and Punitive Immigration Policy in the American States, 2005–2012," *State Politics and Policy Quarterly* 16 (2016): 313–339; R. Michael Alvarez and Tara L. Butterfield, "The Resurgence of Nativism in California? The Case of Proposition 187 and Illegal Immigration," *Social Science Quarterly* 81 (2000): 167–179.

14 Sarah Ghatak and Vincent Ferraro, "Immigration Control and the White Working Class: Explaining State-Level Laws in the US, 2005–2017," *Sociological Spectrum* 41(2021): 457–477.

15 Gary P. Freeman, "Immigration, Diversity, and Welfare Chauvinism," *The Forum* 7 (2009): 1–16.

16 Joel S. Fetzer, "Economic Self-Interest or Cultural Marginality? Anti-Immigration Sentiment and Nativist Political Movements in France, Germany, and the USA," *Journal of Ethnic and Migration Studies* 26 (2000): 5–23; Hans-Georg Betz, "Facets of Nativism: A Heuristic Explanation," *Patterns of Prejudice* 53 (2019): 111–135.

determinants of restrictionist attitudes. High levels of racial resentment, a subject I will return to in Chapter 6, has a much stronger effect on these attitudes than any economic characteristic.[17] Other research suggests that views about the economy can influence attitudes toward immigrants, but the relationship is indirect; a weakening economy is viewed by many people as evidence of cultural decline, which results in higher levels of nativism.[18]

I am well aware of the appalling acts of anti-immigrant violence that have occurred over the last years. I furthermore know that right-wing radicals are engaged in a persistent persuasion and recruiting campaign online and elsewhere. I would never endorse some of the more irresponsible fearmongering about immigrants that we often see or hear from conservative media. However, there is a difference between the tiny minority of radicals that engage in hate crimes, and the typical Republican in the electorate. The data I see do not indicate that the ordinary Republican voter is becoming more anti-immigrant. It is true that they are not moving in a progressive direction as quickly as Democrats, but what little movement we do see appears to be in a more pro-immigrant direction.

In my conversations with Republicans, immigration was an issue that came up again and again, but it was rarely the first issue people mentioned. Overall, I heard more negative comments about immigration than positive ones, but nativism was not the major unifying characteristic of the Republican Party. I did notice a class divide on the immigration issue. Only among wealthier Republicans, especially those people I would consider policy-oriented, free-market Republicans, and those that lean toward the libertarian element of the Republican electorate, were views toward immigrants generally positive.

To get a sense of whether my qualitative discussions matched the quantitative data, I revisited the question about the proper number of immigrants on the 2020 ANES.[19] I divided the Republican respondents up according to income – those making less than $50,000 in household income per year, those making between $50,000 and $100,000, and those making more than $100,000. I found only small differences in immigration attitudes among these groups. For the first two categories, the difference in the mean views toward immigration numbers was negligible. In this case, the class divide was more apparent in personal conversations than it was

---

17 Steven V. Miller, "Economic Anxiety or Racial Resentment? An Evaluation of Attitudes Toward Immigration in the U.S. from 1992 to 2016," *Immigration Research* 1 (2018): 1–29.
18 Nicholas T. Davis, Kirby Goidel, Christine S. Lipsmeyer, Guy D. Whitten, and Clifford Young, "Economic Vulnerability, Cultural Decline, and Nativism: Contingent and Indirect Effects," *Social Science Quarterly* 100 (2019): 430–446.
19 I used the 2020 ANES for this analysis rather than the 2021 GSS because the ANES had the larger number of observations.

in the quantitative data. This may be because wealthier Republicans are more likely to self-censor in interviews.

Immigration restrictionists will be quick to point out that they have public opinion, or at least public opinion among the Republican electorate, on their side. There is a problem with this idea, however: the existing polling data indicate that the claim that the public is overwhelmingly opposed to large-scale immigration is simply mistaken. The overall national trend has been toward lower levels of nativism.

Immigration is an important issue, and one that should be discussed frankly as part of democratic deliberation. Based on the data I see, however, it is not at all obvious that public opinion, even within the Republican Party, is aligned with the most nativist element of the American right. At the very least, the notion that ordinary Republican voters are intolerant, xenophobic, nativists appears discordant with reality.

The best argument against the claim that nativism is a powerful force in the US electorate, and a dominant force among Republicans, can be found in the book, *Immigration in the Court of Public Opinion,* by Jack Citrin, Morris S. Levy, and Matthew Wright.[20] That book takes a deep dive into many different questions relating to immigration, finding that high levels of nativism are rare, even among Republican voters. Although elites, as well as the loudest voices on social media, may seem polarized, the American public tends be ambivalent on this issue, rejecting both open borders and policies such as sanctuary cities, but also opposed to mass deportations and immigration moratoriums. The current political climate in Washington, DC, makes major overhauls to the US immigration system relatively unlikely, but the truth is that incremental changes, some expanding immigration and others restricting it, will probably get us closer to the public's true preferences on these issues.

Republican views on feminism

The Republican Party has not historically maintained a consistent approach toward feminism. As recently as the 1970s, Republican presidents supported the Equal Rights Amendment (ERA), which would have added language ensuring gender equality into the US Constitution. The organized conservative movement, for its part, had little to say about questions of gender equality during its early years. It

---

20 Jack Citrin, Morris S. Levy, and Matthew Wright, *Immigration in the Court of Public Opinion* (Hoboken, NJ: Polity Press, 2023).

was not until Phyllis Schlafly led her successful grassroots uprising against the ERA, and the subsequent rise of the Christian Right, that rejection of feminist claims and demands became a major plank of the Republican Party and conservatism more broadly.[21] Even as Republicans became more overtly hostile to feminism, however, its critiques were not consistent. Some critics of feminism emphasized cultural traditionalism, whereas others argued that women's liberation is a laudable goal, but it is best accomplished via free market capitalism, rather than government intervention.[22]

Anti-feminism seemed to take an especially vitriolic turn in the 1990s, when populist rabble rousers such as Rush Limbaugh introduced terms such as "femi-Nazi" into the conservative lexicon, and attacks on so-called political correctness became largely focused on feminists. Over time, however, this overt, consistent hostility toward feminism seemed to wane. Former Alaska Governor Sarah Palin, for example, described herself as a feminist and began calling for what she termed "conservative feminism."[23] It seemed plausible that feminism could lose its negative connotations for US conservatives.

Donald Trump's decision to enter the 2016 presidential election contest led to new concerns about misogyny in the Republican Party and American culture more broadly. His comments about women throughout that campaign, as well as comments he made earlier in life that came to light, combined with the fact that he was not apparently punished by Republican voters or the broader electorate, seemed to indicate that attitudes toward women and gender equality were not as progressive as many feminists would have hoped.

One simple measure of Republican attitudes toward feminism is simply to ask them whether they consider themselves to be feminists. Fortunately, the 2020 ANES had this question, asking, "Do you consider yourself a feminist, an anti-feminist, or neither of these?" Among Republicans, only about six percent described themselves as feminists. This is a far smaller percentage than we see among Democrats – about 37 percent. However, it is worth noting that, regardless of partisan affiliation, the overwhelming majority of Americans do not describe themselves as feminists or anti-feminists. Even among Republicans, only about eight percent believed "anti-feminist" was an accurate self-description. There was a slight gender gap among Republicans on this question. About three percent of Republican

21 George Hawley, *Conservatism in a Divided America* (Notre Dame, IN: University of Notre Dame Press, 2022), 143–162.
22 Ronnee Schrieber, *Righting Feminism: Conservative Women and American Politics* (New York: Oxford University Press, 2012)
23 "Is Sarah Palin a Feminist?," *The Week*, January 8, 2015, https://theweek.com/articles/493960/sarah-palin-feminist.

men and about nine percent of Republican women described themselves as feminists.

It is notable, however, that Republican feelings toward feminists have apparently declined slightly over the last two decades, though the baseline was already quite low. In the 2000 ANES, the mean feeling thermometer score for feminists was about 48. In 2020, this had dropped to about 44. Democrats, however, have shifted over that same period toward having considerably warmer feelings toward feminists, jumping from about 60 to about 70. Once again, we see some evidence of growing polarization, but it is driven more by movement among Democrats than among Republicans.

One major feminist complaint about contemporary American society is the pervasiveness of sexual harassment throughout the culture. This was a major theme of the #MeToo movement. Conservatives often push back, saying that efforts to deal with sexual harassment often lead to unjust outcomes for men who did nothing wrong. The 2020 ANES included a question on this subject, asking if "attention to sexual harassment has gone too far, has not gone far enough, or has been about right?" Among all respondents, about 22 percent thought it had "gone too far." A larger percentage (about 34 percent) of Republicans felt this way. Republicans are much less concerned about sexual harassment than Democrats or independents, but a large majority nonetheless felt that current attention to the subject was "about right" (about 45 percent) or "had not gone far enough" (about 20 percent). That survey also asked respondents to react to the statement, "Many women interpret innocent remarks or acts as being sexist." Here we again see a sizable partisan gap. About 39 percent of Republicans either somewhat or strongly agreed with that statement, compared to about 26 percent of Democrats. We also see partisan polarization when it comes to attitudes toward the #MeToo movement. The 2020 ANES shows that, of all respondents, the mean feeling thermometer score was about 58. The partisan difference in feelings toward the movement was large, however. Among Republicans, it was about 41, whereas it was about 74 among Democrats. When it comes to attitudes about how American society treats women, we see considerable evidence for partisan polarization. Given that Republican attitudes toward feminism have grown colder since 2000, this is one case where Republican movement to the right is at least partly to blame for that development.

The 2017 Baylor Religion Survey also included some questions that provide information on gender attitudes. It asked, for example, if they agreed or disagreed with the statement, "Men are better suited emotionally for politics than women." A large majority of both parties disagreed, but Republicans were less likely to do so – about 71 percent compared to about 92 percent. We see a much smaller difference in the percentage disagreeing with the statement, "A husband should earn a larger salary than his wife" – about 91 percent of Democrats compared to about 85 percent of Republicans. At least on these kinds of measures of gender traditionalism, we see that large majorities of Republicans hold a relatively progressive view.

Republican views on LGBT people

In the last chapter, I discussed the subject of same-sex marriage in some detail, and I will not revisit the issue here. As we saw, Republican views on same-sex marriage have shifted dramatically in a more progressive direction over the last two decades. There are other questions related to LGBT issues that deserve more scrutiny, however. One notable difference between Republicans and Democrats is that, at least according to the 2020 ANES, Republicans are less likely to have friends or family members that identify as gay, lesbian, or bisexual – about 59 percent compared to about 70 percent of Democrats. The survey shows a much larger gap in perceptions about discrimination toward gays and lesbians. Republicans, on average, express a lot of skepticism toward the idea that LGBT people in contemporary America suffer high levels of discrimination. About 26 percent of Republicans say they suffer "a lot" or "a great deal" of discrimination, compared to about 68 percent of Democrats. The question of anti-transgender discrimination is similarly polarized. About 38 percent of Republicans say that transgender people face "a lot" or "a great deal" of discrimination, compared to about 79 percent of Democrats.

Unsurprisingly, there is also a partisan difference when it comes to personal sexual identity. About 98 percent of Republicans in the 2020 ANES identified as "straight," compared to about 90 percent of Democrats. Discerning partisan differences among transgender people is more difficult because of their comparatively smaller percentage of the population, but the large sample size of the 2022 CES can give us some hints (that survey had 839 trans respondents). That survey showed that about 13 percent of trans respondents identified as Republican. This was similar to what we see among other sexual minorities. Republican identification was about 11 percent for lesbians, 16 percent for gay men, and about 13 percent among bisexuals.

In my interviews, I noted a clear generational divide among Republicans. Among younger Republicans, the norm was more toward tolerance. As one person described the last decades of politics around LGBT issues, "We're going to look back on that just like we look back on race and the conservative movement and the [Republican] Party, and when we look back it's going to be kind of a black mark on the party."

Republican views on religion

Frustration with the decline of religion was a common denominator among the older Republicans I spoke with. In their view, America was founded as a Christian nation, and the decline of Christianity is analogous to the decline of America itself. This seems to confirm the fears of scholars and pundits sounding the alarm about Christian nationalism. As a counterpoint to this, however, I must also note that I never heard anyone say that the government should do anything about it at all. That is, they viewed this as a cultural trend that was disconnected from government. To the extent that they thought it was reflected in politics and policy, they viewed political developments they considered detrimental to be downstream from the decline of Christianity. To paraphrase a few different interviewees: America turned away from God, and then politics went crazy; if America rediscovers God, its politics will become sound again.

Other scholars have examined how US Christians[24] have responded to news of the declining percentage of Americans that identify with the religion. One recent study indicates that Christians, upon learning that Christians are on track to be a minority in the US, respond defensively, becoming more conservative. They were also more likely to express support for Donald Trump.

One of the younger Republicans I spoke with argued that the party can perform well in an era of secularization with just minor changes to its approach to these questions. He argued that most people still embrace the morals and ideals found in the Bible, and pushing for basic decency and traditional values should still be a winning message. He argued that few people are going to disagree with the Ten Commandments, and, just because people no longer literally believe "the Jesus thing," the GOP can still be appealing as a party of morality.

Surveys can help discern the degree to which Christian nationalism is common in the electorate, as well as whether there is a partisan divide on this question. The 2017 Baylor Religion Survey asked respondents, "Some people think that the United States is a Christian nation and some people think that the United States is not a Christian nation. Which statement comes closest to your view?" Among Republicans, about 38 percent believe the US has always been a Christian nation (compared to about 21 percent of Democrats), about 41 percent believe it used to be a Christian nation, but it is not one now (about 27 percent of Democrats), and about six percent say it was never a Christian nation (about 28 percent of

---

24 Rosemary L. Al-Kire, Michael H. Pasek, Jo-Ann Tsang, Wade C. Rowatt, "Christian No More: Christian Americans are Threatened by their Impending Minority Status," Journal of Experimental Social Psychology 97(2021): 104223

Democrats). The rest said they did not know. The question of whether the US is a "Christian nation" is open to interpretation. Some may interpret it as an entirely empirical question, determined by whether a majority of the country identifies as Christian. Others may assume being a Christian nation requires the public or the government exhibit certain Christian principles. Regardless of the interpretation, however, it is notable that a plurality of Republicans believe there was a time when the US was Christian, but that time has passed.

The more interesting question, in my view, is what kind of relationship people want the government to have with religion. More than three quarters of Republicans in the Baylor survey "agree" or "strongly agree" that "[t]he federal government should advocate Christian values." Only about 30 percent of Democrats shared this view. Republicans, on average, were less convinced that "[t]he federal government should declare the United States as a Christian nation" – about 55 percent of Republicans (and about 16 percent of Democrats) agreed in any way with this statement.

About 47 percent of Republicans (compared to about 15 percent of Democrats) agreed in any way with the statement, "Muslims hold values that are morally inferior to the values of people like me." It is notable that Democrats were somewhat more willing to declare their moral superiority to "conservative Christians" – about 29 percent of Democrats said conservative Christian values were morally inferior to their own. On this question, Republicans were more hostile toward atheists than toward Muslims. A near majority of Republicans (compared to about 18 percent of Democrats) believed atheists held morally inferior values.

Although this can be overstated, and we should not exaggerate the degree to which Republicans maintain reactionary views on these issues, it would be reasonable to say that the two parties are becoming increasingly polarized along religious lines. Republicans are very distrustful of atheists (something that has been a consistent element of American political culture for a very long time), but Democrats have also, on average, developed increasingly negative views toward conservative Christians. The latter is certainly a more recent development, and would not have been true before the Christian Right became a major part of the political scene and a large constituency within the GOP.

I am skeptical that the Republican Party will ever become a vehicle for Christian nationalism. Religious disbelief has reached too great a level for anything resembling a theocratic government to be a reasonable concern. It is true, however, that Republican attitudes toward religious minorities and atheists are relatively negative. This is a concerning finding, and it will continue to be a major element of affective polarization in the electorate going forward. Once again, however, it is important to think about the direction of the trend.

Much of the recent literature on Christian nationalism relies primarily on cross-sectional analyses (looking at data that provides information about a recent snapshot in time). One scholar, however, has conducted useful work looking at how some of these sentiments have changed in recent decades. Ryan Burge has helpfully looked at how attitudes toward Christian nationalism changed between 2007 and 2021, examining the same survey questions to see where things have been heading.[25] He found that, across questions such as whether "[t]he federal government should advocate Christian values" and "[t]he federal government should declare the United States a Christian nation," the Christian nationalist responses have become less common. Some of this may be driven by declining rates of religiosity, but the trend was there even when the analysis was restricted to Christians. When he restricted the analysis further, looking exclusively at Republicans, the results became more mixed. On one question, there was a dramatic decline in Christian nationalist sentiments, and a modest increase in another. Although he noted that the results for Republicans and Christian nationalism were a "mixed bag," I saw nothing in his analysis that warrants alarmism.

Another reason I am not especially concerned about Christian nationalism as a potent political force is that it, for now, seems to only represent an inchoate set of attitudes. It is not an organized movement. A few people have written books in favor of the concept, but it lacks significant political entrepreneurs trying to make this idea a political reality. Compared to its halcyon days in the 1990s, the religious right is a shadow of its former self, at least in its capacity to mobilize large numbers of people for political causes. It is true that the religious right arguably won its greatest victory when *Roe v. Wade* was overturned in 2022, but this was the result of a Supreme Court decision, not grassroots activism or roll call votes in Congress. Organized groups remain a powerful force in American politics, and, at this point, Christian nationalists are severely lacking in this regard.

Republican trust in the media

Conservatives have long distrusted mainstream sources of news.[26] Richard Nixon famously hated journalists. Vice President Spiro Agnew was renowned for his

---

25 Ryan Burge, "Has Christian Nationalism Intensified or Faded?," *Graphs About Religion*, February 22, 2024, https://www.graphsaboutreligion.com/p/has-christian-nationalism-intensified.
26 In fact, dislike of the "liberal media" is largely the reason conservative media, and by extension, the conservative movement came into being. For a longer discussion of this history, see Mark Major, "Objective but Not Impartial: Human Events, Barry Goldwater, and the Development of the "Liberal Media" in the Conservative Counter-Sphere," *New Political Science* 34 (2012): 455–

anti-media zingers.[27] Talk radio personalities have focused their hostility on the nation's most prestigious newspapers and television news programs for decades. Fox News marketed itself as the only "fair and balanced" source of political information. In the Trump era, Republican hostility toward the media reached unprecedented levels. Throughout his presidency, Donald Trump took an overtly hostile approach to the conventional media, decrying unfavorable coverage as "fake news" and the media an "enemy of the American people."[28] For their part, many mainstream journalists and commentators responded in kind, either declaring outright that Trump was a fascist, or at least seriously considering whether the label was appropriate.[29]

Republicans are the main group in the electorate that is increasingly distrustful of the media. Not long ago, Gallup showed that confidence in television news and newspapers has sunk to an all-time low.[30] That decline was driven primarily by Republicans, however. Among Democrats, trust in the media actually increased quite a bit during the Trump years.

Although only tangentially related to the question of Republican trust in the media, it is worth knowing what kinds of news media Republicans consume and compare them to Democrats and independents. Are we really retreating into different political worlds, where people in different camps receive completely different sets of facts? Fortunately, the 2022 CES can shed some light on this question, as it included many questions about media use. It asked respondents which kind of media they consumed, and then asked about specific channels and publications. Unsurprisingly, Republicans disproportionately watched Fox News when they watched television news. In fact, about 76 percent of Republicans that watch television news reported watching Fox News. Republicans were less likely to report listening to radio news than I anticipated – about 33 percent of Republicans said they had listened to radio news within the last 24 hours.

468; Mark Major, "Conservative Consciousness and the Press: The Institutional Contribution to the Idea of the 'Liberal Media' in Right-Wing Discourse," *Critical Sociology* 41 (2015): 483–491.

27 Thomas Alan Schwartz, "He was Trump before Trump: VP Spiro Agnew Attacked the News Media 50 Years Ago," *The Conversation*, November 8, 2019, https://theconversation.com/he-was-trump-before-trump-vp-spiro-agnew-attacked-the-news-media-50-years-ago-122980.

28 Michael M. Grynbaum, "Trump Calls the News Media the 'Enemy of the American People,'" *The New York Times*, February 18, 2017, https://www.nytimes.com/2017/02/17/business/trump-calls-the-news-media-the-enemy-of-the-people.html.

29 See, for example, Ishaan Tharoor, "Is it Time to Call Trump the F-Word?," *The Washington Post*, June 3, 2020, https://www.washingtonpost.com/world/2020/06/03/trump-protests-fascism/; Dylan Matthews, "Is Trump a Fascist? 8 Experts Weigh In," *Vox*, October 23, 2020, https://www.vox.com/policy-and-politics/21521958/what-is-fascism-signs-donald-trump.

30 Sara Fischer, "Trust in News Collapses to Historic Low," *Axios*, July 8, 2022.

It would, however, be wrong to infer that Republicans only get information from Fox News and conservative talk radio show hosts. Just under 30 percent of Republicans reported that they read a newspaper in the last 24 hours. Democrats were somewhat more likely to report reading a newspaper – about 40 percent. A small minority of Republicans also reported that they watch television news stations with a more liberal reputation. About eight percent of Republicans reported that they watch MSNBC, and about 16 percent reported that they watch CNN. This may seem quite lopsided, but Democrats are no less tribal when they consume news and opinion television programs. Fewer than one in five Democrats say they watch Fox News, preferring instead to watch TV news stations aligned with their own partisan and ideological preferences. Democratic viewers tend to be more spread out across various news networks, but that is largely a function of them having more options when it comes to networks that promote a more progressive perspective. This may be starting to change with the arrival of new right-wing television news networks such as Newsmax TV, but at present it appears unlikely that any upstart is on track to take Fox News's place as the leading source on television for conservative news and opinion.[31]

Media bias is a perennial complaint among conservative pundits. It is not surprising that we find similar sentiments among Republican voters. The most straightforward ANES question on this subject was simply, "In general, how much trust and confidence do you have in the news media when it comes to reporting the news fully, accurately, and fairly?" Subjects were given the choices of "none," "a little," "a moderate amount," "a lot," or "a great deal." The electorate overall has a very negative view of the new media. A bit more than 30 percent of ANES respondents reported no or little trust in the media. When we focus just on Republicans, however, we find that trust in the media has reached shocking lows. A majority of Republicans (about 55 percent) reported having no trust in the media whatsoever. Four-fifths of Republicans either had no trust or a little trust in the media. Less than two percent of Republicans said they had "a great deal" of trust in the media.

The 2021 GSS also asked a very similar question: "How much do you trust the news media?" Respondents were asked to place themselves on a 0–10 scale, with zero indicating "no trust at all" and ten signifying "total trust." Among Republicans, a significant plurality (about 40 percent) provided the lowest possible score. Less than one percent gave the highest possible score. On the ten-point

31 Justin Baragona, "Newsmax's Ratings Have Crashed From Its Post-Tucker Carlson Sugar High," *The Daily Beast*, May 8, 2024, https://www.thedailybeast.com/a-year-later-newsmaxs-ratings-have-crashed-from-its-tucker-carlson-sugar-high.

scale, the mean score was only about 1.7. Republicans today seem to take it for granted that media is dominated by liars pursuing an ideological agenda they despise.

Among the people I interviewed, frustration with the media was another one of the few truly consistent themes, which I encountered over and over. Both political elites and ordinary voters insisted that today's mainstream journalists are not to be trusted, suggesting their commitment to their left-wing ideologies precludes them from treating Republicans in a fair and even-handed manner. One of the people I spoke with put it this way:

> The media has done a real disservice to the political discourse. I stopped watching TV news on the regular after the 2012 election. I still watch a clip here or there via Twitter, etc. but I don't even watch Fox News on the regular [. . .]. Long gone are the days of reporting the news without injecting bias and letting people decide what they think. That said – I feel like 90% of media is skewed to the left [. . .]. You simply cannot get a fair shake. Same thing can be said for a lot of print journalists.

Whatever one thinks of conventional journalism – perhaps Republican distrust of mainstream journalists is justified – one can consider this an ominous trend. It may become increasingly difficult for Americans to develop a widely shared narrative over any significant event. Everyone may simply retreat into information silos that consider everything through a partisan lens, with partisan pundits primarily focused on how any event can be spun in a way that makes the other party look bad. The Republican retreat from mainstream news sources may be concerning for other reasons. Media sources such as *The New York Times* or *The Washington Post* may have a liberal bias, but at least they are expected to maintain certain journalistic standards (fact checking, etc.). Most right-wing alternatives to the mainstream media often lack these basic journalistic norms. It would be one thing if Republicans were rejecting *The New York Times* in favor of a newspaper that, while perhaps giving a conservative spin to the news, nonetheless endeavored to provide accurate and carefully sourced information. Currently, however, few such conservative newspapers exist. There are plenty of conservative journals of opinion, but they are focused more on commentary than journalism. I fear Republicans are increasingly reliant on less reliable information sources, ones lacking journalistic ethics and some promoting dangerous conspiracy theories.

Republican trust in government

Modern conservatism in the US is inherently distrustful of government. For many generations now, Republican leaders and the conservative intelligentsia have consistently argued that government is inherently bad, that it is incompetent and perhaps even malevolent. Ronald Reagan famously declared, "[t]he nine most terrifying words in the English language are: I'm from the Government, and I'm here to help."[32] According to conservatives, even if everyone involved had the best of intentions, central planning of the economy is unworkable. Smaller-scale government interventions, such as a progressive welfare state, are possible, but they can create unhealthy incentives and they can undermine economic vitality. Democrats, on the other hand, are more inclined to believe that government is, or at least can be with the right leadership, a force for good.

Although we should not expect every Republican in the electorate to have a thorough knowledge of conservative political philosophy, or to agree with every element of that philosophy even if they understand it, Republican distrust of government has been a consistent theme of US politics. We can reasonably expect to find a partisan divide on this subject. Once again, we can turn to the cumulative ANES for insights into this subject. For many years, the survey has had questions that allow researchers to create a trust in government index and see its trend over time.[33] Unfortunately, the population's trust in the federal government has tanked in recent decades.

In 2000, the mean score for the trust in government index was already cool, about 36 (on a scale of 0–100). In 2020, however, this had declined to about 17. This is a non-partisan development, however. There was barely a one-point difference between Republicans and Democrats on this question in 2020. Since 2000, however, Democrats have fallen slightly farther on this measure – for Democrats in 2000, the mean was about 38, compared to Republicans at about 35.

Although Republicans have traditionally been the party to express distrust of government, this result may not be entirely surprising for a few reasons. To begin with, progressive Democrats have their own ideological reasons to be mistrustful of government, at least as it currently functions. The idea that government officials are corrupt or bigoted is a consistent theme in progressive discourse. Like many conservatives, some progressives are frustrated by the limited choices in American

---

32 Ronald Reagan, "August 12, 1986: Reagan Quotes and Speeches," Ronald Reagan Presidential Foundation and Institute, https://www.reaganfoundation.org/ronald-reagan/reagan-quotes-speeches/news-conference-1/.

33 The trust in government index results from a question asking respondents whether they "trust the federal government to do what is right," whether "the government is pretty much run by a few big interests looking out for themselves or that it is run for the benefit of all the people," whether "people in the government waste a lot of money we pay in taxes, waste some of it, or don't waste very much of it," and whether "the government is pretty much run by a few big interests looking out for themselves or that it is run for the benefit of all the people."

democracy, believing that there are insufficient differences between the two parties. Sometimes certain issues or scandals can damage trust in government – the Vietnam War and the invasion of Iraq being classic examples of this phenomenon.[34]

Does low trust in government matter? From a conservative perspective, distrust in government is not necessarily bad. Indeed, such a trend might be viewed as evidence that conservative arguments against government are gaining ground throughout the electorate. Political scientists have argued, however, that trust in government is an important element of effective government. Insufficient trust in government may also threaten democracy itself. Trust in government can also influence attitudes about specific policy issues. Low trust in government is associated with lower levels of support for immigration, for example.[35]

Political scientists first began noticing the electorate was rapidly losing trust in government in the 1970s. There were many possible causes for rising cynicism during that period. The Vietnam War, racial violence, and frustration with both political parties were significant factors in kicking off this trend. Political scientist Arthur Miller argued that policy dissatisfaction was largely responsible for declining trust.[36] According to his view, a lack of trust in the electorate could stymie political leaders pursuing new policies. He was concerned that this discontent, if it caused frustrated elements of US society to lose faith in the political system, could be a precursor to civil disorder. Other scholars raised similar concerns at that time.[37]

In the late 1990s, political scientist Marc Hetherington revisited the subject of political trust, also arguing that low trust makes it much harder for politicians to succeed.[38] He found that political trust had been steadily declining since the 1960s, and this was only going to make it harder for politicians to tackle looming problems, threatening a negative spiral. Lack of trust makes it harder to solve problems, eventually making problems worse, causing trust to decline further.

---

34 Arthur H. Miller, "Political Issues and Trust in Government: 1964–1970," *American Political Science Review* 68 (1974): 951–972.

35 David MacDonald, "Political Trust and Support for Immigration in the American Mass Public," *British Journal of Political Science* 51 (2021): 1402–1420.

36 Arthur H. Miller, "Political Issues and Trust in Government," *The American Political Science Review* 68 (1974): 951–972.

37 Edward N. Muller, "A Partial Test of a Theory of Potential for Political Violence," *American Political Science Review* 66 (1972): 928–959.

38 Marc J. Hetherington, "The Political Relevance of Political Trust," *The American Political Science Review* 92 (1998): 791–808.

Not every political scientist was greatly alarmed by declining trust as such. In 1974, political scientist Jack Citrin argued against alarmism about political trust.[39] He suggested declining trust could be partially explained by growing sophistication among US voters. Distrusting the government can also help to keep government leaders accountable. He furthermore argued that the empirical evidence for the claim that declining trust resulted in withdrawal from political activity was weak.

Republican external efficacy

Feelings of external personal efficacy are related to trust in government. Among political scientists, political efficacy is defined as "the feeling that individual political action does have, or can have, an impact on the political process, i. e., that it is worthwhile to perform one's civic duties."[40] A lack of efficacy can lead to cynicism and a withdrawal from the political process.

The ANES has also asked a number of questions relating to external efficacy for many decades, allowing for the creation of an efficacy scale that we can examine over time.[41] In the cumulative file, the ANES categorized people's efficacy on a scale from 0 (least efficacious) to 100 (most efficacious), with 25, 50, and 75 representing midpoints. As with trust in government, the general trend has been toward lower feelings of efficacy, and this is true for both parties. However, the downward trend has been steeper for Republicans. In 2000, only about 31 percent of Republicans were in the least efficacious category, and a similar percentage was classified as most efficacious. By 2020, about 59 percent were in the least efficacious category, and about nine percent felt most efficacious. Democrats showed a smaller decline in efficacy. Among Democrats, about 37 percent exhibited the lowest level of efficacy in 2000, compared to 47 percent in 2020.

It is notable that these extraordinary low levels of Republican efficacy were recorded at a time their party controlled the presidency and the US Senate, and Republicans had enjoyed united control of government as recently as 2018.

---

39 Jack Citrin, "Comment: The Political Relevance of Trust in Government," *The American Political Science Review* 68 (1974): 973–988.

40 Angus Campbell, Gerald Gurin, Warren E. Miller, Sylvia Eberhart, and Robert O. McWilliams, *The Voter Decides*, (Evanston, IL: Row, Peterson, 1954), 187.

41 The ANES external efficacy scale consists of questions about whether respondents agree that people like themselves can influence government. One question asks whether they believe "public officials care much about what people like me think." The other question asks respondents whether they agree or disagree with the statement, "People like me don't have any say about what the government does."

Given Trump's commentary on his political enemies, this is not entirely surprising. Trump, for example, insisted that he was being stymied by an unaccountable "deep state" that sought to thwart his agenda. He insisted Washington, DC, was a "swamp" that needed to be "drained." Although only a small percentage of Trump supporters supported the most outlandish conspiracy theories, in my interviews, I noted a pervasive sense of cynicism, even from Republicans that seemed otherwise moderate in their opinions. In their view, government was controlled by the elites, and politicians gave little weight to the views of "ordinary people."

As was the case for trust in government, there may be good reasons for the electorate to have a low-level of political efficacy. Although the media and partisan activists often play up the importance of each election cycle, one could argue that even elections that change the majorities in congress often have few tangible effects on most people's lives. Figures on the radical left and the radical right are, of course, especially likely to be frustrated by the two major parties. Even centrists who are generally satisfied with government may nonetheless feel a low level of efficacy if they perceive that political leaders are not responsive the public's desires.

Conservatives could of course retort that the public should not be efficacious when it comes to policy. A traditionalist conservative perspective holds that elected representatives are not supposed to make decisions based on their constituent's desires. Edmund Burke, considered by many the father of modern conservatism in the English-speaking world, was quite emphatic during his time as a legislator that he would listen attentively to the people in his district, but he was elected to use his best judgment. He was not elected to follow the whims of a fickle public.[42] Many of today's conservatives may agree with Burke's sentiments. The Republican Party, as I showed in Chapter 3, has historically taken positions on economic issues far to the right of the median voter, and even to the right of Republican voters.

Whether this approach to legislative behavior results in the best policy outcomes, however, the electorate's loss of efficacy may create problems. Again and again, studies have shown that low levels of efficacy are associated with lower rates of political participation, including basic civic responsibilities like voting.[43] If feelings of efficacy are declining faster for one partisan group than another, it may put that party at a disadvantage. President Trump, along with many of his

---

42 Edmund Burke, "Speech to the Electors of Bristol," November 3, 1774, https://press-pubs.uchi cago.edu/founders/documents/v1ch13s7.html.
43 Gabriel A. Almond and Sidney Verba, *The Civic Culture* (Princeton, NJ: Princeton University Press, 1963); Karen Stenner-Day and Mark Fischle, "The Effects of Political Participation on Political Efficacy: A Simultaneous Equations Model," *Australian Journal of Political Science* 27(1992): 282– 305;

vocal supporters, continuously suggested that the system was unfair and rigged against him and his voters. Republicans can be reasonably concerned that such talk could have a demoralizing effect on their own supporters, driving down turnout in elections where they desperately need their voters to show up.

The geographic distribution of voters may benefit Republicans' sense of efficacy, however. Because Republicans tend to live in smaller municipalities and more rural communities compared to Democrats, their local governments also tend to be smaller, cover fewer people, and be more responsive to constituent demands. A resident of a small town in Indiana is more likely to have a meaningful conversation with her community's mayor or city council than, say, a resident of New York City or Los Angeles. Recent research suggests that living in smaller municipal areas is associated with both stronger feelings of efficacy and higher levels of political participation.[44] We of course should not overstate this finding. Even as Republicans have come to dominate rural areas and lose ground in heavily populated urban and suburban areas, their feelings of efficacy have continued to decline.

Republican activism

There are many reasons to be concerned about distrust in government and low levels of political efficacy, but from the standpoint of partisan politics, political parties have practical reasons to be concerned about the direction of trends. Feelings of external efficacy are positively related to multiple forms of political participation beyond voting.[45] A party dominated by cynics, convinced that nothing they do will change political outcomes in any meaningful way, will have a harder time convincing its supporters to engage in meaningful political activism.

Unfortunately for the Republican Party, its supporters are much less likely to engage in any kind of meaningful political activity. Protesting is one of the more common forms of activism, and the political science literature demonstrates that protests have a meaningful impact on election outcomes.[46] When it comes to mobilizing protesters, however, Democrats have a decided advantage. Although only a minority of Democrats in the 2020 CES reported attending a protest in the past

---

44 Joshua McDonnell, "Municipality Size, Political Efficacy and Political Participation: A Systematic Review," *Local Government Studies* 46 (2020): 331–350.

45 Jennifer Oser, Amit Grinson, Shelley Boulianne, and Eran Halperin, "How Political Efficacy Relates to Online and Offline Political Participation: A Multilevel Meta-Analysis," *Political Communication* 39 (2022): 607–633.

46 Daniel Q. Gillion, *The Loud Minority: Why Protests Matter in American Democracy* (Princeton, NJ: Princeton University Press, 2020).

year (about 12 percent), this was more than double the rate for Republicans (about five percent). The 2020 ANES found a similar gap (about 13 percent versus five percent). Republicans in 2020 were also only about half as likely as Democrats to report working for a campaign (about four percent compared to about eight percent, according to the CES). Republicans and Democrats were about equally likely to put up political signs, however (about 21 percent of both groups reported doing so, also according to the CES).

That same survey also showed that Republicans were slightly less likely to have given money to a political party over the previous year (about 10 percent compared to about 13 percent). We see a larger gap on the question of whether they gave money to specific candidates (about 22 percent of Democrats compared to about 14 percent of Republicans). The CES worded the question slightly differently, asking if they had donated to any candidate, campaign, or political organization, but the gap was similar – about 37 percent of Democrats compared to about 25 percent of Republicans. This is not to say that Republicans are less likely to donate to causes. Unsurprisingly, the ANES showed that Republicans were much more likely than Democrats to have donated to a religious organization over the previous year (about 43 percent compared to about 24 percent).

Beyond protests and donating money, the ANES shows Republicans were also less likely to engage in other forms of civic engagement. The survey asked the question, "During the past 12 months, have you worked with other people to deal with some issue facing your community?" About 19 percent of Republicans responded that they had, compared to about 25 percent of Democrats.

Republicans are not necessarily less likely to have engagement of any kind with their community, but their engagement largely occurs through religious institutions. They are much more likely to be involved with a church or other religious organization. From the perspective of building their own social capital and remaining involved in their community, this may be no less valuable than engaging directly in politics. Given the increasing religious divide in partisanship, this may furthermore have downstream political effects that benefit the GOP. Overall, however, when it comes to expressly political activity, the Democrats have recently had an advantage. The Democratic Party's edge in its ability to organize and mobilize a large percentage of its supporters is impressive, and it may have important long-term political effects.

Republican feelings about upward mobility

Social mobility is a key element of the "American Dream." Americans want to believe that, through hard work, they can enjoy more economic success than their parents, and their children can achieve even higher levels of success. Optimism about the country and its future has been a hallmark of the most successful Republican presidents. President Reagan, for instance, was a paragon of optimism about the country He rejected President Carter's suggestion that Americans needed to learn to live with austerity. Instead, Reagan insisted, America's best days were still ahead. If the government got out of the way, got rid of burdensome regulations, and lowered the tax rates, the hard work and creativity of the American people could achieve new heights of prosperity.

The 2020 ANES gives us an indication of how contemporary Republicans feel about the state of country economically. It asked, "When it comes to people trying to improve their financial well-being, do you think it is now easier, harder, or the same as it was 20 years ago?" Unfortunately, on this question, a significant majority of the public believed it had become harder to improve one's economic standing. About 61 percent of respondents believed it had gotten harder.

As of 2020, Republicans were more optimistic than Democrats about the ability of Americans to improve their economic status. About 47 percent of Republicans said that, compared to the past, it is now harder to improve one's status. For Democrats, it was about 73 percent. Although Republicans may have very negative attitudes toward other elements of the culture, they remain more optimistic than Democrats that the dream of upward mobility is still alive in the US. Even among Republicans, however, a near majority believe that the situation has gotten worse in recent decades, and they did so even at a time when a Republican was in the White House, constantly reiterating his economic achievements.

Conclusion

Republican attitudes toward cultural issues remain, unsurprisingly, sharply to the right of Democrats. The gap on these issues furthermore appears larger than it does for economic concerns, where the Republican Party in the electorate typically holds less conservative positions than the Republican Party in government. Republicans are far more likely than Democrats to hold nativist views on immigration, skeptical attitudes toward advances in LGBT rights, and negative views toward non-Christians. Progressive pundits are not wrong to note that fear and hostility toward cultural change is common in today's Republican Party in the electorate. The real question, in my view, is the direction of the trend. It does appear that Republicans have become more negative toward feminism over the last two decades. On the other hand, we see little evidence that they are becoming more anti-immigrant, and they have shifted in a more progressive direction on questions related to the LGBT community – though they are much less progressive than Democrats on these issues, which likely explains the very low level of Republican identification we see from that group.

Republican negativity is not entirely focused on changing cultural norms and growing diversity. Indeed, the evidence that they are becoming more reactionary on these issues is rather weak. Their growing sense of cynicism about the government is undeniable, however. They overwhelmingly, and intensely, dislike the mainstream media and doubt they can personally have any impact on the government. They, furthermore, compared to their Democratic counterparts, are extremely unlikely to engage in political activism to change any of this. Republicans may not be radicalizing in an ideological or policy sense, but they are becoming disenchanted with mainstream institutions that they consider hostile to their interests or identities.

There is a major issue that is largely absent from this chapter: race, especially attitudes toward African Americans. The protests that followed George Floyd's murder in 2020 were among the leading stories of that year. The salience of systemic challenges facing the African American community seemed to be leading toward what many commentators were calling a "racial reckoning." In subsequent years, however, there seems to be a growing backlash against new efforts to promote the wellbeing of black Americans. There was a brief period where there seemed to be a bipartisan consensus that, for example, criminal justice needed serious reforms – Donald Trump, for his part, was a proponent of significant progressive changes in this regard. Now, however, partisan polarization on racial questions seems to again be on the rise. In the next chapter, I examine Republican attitudes about race in greater detail.

Chapter 6
Racism, conspiracy theorists, and affective polarization

For several years, progressive media, as well as much of the mainstream news media, has been sounding the alarm that the Republican Party has been thoroughly conquered by extremists. According to this view, President Trump unleashed the most extreme and illiberal forces in the electorate. It is not that these trends did not exist before Trump launched his presidential campaign in 2015, but that they were not treated as an ordinary part of US politics. Many critics persuasively argued that Trump normalized explicit racism and antisemitism, and he helped bring them into the mainstream of American life.

During the 2016 presidential campaign, many right-wing radicals agreed with those progressives who feared Trump prefigured a change in US politics. The so-called Alt-Right, which was a recent manifestation of the white nationalist movement, was almost uniformly enthusiastic about Donald Trump.[1] US white nationalists had, in previous decades, shown little interest in US Presidential campaigns. They did not organize in favor of George H.W. Bush, Bob Dole, George W. Bush, John McCain, or Mitt Romney. In fact, many white nationalists argued that the Republican Party was one of the movement's primary stumbling blocks, one that channeled right-wing energy away from the issues they cared about and toward non-racial policies such as tax cuts. Trump's campaign-trail comments about Mexican immigrants, his call for a ban on Muslims entering the country, and his general combativeness with progressive media indicated to the far right that Trump would be a different kind of president.

The racist right was not the only group that exhibited extraordinary support for Trump. The Trump era was also a boon to conspiracy theorists, many of whom believed the most outlandish things about Trump's secret, behind-the-scenes war on the deep state's satanic cabal of pedophiles. The bizarre QAnon conspiracy theory and its followers received much less media attention than the Alt-Right throughout most of the Trump Administration. In retrospect, however, it appears that the QAnon movement was much larger than the Alt-Right, at least in terms of the number of people it could mobilize for real-world action, and on January 6th we saw that it could be a very destructive force. Until that point, I will admit that I viewed these kinds of conspiracy theorists as a curiosity, rather than something that need-

---

1 George Hawley, *Making Sense of the Alt-Right* (New York: Columbia University Press, 2017).

https://doi.org/10.1515/9783111469720-006

ed to be treated as anything serious. I now agree that the subject warrants serious scholarly analysis.

Throughout this book, I have argued that claims about the Republican Party's radicalization are not aligned with reality. Most Republicans are just ordinary people who do not think about politics very much, nor do they spend their time hating minorities or piecing together conspiracy theories on the internet. That does not mean, however, that radicalism is absent within the Republican electorate. In this chapter, I will consider the right-wing radical fringe in the party and attempt to discern their size and influence.

The number of extreme racists and conspiracy theorists, who earned so much media attention in recent years, is fortunately small. However, more typical Republican voters have shown, in my view, a concerning willingness to excuse the excesses of Donald Trump's presidency and post-presidency, always finding a way to justify his worst behavior. Their insistence on circling the wagons around one man, always finding a way to justify their continued support, is concerning, and deserves our attention. Some of this partisan defensiveness can be explained by the growth of negative partisanship. The two major parties intensely dislike each other, and their disdain has grown over the last decades. Although we can find little evidence that Republicans are becoming more prejudiced toward racial, ethnic, or religious minorities, affective polarization is very real.

Explicit racism in the twentieth century

During the last century, openly racist movements of different varieties sprang up with some regularity. The Ku Klux Klan (KKK), with roots in the Reconstruction-era South, is unquestionably the most significant of these, though its size and influence declined drastically after the 1920s.[2] During the first half of the twentieth century, there was not a clear partisan dividing line when it came to racial issues. Some contemporary conservatives are eager to point out that major figures of the early KKK would have uniformly supported the Democratic Party. When Strom Thurmond first exited the Democratic Party over the issue of segregation in the 1940s, he did not make the immediate jump to the Republican Party, instead running on a new, third-party ticket.

On the other hand, we should not overstate the Republican Party's commitment to its identity as the "Party of Lincoln," even in the early twentieth century

---

2 Darren Mulloy, *Years of Rage: White Supremacy in the United States from the Klan to the Alt-Right* (Lanham, MD: Rowman and Littlefield, 2021).

when the Civil War was still a relatively recent memory. As I noted in Chapter 2, The "Lily white movement" in the GOP sought to wrest control of the party in Southern states, where African Americans had previously taken leading roles. The Republican Party's approach to the Civil Rights Movement was complicated but, overall, it held a less progressive position than the Democratic Party. Barry Goldwater's presidential run is largely remembered because of his opposition to the Civil Rights Act, which played a major role in causing white Southerners to break away from the Democratic Party. It is true that many Republicans in congress were in favor of that legislation, but by that time the party had clearly established itself as the party of racial conservatism. Many of the Democrats that remained opponents of civil rights legislation at that time subsequently switched parties, or they left office and were replaced by more progressive Democrats or more conservative Republicans.

Thinking about racist movements in the US from a partisan perspective can be misleading, however. In some ways, majorities in both parties took a degree of white supremacy for granted during much of the twentieth century. Those with the most extreme racial views, especially those organizing for explicit white nationalism, tended to look upon both major parties with great suspicion. Of the major white nationalist organizations that emerged in the latter decades of the twentieth century, such as the American Nazi Party, the National Alliance, the Church of the Creator, the Aryan Nations, and the many other small racist groups, none looked to the Republican Party as the organization that would save the white race. Indeed, white nationalists tended to view mainstream conservatism as an obstacle, rather than a movement working toward similar ends.

Progressives have long complained, often for good reason, that the conservative movement and the Republican Party frequently engage in "racial dog whistling" to gain support from white people. Racial extremists make a similar complaint, but from a different perspective. In their view, the Republicans have been very good at activating white racial resentments to win votes, but they then fail to actually do anything substantive to advance white interests. Despite controlling the presidency more often than not, Republicans made little effort to restrict immigration from non-white countries. In fact, Ronald Reagan signed legislation giving amnesty to a large number of undocumented immigrants. George W. Bush attempted to do the same.

Explicit racism in the Trump era

Most of the explicitly racist right viewed Donald Trump, at least during the 2016 campaign and the early days of his presidential administration, as a boon to their cause. It is not coincident that the Alt-Right first began breaking out of its narrow internet confines and making a mark on the broader public consciousness during this period.[3] To some extent, however, the Alt-Right's rapid ascent in this regard can be blamed on its opponents. Hillary Clinton, for example, dedicated an entire speech in 2016 to denouncing the Alt-Right, and did so at a time when the movement was still not widely known. The logic of the speech, I assume, was to drive a wedge in the Republican Party between Trump's enthusiastic racist supporters, and more moderate, traditional Republicans who may have been on the fence about supporting the GOP nominee.[4] Whether her speech had its intended effect is impossible to know; I think it is possible that efforts to link Trump to the Alt-Right did cost him some votes from moderates who would otherwise consider voting Republican. However, the speech also brought the Alt-Right unprecedented media attention, bringing fame to some of its leading figures.

Most of the Alt-Right was understandably jubilant after Trump's victory, but, at least among many leading Alt-Right figures, that enthusiasm was short lived. Donald Trump denounced the Alt-Right for the first time a few weeks after Election Day after some of his supporters at an Alt-Right conference were filmed making Nazi salutes.[5] The Alt-Right suffered further setbacks in the following months, as the movement divided between more moderate factions that sought to work within the existing political framework and build arguments that would appeal to a broader swathe of the public, and the explicit radicals that wanted to maintain a clear distinction between themselves and the more traditional conservative movement and the Republican Party.

The movement was hindered even further when it attempted to move out of the online sphere and began conducting real-world events. In the early months of 2017, Alt-Right groups conducted a number of small rallies. In August of that year, the "Unite the Right" rally, an event to support maintaining Confederate monuments in Charlottesville, VA, was the largest gathering of the Alt-Right to date. The event proved disastrous for the movement. Fights between the event's attendees and left-wing counter protesters began before the rally started, leading to the event's cancellation, which resulted in yet more violence, ultimately ending with

---

3 For a longer description of the Alt-Right's early years, see George Hawley, *Making Sense of the Alt-Right* (New York: Columbia University Press, 2017).

4 Abby Ohleiser and Caitlyn Dewey, "Hillary Clinton's Alt-Right Speech, Annotated," *The Washington Post*, August 25, 2016, https://www.washingtonpost.com/news/the-fix/wp/2016/08/25/hillary-clintons-alt-right-speech-annotated/.

5 Eric Bradner, "Alt-Right Leader: 'Hail Trump! Hail our people! Hail victory!'" *CNN Politics*, November 22, 2016, https://www.cnn.com/2016/11/21/politics/alt-right-gathering-donald-trump/index.html.

the death of a counter protester, killed by white nationalist who drove his car into a crowd.[6]

Unite the Right resulted in hugely negative publicity, and eventually led to successful lawsuits against the event's organizers, effectively wiping out their ability to organize in the future. Public opinion turned sharply against the Alt-Right, and the movement further splintered internally. By mid-2018, the Alt-Right had largely ceased to exist as a political movement.[7] Public opinion data demonstrated that, by 2018, the Alt-Right was one of the most disliked social groups in the country.[8]

Since the Alt-Right's decline, we have seen a few groups attempt to pursue explicit white identity politics under different brands and strategies. The so-called Groypers, led by a young right-wing activist named Nick Fuentes, have thus far been the most successful successor to the Alt-Right.[9] A number Republican members of congress have begun associating with fringe, radical figures. Congressional Republicans such as Paul Gossar (AZ) and Marjorie Taylor Greene (GA) have openly aligned themselves with the far-right.[10] These figures are not leaders within the Republican Party, and I consider it unlikely that politicians with similar views will come to dominate the party in congress. Yet, it is true that they represent a far-right element of the party, and threaten to destabilize a movement that already contains many fissures.

To get a sense of whether far-right politicians represent the Republican Party's likely future, we should investigate the degree to which their racist and conspiratorial views are concordant with the party in the electorate. Survey data can provide us with some meaningful measures of explicit racism. Results from these types of surveys should be viewed with caution, as they are especially susceptible to social desirability bias. They are nonetheless worth examining, especially if we

6 George Hawley, *The Alt-Right: What Everyone Needs to Know* (New York: Oxford University Press, 2018)

7 For a more detailed explanation for why I say this, see George Hawley, "The Alt-Right's Moment has Come and Gone," *The American Conservative*, December 6, 2018, https://www.theamer icanconservative.com/articles/the-alt-rights-moment-has-come-and-gone/.

8 Jack Thompson and George Hawley, "Does the Alt-Right Still Matter? An Examination of Alt-Right Influence between 2016 and 2018," *Nations and Nationalism* 27 (2021): 1165–1180

9 George Hawley, "The 'Groyper' Movement in the U.S.: Challenges for the Post-Alt-Right," in *Contemporary Far-Right Thinkers and the Future of Liberal Democracy*, edited by A. James McAdams and Alejandro Castrillon (New York: Routledge, 2021).

10 Robert Draper, "The Problem of Marjorie Taylor Greene," *New York Times Magazine*, October 17, 2022, https://www.nytimes.com/2022/10/17/magazine/marjorie-taylor-greene.html; Catie Edmondson, "Far-Right Extremist Finds an Ally in an Arizona Congressman," *The New York Times*, July 5, 2021, https://www.nytimes.com/2021/07/05/us/politics/paul-gosar-republicans-con gress-extremism.html.

are looking at trends over time. Even if results are incorrect because people are less willing to express prejudiced views, even to anonymous pollsters, changes in these scores over time can nonetheless suggest meaningful changes in US public opinion on these attitudes. Throughout the Trump years, we heard from journalists and some scholars that Trump was normalizing racist attitudes, making people feel comfortable expressing racist views that they might have previously kept hidden. Is this true?

In my interviews, subjects rarely brought up the subject of race unprompted. They tended to be defensive about the issue, insisting that Republicans were unfairly portrayed by the media when it comes to racial issues. As one interviewee put it, "I think one of the misleading things that is perpetuated in the media about the GOP, especially about race, is that we don't care about voting or voting rights." Another similarly argued:

> I think the Republican Party as a whole constantly get a rap about being white supremacist and white nationalist. I don't doubt that there are certainly people, on either side, who are white supremacist or truly a nationalist, but I think a mass misconception is that Republicans are racist. I genuinely believe in the conservative movement, the platform of the Republican Party, for example the principle of abolishing Critical Race Theory, not because, you know, we're racist, but because [policies like teaching Critical Race Theory] themselves are racist. Critical Race Theory is racist. Affirmative action being racist. So I think that if people really looked at the policies that conservative Republicans are pushing at length, they would notice that they aren't actually racist, they're trying to repeal racism.

Comments like this demonstrate the gap between how conservatives and progressives generally understand racism. For conservatives like the one quoted above, anything other than official color-blindness, implemented immediately, would be a form of racism – regardless of which group benefited from race-conscious policies. Much of the contemporary left, however, now rejects this approach, arguing that pursuing color-blindness before equity has been achieved will only serve to reinforce existing racial inequalities. Some progressives would go further and argue that racism against white people is literally not possible because of the nation's existing power structures. The ideological and partisan divide in how these concepts are understood can make fruitful dialog on these issues challenging.

Republican feeling thermometer scores for racial/ethnic groups

The simplest way to measure attitudes toward different racial groups is to look at feeling thermometer scores. Have attitudes toward racial minorities become notably warmer or cooler over the last several decades? Once again, the cumulative ANES can give us some insights into this. We should keep in mind that some changes in their attitudes may be driven by changes in the racial compositions of the two major parties. Although the Republican Party remains overwhelmingly white, it is slightly less white than it used to be. For this reason, for this part of the analysis, I will restrict my sample to non-Hispanic white Republicans.

According to this data set, in 2000, the mean feeling thermometer score toward blacks among white Republicans was about 63. In 2020, it had increased slightly, to about 67. That is not a dramatic difference, but the direction of the trend was toward more positive feelings toward African Americans. The score for Asian Americans was almost identical to that of African Americans in both years. We see a similar result for Hispanics, who had a mean score of about 61 in 2000 and about 67 in 2020. Non-Hispanic white feelings toward Jewish people made a more significant jump over this period, rising from about 65 to about 73. Despite the efforts of explicitly antisemitic movements like the Alt-Right to push an anti-Jewish message into mainstream discourse, it does not appear that it had any effect on the Republican electorate overall. White attitudes toward their own group remained virtually unchanged. At least in terms of subjective feelings of warmth, we see no evidence that white Republicans are becoming more hostile toward racial minority groups, or more favorable toward their own race.

Republican beliefs in racial stereotypes

The ANES has also included questions relating to racial stereotypes. For example, it asks respondents the degree to which different groups can be characterized as hard working or lazy. It is a seven-point scale, with higher values indicating that the respondent thinks the group is characterized by greater laziness.[11] Between 2000 and 2020, white Republicans became somewhat less likely to describe blacks as "lazy," dropping from about 4.2 to about 3.8. The decline in these views was larger for Hispanics, decreasing from about 3.6 to about 2.9. For Asians, there was very little change, shifting from about 2.9 to about 2.7. For their own group, there was almost no change at all – about 3 in 2000 and about 2.9 in 2020. It is worth noting

---

11 Specifically, the questions are written as follows: "Now I have some questions about different groups in our society. I'm going to show you a seven-point scale on which the characteristics of the people in a group can be rated. In the first statement a score of 1 means that you think almost all of the people in that group tend to be "hard-working." A score of 7 means that almost all of the people in the group are "lazy." A score of 4 means that you think that most people in the group are not closer to one end or the other, and of course you may choose any number in between."

that white Republicans did not uniformly describe their own group as the most hardworking. In 2020, they scored their own group a little lower than Hispanics. From this, we do see that white Republicans are more likely to believe this negative stereotype about blacks than toward other groups, but the trend has been toward less prejudice and stereotyping.

The 2020 ANES provides other measures of beliefs in negative racial stereotypes. For example, it asked the degree to which respondents believed different racial groups were "peaceful" or "violent," again using a seven-point scale, with higher scores indicating a greater belief that a group is violent. For blacks, the mean score on the violence stereotype scale was a relatively high 4.1 (among white Democrats, it was about 3.7). It was much lower for Hispanics, at about 3.2 (Democrats had a very similar mean for this group, at about 3.3). Asians scored the lowest on the violence scale among white Republicans, at about 2.6. In fact, compared to Republicans, Democrats were slightly more likely to describe Asians as violent; the mean score for Asians among white Democrats was about 2.8. When asked this same question about whites, white Republicans provided a mean score of about 2.9 – white Democrats rated whites, on average, about 3.7, similar to their mean score for blacks. Once again, Republicans were more likely to believe this negative stereotype about blacks compared to other groups, but they did not, on average, give their own group the most positive score.

The 2017 Baylor Religion Survey asked questions relating to racial or ethnic stereotypes. Respondents to that survey were asked how much they agreed that "Illegal immigrants from Mexico are mostly dangerous criminals." Among Republicans, 82 percent either disagreed or disagreed strongly with this statement. That survey also provided the statement, "Police officers in the United States shoot blacks more often because they are more violent than whites." About 60 percent of Republicans disagreed or disagreed strongly with this statement.

Republican racial resentment

As I mentioned, there is a problem with survey questions asking questions with explicitly racist options: we may reasonably question whether respondents are giving sincere answers. The phenomenon of social desirability bias has been well documented in the social sciences.[12] People with unpopular opinions may hesitate to share them with pollsters, even in situations where anonymity is guaranteed. As

---

12 Ivar Krumpal, "Determinants of Social Desirability Bias in Sensitive Surveys: A Literature Review," *Quality and Quantity* 47 (2013): 2025–2047.

a result, changing attitudes on questions of race, as measured by opinion polling, may be misleading. Rather than representing an actual move toward racial egalitarianism, apparently shifting racial attitudes may simply reflect changes in what is considered socially acceptable. I contend that asking people about explicitly racist attitudes is nonetheless valuable, even if we cannot immediately gauge the sincerity of respondents. Though changes over time can be entirely explained by changes in what is considered taboo, the shift is nonetheless important – but understanding the real source of the change can be difficult.

To partially get around this problem, social scientists have developed questions that indicate important feelings about race but are less explicit in terms of racial prejudice – and thus more likely to garner honest answers from the people being polled. Public opinion scholars now often use a battery of questions measuring what is called "racial resentment." Political scientists Donald Kinder and Lynn Sanders described it this way: "A new form of prejudice has come to prominence [...]. At its center are the contentions that blacks do not try hard enough to overcome the difficulties they face and they take what they have not earned. Today, we say, prejudice is expressed in the language of American individualism."[13]

Kinder and Sanders furthermore argue that racial resentment is a powerful predictor for many important political attitudes and behaviors. It is now a very popular tool for political scientists. Racial resentment, for example, was a strong predictor of support for Donald Trump in 2016,[14] as well as feelings toward the Black Lives Matter movement.[15]

For many election cycles, the ANES has used several questions to measure levels of racial resentment. Specifically, the ANES has asked respondents the degree to which they agreed with the following statements: "Irish, Italian, Jewish and many other minorities overcame prejudice and worked their way up. Blacks should do the same without any special favors." "Generations of slavery and discrimination have created conditions that make it difficult for blacks to work their way out of the lower class." "Over the past few years, blacks have gotten less than they de-

---

13 Donald R. Kinder and Lynn M. Sanders, *Divided by Color: Racial Politics and the Democratic Ideal* (Chicago: University of Chicago Press, 1996), 105–106.
14 Alan Abramowitz and Jennifer McCoy, "United States: Racial Resentment, Negative Partisanship, and Polarization in Trump's America," *The ANNALS of the American Academy of Political and Social Science* 681(2019): 137–156; Kevin K. Banda and Erin C. Cassese, "Hostile Sexism, Racial Resentment, and Political Mobilization," *Political Behavior* 3(2022): 1317–1335; Caroline J. Tolbert, David P. Redlawsk, and Kellen J. Gracey, "Racial Attitudes and Emotional Responses to the 2016 Republican Candidates," *Journal of Elections, Public Opinion and Parties* 28 (2018): 245–262.
15 Emmitt Y. Riley and Clarissa Peterson, "I Can't Breathe: Assessing the Role of Racial Resentment and Racial Prejudice in Whites' Feelings toward Black Lives Matter," *National Review of Black Politics* 1 (2020): 496–515.

serve." And finally, "It's really a matter of some people not trying hard enough; if blacks would only try harder they could be just as well off as whites."

Republicans overwhelmingly agree with the sentiment that blacks should work harder to succeed "without any special favors." The surveys show very little change in between 2000 and 2020. In 2000, about 70 percent of all Republicans "strongly" or "somewhat" agreed with this perspective; in 2020, about 68 percent held one of those positions. We see similar results when we look at Republican attitudes on the question of whether blacks must try harder to succeed. In 2000, about 57 percent of Republicans agreed, and in 2020, about 49 percent agreed. On the other hand, on the other questions, there appears to have been small movement in the other direction. In 2000, about 17 percent agreed that blacks have gotten less than they deserve over the past few years, compared to about 15 percent in 2020. For the question of whether historical discrimination has made it harder for blacks to succeed, between 2000 and 2020 the percentage that agreed dropped from about 30 percent to about 27 percent.

None of this is to say that progressives should not be discouraged by the relatively high levels of racial resentment that Republicans exhibit on these surveys. The fact that most Republicans have not been persuaded by arguments about racial injustice may be a demoralizing finding. It is nonetheless also the case that Republicans are not exhibiting notably higher levels of racial resentment. Once again, if the Republican Party in the electorate is moving in a more racist direction, it is not showing up in the data.

The concept of racial resentment, or at least the questions used to measure it, has been criticized by conservatives. Some have argued that the positions associated with racial resentment are, in fact, perfectly reasonable statements that reflect reality, and it is not fair to suggest that holding these views signals bigotry. Writing in *National Review,* Robert Cherry pushed back against the idea that believing blacks have any responsibility for their own economic standing is itself an inherently racist proposition.[16]

Despite its continued popularity, some scholars have also raised questions about the validity of racial resentment scores. One potential problem is that, because the racial resentment questions specifically mention blacks, we usually take it for granted that these attitudes specifically measure attitudes toward African Americans. However, if the questions are slightly reworded, switching out African Americans for other groups – including white ethnic groups like Lithuanians

16 Robert Cherry, "The Problem with Trying to Measure 'Racial Resentment,'" *National Review,* January 24, 2019, https://www.nationalreview.com/2019/01/measuring-racial-resentment-problems/.

– the results are very similar.[17] This seems to indicate that racial resentment questions are likely picking up attitudes associated with economic conservatism or the Protestant work ethic, rather than with racial animosity as such. The interpretation of racial resentment scores is therefore debatable. Although the scale's opponents make trenchant critiques, I am inclined to keep using them, simply because they often prove to be such important predictors of other attitudes and behaviors. Scoring high on these scales is understandably associated with holding more conservative positions on race, but they also predict attitudes seemingly unrelated to racial issues.

Republican feelings of white identity

Beyond overt, old-fashioned racism and feelings of racial resentment, scholars of race in American politics have discovered an additional, separate source of racial attitudes: racial identity. That is, the degree to which people view their race as an important source of personal identity. Political scientist Ashley Jardina has been the leading scholar demonstrating the importance of white identity to many kinds of political attitudes and behaviors. In Jardina's analysis, white identity manifests as "a sense of commonality, attachment, and solidarity with their racial group."[18] She argues that, especially during a period of rapid demographic change, when people no longer view whiteness as the default in America, "we must, to some extent, think about white identity in the same way we think about black identity."[19] Strong feelings of white identity, she found, are not synonymous with out-group animus, but they are associated with more conservative views and support for the Republican Party. She found, for example, that white identity was not associated with opposition to affirmative action. It also did not seem to predict opposition to government spending designed to help minorities, but it was associated with greater opposition to immigration. Jardina argued the following questions can be used to measure feelings of white identity: the importance of whiteness to one's identity, the extent to which white Americans have much to be proud of, and how much American whites have in common with each other.[20]

The ANES has only recently begun to use questions directly related to white identity (feeling thermometers can act as a proxy, but an imperfect one). We

17 Riley K. Carney and Ryan D. Enos, "Conservatism and Fairness in Contemporary Politics," *NYU CESS Experiments Conference*, 2017.
18 See Ashley Jardina, *White Identity Politics* (New York: Cambridge University Press, 2019).
19 Ibid, 34.
20 Ibid, 58.

can nonetheless compare how these attitudes changed between 2016 and 2020. In answer to the question, "How important is being white to your identity?," about 33 percent of white Republicans in 2016 reported that it was "extremely important" or "very important." In 2020, this dropped to about 24 percent.

We can also get a sense of feelings of white solidarity from the question, "How important is it that whites work together to change laws that are unfair to whites?" In 2016, about 41 percent of white Republicans responded that it was "extremely important" or "very important." This also dropped in 2020, down to about 33 percent. Both surveys also asked, "How likely is it that many whites are unable to find a job because employers are hiring minorities instead?" In 2016, about 26 percent of white Republicans considered this very or extremely likely; in 2020, it was about 18 percent.

To be clear, white Republicans consistently show much higher levels of white identity than white Democrats. Yet again, however, only a minority of whites exhibit the highest levels of these feelings, and those attitudes seem to have declined during President Trump's time in office.

Republican antisemitism

Over the last decade, many Americans expressed reasonable concern about rising antisemitism.[21] We witnessed cases of horrific antisemitic violence, especially the rampage at the Tree of Life synagogue in Pittsburgh, PA in 2018, which killed eleven people.[22] The Alt-Right movement was, for the most part, intensely antisemitic. During a torchlit rally in Charlottesville, VA, in 2017, Alt-Right protesters shouted the slogan, "Jews will not replace us!" In fact, antisemitism may have been more central to the Alt-Right's ideology than racism or nativism.

According to a 2020 Pew study of Jewish Americans, an overwhelming majority of US Jews believes antisemitism is still present in the US. A majority also claimed that antisemitism had gotten worse over the previous five years.[23] On the other hand, the antisemitism of the American right should not be overstated. The Amer-

---

21 Jonathan Weisman, (((Semitism))): Being Jewish in America in the Age of Trump (New York: St. Martin's Press, 2018)

22 Campbell Robertson, Christopher Mele, and Sabrina Tavernise, "11 Killed in Synagogue Massacre; Suspect Charged With 29 Counts," *The New York Times*, October 27, 2018, https://www.nytimes.com/2018/10/27/us/active-shooter-pittsburgh-synagogue-shooting.html.

23 "Jewish Americans in 2020," Pew Research Center, May 11, 2021, file:///C:/Users/ghawley/Downloads/PF_05.11.21_Jewish.Americans.pdf.

ican conservative movement explicitly sought to rid itself of antisemitism.[24] William F. Buckley, founder of the *National Review* and arguably the most important post-war conservative journalist, wrote an entire book about his effort to extirpate anti-Jewish attitudes from the mainstream right.[25]

In my conversations with Republicans, my main takeaway on this subject was that most of them do not think about Jewish people very often. Only one person I spoke with (a very conservative man in his 80s who had spent his entire life in a Western state) brought up the subject without any prompting. He began with the statement, "So what's the deal with the Jews?" I expected he would follow up that statement with some kind of antisemitic trope. Instead, however, he clarified the question: "I mean, why do some people not like them? What's the problem?" He seemed genuinely curious, indicating he did not even know what the anti-Jewish stereotypes were. To the extent that he ever thought about Jews at all, he knew they had some connection to the people in the Bible, and that Israel is a Jewish state. On the other rare occasions that the subject of Jews came up in my interviews at all, it was usually in connection with Israel.

As always, some skepticism about these kinds of poll questions is warranted. However, it is worth knowing how Republicans respond when asked their feelings about Jewish people. As I noted earlier, according to the 2020 ANES, the mean feeling thermometer score Republicans gave Jewish Americans was about 72 – a very warm number. This was almost identical to the mean Jewish feeling thermometer score among Democrats, which was just under 73. To put that number in context, it is less than one integer lower than Republicans' average feelings toward white people. It is also considerably higher than the mean score Republicans give to Christian fundamentalists, which is a just below 60, and far higher than their mean score for Muslims (about 50).

Looking at the mean score at one point in time may not be the best measure. We should also look at the direction of the trend. Although Republican attitudes toward Jewish people seems quite high, perhaps it is nonetheless moving in the wrong direction and will drop considerably further. As of 2016, however, according to the ANES, the mean feeling thermometer score for Jews was about 72, just under what it was in 2020. To get a better sense of the direction Republican attitudes have been trending, we can look over a longer period. As of 2000, the mean feeling thermometer toward Jews among Republicans was about 66. That is, Republican warmth toward Jews appears to have increased over the last two decades.

---

24 George Hawley, *Right-Wing Critics of American Conservatism* (Lawrence, KS: University Press of Kansas, 2016).

25 William F. Buckley, *In Search of Anti-Semitism* (New York: Continuum, 1993).

Perhaps mean scores are misleading. For this issue, the distribution may be just as important as the mean. It is possible for the mean feeling thermometer score to be high even though a significant minority of respondents has very negative views toward the group in question. What percentage of Republicans have an extremely negative view of Jewish people? I will define that as a feeling thermometer score of 10 or less. In the 2020 ANES, about one percent of Republicans had views of Jewish people that were this negative. This was similar to what we find among Democrats – just under two percent of Democrats had views of Jewish people that were this negative.

Although I hope readers will take comfort in knowing that open anti-Jewish attitudes are relatively rare among Republicans in the electorate, I must be clear that I am not attempting to downplay antisemitism. The contemporary extreme right's hostility toward Jews is unquestionably real, as it was for earlier white nationalist movements. The number of Neo-Nazis in the US is infinitesimally small, but they do exist. It only takes one deranged person to inflict massive horror, and it is therefore important to monitor antisemitic rhetoric online and the behavior of antisemitic groups in the real world. Nonetheless, the odds of a significant antisemitic turn among the Republican electorate is exceedingly unlikely.

Republican support for political violence

Political violence has unquestionably been a major problem in the US in recent years. Beyond the January 6th riots and the violence in Charlottesville, VA in 2017, we have witnessed horrific acts of violence committed by white supremacist terrorists in places like Pittsburgh, PA, and El Paso, TX. At a lower level, groups like the Proud Boys seem to exist for no other reason than to engage in street fights with left-wing groups such as Antifa, which is short for "anti-fascist."[26] Political violence is especially concerning if we find evidence that it is supported by a wide swathe of the population. Even if large majorities would never personally engage in violence, they may be willing to excuse it. Are Republicans in the electorate willing to support, or at least rationalize, political violence?

The political science literature may give us reasons to be worried about rising support for political violence. Although Republicans are not becoming more radical in their policy preferences, and they are not apparently becoming more hostile to minority groups, political anger in the electorate is a real phenomenon. Negative

---

26 Shannon E. Reid and Matthew Valasik, *Alt-Right Gangs: A Hazy Shade of White* (Berkeley, CA: University of California Press, 2020)

partisanship, the loathing of the opposing political party, is distressingly high, as I will discuss shortly. Republicans and Democrats may not be all that different from each other when it comes to political differences, but they can still hate each other and, perhaps, even wish each other harm.

When the subject of right-wing violence comes up in discussion, conservatives often retort that the right-wing of the political spectrum is not the only, or even the leading, source of political violence in the US. Indeed, the question of which side is to blame for an apparent increase in violence is one of the most polarizing questions in politics right now. The ideological and partisan gap in views on political violence arguably reached a recent historical peak in 2020 and 2021. Throughout the summer of 2020, protesters took to the streets across the nation, calling for racial justice. Some of these protests included acts of violence, including arson and assault – though the overwhelming majority of protesters did not engage in these acts. While not every act of vandalism or assault was associated with a particular group, conservatives zeroed in on Antifa activists as the source of riots and violence. Antifa famously does not disavow violent actions as part of their political toolkit, though they insist that they are only seeking to protect vulnerable populations.[27] Republicans, whether moderate or more radical, are eager to denounce Antifa, and I found they brought up Antifa almost every time the question of violence came up during interviews.

During discussions of political violence, Republicans are eager to return to a perennial subject: media bias. Conservative media was quick to argue that mainstream and progressive journalists and pundits always turned a blind eye to violence committed by the left, arguing that left-wing protesters and rioters had transformed many large American cities into very dangerous places. The media, from their perspective, was deliberately keeping left-wing extremism out of public view for ideological reasons. According to conservative commentator Sean Hannity, "[t]hey know about Antifa. They know about these anarchists. They know the risks they pose. They have let this build and build and build and do nothing to stop the violence."[28]

Have high levels of negative partisanship resulted in a growing willingness to accept violence as a legitimate political tool, on either side of the political divide? Once again, survey data may be able to provide some clues. The 2020 ANES asked respondents the following question: "How much do you feel it is justified for people to use violence to pursue their political goals in this country?" We see that over-

---

27 Mark Bray, *Antifa: The Anti-Fascist Handbook* (Brooklyn, NY: Melville House, 2017)

28 Charles Creitz, "Sean Hannity calls out Dem Leaders of Cities Ravaged by Riots: 'Spectacular Failure on Every Level,'" Fox News, June 1, 2020, https://www.foxnews.com/media/sean-hannity-george-floyd-cities-ravaged-riots.

whelming majorities of both parties completely reject political violence as a legitimate tool. Fortunately, almost 84 percent of all ANES respondents believed that political violence was "not at all justified." About seven percent believed it was "a little justified"; about six percent claimed it was justified "a moderate amount"; under two percent thought it was "a lot" justified, and a similar percentage thought it was justified "a great deal." At least when it comes to survey responses, the norm against political violence remains strong in the US, even during a period of comparatively high civil unrest.

Although these percentages indicate that large majorities of both parties categorically reject political violence as a tactic, we may nonetheless discern partisan differences indicating that one side is more likely to justify the use of violence to attain political ends. In the 2020 ANES, we do see a partisan gap, but it indicated that Republicans were less likely that Democrats to justify political violence. Among Republicans, almost 91 percent argued that violence was "not at all justified." Among Democrats, this was about 78 percent. Overwhelming majorities of both parties reject political violence, but support for political violence is especially weak among Republicans – only about one percent of whom thought it was justified "a great deal."

To be clear, although overwhelming majorities of both parties reject political violence as a tactic, we should nonetheless treat the issue very seriously. Even one percent of either party enthusiastically engaging in serious political violence could cause disastrous harm. Indeed, a single lone-wolf actor can cause extraordinary levels of death and destruction. Nothing I have written should be interpreted to mean that law enforcement should not treat political violence as a very serious matter. However, political violence would be especially concerning if there was a wide swathe of the population willing to excuse it or perhaps even cheer it on. Fortunately, I have seen little compelling evidence that this is the case.

I must add a caveat to the finding that Democrats appear slightly more likely than Republicans to justify violence. These differences may be driven somewhat by political context. At the time the 2020 ANES was being conducted, left-wing political violence was the major news story, especially violence on the part of a very small percentage of Black Lives Matter protesters. Given that violence in service of left-wing causes dominated the news during that period, it may not be surprising that Americans on the left were somewhat more sympathetic to left-wing violence than right-wing voters. It is therefore worth looking at the same question during a different year. Fortunately, the ANES also asked this question in 2016, when partisan polarization was unquestionably high, but real-world political violence did not dominate the news. In that year, there was still a partisan gap, but it was smaller. In 2016, the aggregate percentage that opposed all political violence was nearly identical (about 84 percent). However, Republican opposition to violence was slightly lower than in 2020 (about 87 percent) and Democratic unequivocal opposition was slightly higher (about 83 percent). We therefore see that, on the margins, these percentages will vary in different contexts, but the data nonetheless showed that huge majorities of Americans of all partisan loyalties reject political violence, and the idea that Republicans are particularly likely to excuse political violence is not backed up by survey data.

Republican belief in QAnon and other conspiracy theories

The American right has always had a problem with conspiracy theories. Dealing with the most preposterous and dangerous ideas from a significant contingent of its own supporters has always been a challenge for the mainstream conservative movement.[29] Responsible voices today are justifiably concerned about QAnon and various other wild conspiracy theories that have gained shocking traction among elements of the Republican electorate. However, these theories can be reasonably compared to the crazy ideas promoted by Robert Welch and the John Birch Society many decades ago. From my conversations with ordinary Republicans, I concluded that most of them, even those that strongly reject conspiratorial thinking, nonetheless find conspiracy theorists in their ranks relatively harmless. As one person told me in response to a question about the January 6th riots, "The effects of these groups was vastly overblown. I think it's mostly young men getting a rile, making people upset, who probably have two or three good points to make."

Despite the long history of conspiracy theories across the political spectrum in the US, QAnon really does stand out for its outlandish premises. Whereas many Trump fans chanted for him to "drain the swamp," they were usually talking about getting rid of career politicians and bureaucrats whose agenda did not align with their vision for the country. Sometimes they were complaining about real and perceived corruption, especially as it related to the Clintons. Even complaints about the "deep state" were at least partially grounded in objective reality – there are institutional interests across the government that will resist changes pursued by elected officials, or at least drag their feet and hope that the next election cycle will put someone else in charge. QAnon went several steps further than these controversial, but at least arguable, complaints.

---

29 I cover the history of conservatism's efforts to expunge its most irresponsible elements in George Hawley, *Right-Wing Critics of American Conservatism* (Lawrence, KS: University Press of Kansas, 2016).

QAnon adherents genuinely believed that the Trump administration was engaged in an apocalyptic struggle against actual demonic forces (or at least against enemies that believed they were serving the devil). The basic premise of QAnon was that there was a secret war being waged by Donald Trump and his allies against a ghoulish, corrupt cabal engaged in political corruption and, more disturbingly, child sex trafficking. These villains, who included the highest echelons of the Democratic Party, as well as leading media figures, never believed Donald Trump would be elected president, and his victory sent them into a panic. Trump, as a messianic leader, was going to sweep them all away, clearing out the satanic corruption that had so long controlled America's destiny.

Given its origins, it is surprising that QAnon gained such a large following. QAnon was born on 4chan, which is a mostly unmoderated image board. As is often the case for unmoderated online spaces, 4chan is known as a place to share extreme pornography and extreme politics (especially its infamous board, "/pol/," which is short for "politically incorrect"). As I learned during my research on the Alt-Right, this site is where many far-right memes and tactics are born. On 4chan, and later 8chan, QAnon had a relatively limited reach. These sites are ugly and can be difficult for the uninitiated to make sense of. It was only after QAnon ideas started jumping to other, more mainstream sites, such as Reddit, Twitter, and YouTube, that it gained prominence among Republicans in the electorate.[30]

According to Q believers, the person feeding them information was a member of a secretive military operation. The first Q "drop" occurred in 2017, the first year of the Trump Administration. Responding, apparently, to a cryptic remark President Trump made about "the calm before the storm," an anonymous 4chan commenter declared the time and date that Hillary Clinton would be arrested. This claim went viral, and believers looked forward to this event. Although that date came and went without incident, Q continued to post and gain new followers.[31]

In my personal interviews, I met only one Republican that was fully on board with QAnon and similar conspiracy theories, though another acknowledged that he once bought into these theories, and a few admitted they thought some elements of the theory were plausible. Perhaps they were underrepresented because such people are especially skeptical of academics, but it is more likely that they were only a small percentage of my interviewees because they are a small percentage of Republican voters. In my 2022 survey asking Republicans their top policy priorities,

30 Daniel de Zeeuw, Sal Hagen, Stijn Peeters, and Emilija Jokubauskaite, "Tracing Normiefication: A Cross-Platform Analysis of the QAnon Conspiracy Theory," *First Monday* 25 (2020): https://journals.uic.edu/ojs/index.php/fm/article/view/10643/9998.
31 Mike Rothschild, *The Storm is Upon Us: How QAnon Became a Movement, Cult, and Conspiracy Theory of Everything* (New York: Melville House, 2021), 19–20.

only one mentioned anything even tangentially related to QAnon subjects. An oblique reference to "sex trafficking," which the respondent did not elaborate on, was the closest any of them came to referencing the conspiracy theory – and even this person listed inflation as his first priority.

We should therefore acknowledge that, for all the attention they received, active QAnon supporters are an exceptionally small part of the electorate and only represent a small fraction of the Republican Party. Among those Republicans that do frequent QAnon message boards and other conspiracy sites, the overwhelming majority never do anything beyond passively read online material. Mike Rothschild, who has written the most definitive book to date on QAnon, rejects the claim by some Q supporters that their numbers reach the hundreds of millions, and notes that skeptics think its actual true-believing adherents may be less than 100,000 people.[32]

Of course, one way to determine how many people support QAnon is simply to ask them in a public opinion poll. Fortunately, one online polling organization, Civiqs, has been doing this for several years. According to their most recent poll at the time of this writing, about three percent of Americans reported supporting QAnon.[33] More than three times as many registered voters (11 percent) indicated that they had "never heard of QAnon." Among Republicans, QAnon support was higher, but still in the single digits (seven percent). Those percentages sound extremely small, but it is worth noting that, in a nation as large as the United States, three percent of registered voters still represents more than a million people.

This number may be a bit misleading, however. In the aftermath of the Capitol riots, people may have been hesitant to share the fact that they believe in QAnon theories. QAnon supporters and other right-wing conspiracy theorists may represent a more extreme version of the "shy Trump voters," the Trump supporters that either did not want to talk to pollsters or gave misleading answers about their voting intentions in the run-up to the 2016 and 2020 presidential elections.

The Civiqs data do indicate that there was a drop in QAnon support after January 6th, 2020 (its level of support had previously peaked at about seven percent). On the other hand, even if QAnon support really is just three percent of registered voters, that finding may also be deceptive. Although they are a tiny minority of the population, QAnon supporters have demonstrated that they are disproportionately

---

32 Ibid, 12.
33 "QAnon Support," Civiqs, September 10, 2020-October 24, 2022, https://civiqs.com/results/qanon_support?uncertainty=true&annotations=true&zoomIn=true.

motivated and involved in politics, as indicated by the recent surge of Republican candidates that directly or indirectly indicate support for QAnon.[34]

Scholars and mainstream journalists largely ignored QAnon throughout its early history. In part, this was because, as a distrustful, primarily online community, they were not pursuing attention from journalists and academics. The fact that so many QAnon ideas seemed preposterous to outsiders further made it hard to take seriously. I admit that I was in this category, despite my many years of research on the far right. After January 6th, 2021, however, when a significant contingent of the Capitol rioters repeated slogans or carried banners associated with conspiracies, the theory and its followers suddenly received extraordinary attention, perhaps more than it warrants.

Beyond just asking them if they believe in and support QAnon, other pollsters have attempted to discern how many people can be accurately described as QAnon supporters using different questions. In May 2021, the Public Religion Research Institute conducted a poll that asked subjects questions relating to the QAnon worldview.[35] They argued that three questions can tell us the degree to which a person subscribes to the QAnon perspective: "The government, media, and financial worlds in the US are controlled by a group of Satan-worshipping pedophiles who run a global child sex trafficking operation"; "There is a storm coming soon that will sweep away the elites in power and restore the rightful leaders"; and "Because things have gotten so far off track, true American patriots may have to resort to violence in order to save our country."

The poll found that only a minority of Americans supported any of these positions, and a smaller percentage supported all three. About 15 percent of those polled, and almost a quarter of all Republicans, believed the first statement (the one about Satanic pedophiles). This is a disconcertingly high percentage stating agreement with a ludicrous claim. About 28 percent of Republicans agreed with the second statement (about the coming "storm"). A similar percentage of Republicans agreed that patriotic Americans may need to resort to violence. Many writers expressed extraordinary concern over this poll. One of the people responsible for it suggested that QAnon had as many adherents as the largest religious groups in the

34 Katherine Tully-McManus, "QAnon goes to Washington: Two Supporters Win Seats in Congress," *Roll Call*, November 5, 2020, https://rollcall.com/2020/11/05/qanon-goes-to-washington-two-supporters-win-seats-in-congress/.
35 "Understanding QAnon's Connection to American Politics, Religion, and Media Consumption," The Public Religion Research Institute, May 27, 2021, https://www.prri.org/research/qanon-conspiracy-american-politics-report/.

country, comparable in size to evangelical Protestantism or mainline Protestantism.[36]

Although I do not want to be dismissive of concerns about radicalized conspiracy theorists and the potential security threats they pose, there are a few reasons to be skeptical about these percentages. Intentionally or not, the language about political violence in that question was clearly going to activate different sentiments among people depending on their political loyalties. The line about "true American patriots" calls to mind instances of justifiable political violence in the name of resisting tyranny. It is aligned with the spirit of the Gadsden Flag and other imagery that much of the right, including people who would never engage in any kind of violence, has embraced. I am furthermore willing to take expressions of support for partisan hyperbole with a grain of salt, given our high levels of negative polarization. The notion that the world elite are "Satan worshipers" is of course preposterous, but what percentage of Democrats would agree with a question asking whether they believed Republican or conservative elites were secretly Nazis? The percentage would undoubtedly be depressingly high.

The wording of this question is problematic because it almost inevitably leads to results indicating that Republicans are disproportionately prone to violence. Different wording of the question would have yielded different results. Simply switching out the line "true American patriots" with a more neutral word like "people" would probably make the partisan difference less pronounced. Changing the words further, asking, for example, "If America fails to address systemic inequalities and discrimination, people may have to resort to violence to achieve social justice," we would get extremely different results. None of this is to excuse political violence on any side of the political spectrum, or to suggest that right-wing radicalization is not a problem in the US. I merely want to reiterate that relatively small changes to polling questions can yield very different results, and poorly worded questions can paint a misleading picture.

Another point to note about QAnon is that it was almost an exclusively online phenomenon. Some researchers have pointed out that people who watched conservative television news programs such as Fox News were disproportionately likely to believe in QAnon. This is both true and misleading. Although the hosts of Fox's most popular shows were unquestionably pro-Trump and against his enemies, none of them ever promoted anything as absurd as QAnon. If people believed in the theory, they were learning about it from the internet.

---

36 Giovanni Russonello, "QAnon Now as Popular in U.S. as Some Major Religions, Poll Suggests," *The New York Times*, May 27, 2021, https://www.nytimes.com/2021/05/27/us/politics/qanon-repub licans-trump.html.

Other scholarship has considered what other attributes are associated with support for QAnon. Political scientists Jack Thompson and Sierra Davis Thomander conducted a survey experiment to discern what kinds of information can diminish public support for QAnon.[37] They found that telling people that many online QAnon message boards include racist and antisemitic language weakened support for the movement. Pointing out that some members of congress have expressed support for QAnon increased support. Pointing out that many Q predictions failed to come true, however, did not have any apparent effect on public support.

Readers may be comforted to know that I have not uncovered much evidence that QAnon true believers represent a substantial percentage of the Republican Party. It may be more alarming to some that I also found few Republicans eager to condemn the movement or who believed it was worth worrying about. The overwhelming consensus among interviewees was that the premises of QAnon were silly (though a few thought some claims might have merit), but it was really nothing more than a collection of mostly harmless online eccentrics. They thought all the hype about QAnon was just another example of the mainstream media treating conservatives as unhinged lunatics.

Understanding the basic premises of the QAnon theories helps us understand why so many of the January 6th rioters were confident that they would be vindicated. Even the most ignorant online conspiracy theorists must surely realize that a few hundred, overwhelmingly unarmed civilians rushing the Capitol Building would not overturn the government. Many QAnon believers, however, did not think they would be alone. They had every expectation that they would shortly be joined by special forces troops, operating under President Trump's orders, who would arrest the president's enemies and ensure that the rightful president (Trump) would remain in office. I spoke with one person who told me his father was delighted when he watched the January 6th riots unfold. Throughout the day, he was absolutely convinced that, at any moment, troops would swoop in, join the rioters, and arrest the traitors.

Given that Q's predictions have an abysmal track record, and many of the people who took QAnon seriously and stormed the Capitol were arrested and imprisoned, one might reasonably anticipate that QAnon lost adherents. In my personal interviews, I found anecdotal evidence that failed predictions can eventually weaken support for the movement. As one person I interviewed in 2023 told me, "I admit I got sucked into QAnon, but at some point something had to happen to

---

37 Jack Thompson and Sierra Davis Thomander, "What Drives Support for QAnon? Evidence from a Survey Experiment," Working Paper.

make me believe it isn't bullshit. How many years do you really expect me to 'trust the plan?'"

Other QAnon believers have not updated their beliefs as predictions continuously failed to come true. One Trump supporter I spoke with remained adamant that everything that Q predicted actually has come true, that Donald Trump is still the actual president and in charge of the country, but Trump is keeping his activities mostly hidden for the sake of social harmony. Eventually, he believes, the truth will be known to everyone.

Again, hard numbers are difficult to come by. However, it is clear that QAnon continues to this day. QAnon's failed predictions can always be explained away or, better yet, reinterpreted to show that they actually did come true, but not in the way people initially predicted. Violence committed by QAnon followers can always be called a false flag intended to discredit the movement. In reaction to my questions about the January 6th riots, one interviewee argued that it was all faked by the left:

> I did some research, and from what I found in my research was that – and this could be hearsay – but I found that it was Antifa, that George Soros had paid off Antifa to invade the Capitol, as he had been doing for previous riots. He was paying them $15 an hour, which is way above minimum wage. That was a way to incite violence and have them dressed as conservatives. It could be hearsay, but there were a lot of documents that I found that did confirm that. So, I think that it was definitely a ploy by the left.

Much of the coverage of QAnon has included breathless commentary about the movement's antisemitism and general reactionary approach to politics – attacks on progressive billionaire George Soros, who is Jewish, are sometimes interpreted as veiled expressions of antisemitism. For many prominent voices amplifying the QAnon narrative, this is unquestionably true. It is also true that antisemitic attitudes appear to be correlated with QAnon support.[38] However, we should remember that many people were drawn into the movement by noble intentions. They took seriously the claim that global elites were harming children, and they wanted to play a role in solving the problem. I consider this one of the more insidious aspects of QAnon and related conspiracy theories. Many of the people they prey upon may be gullible, but they are also well meaning. During an interview with a young woman who had only recently switched over to the Republican Party,

---

38 Ines Levin, Alexandra Filindra, and Jeffrey S. Kopstein, "Validating and Testing a Measure of anti-semitism on Support for QAnon and Vote Intention for Trump in 2020," *Social Science Quarterly* 103 (2022): 794–809.

she explained how this kind of material first motivated her to get involved with politics:

> After the election, I started getting into [QAnon] around the time COVID hit. And then it started releasing all the documents about COVID and the Wuhan lab and with Dr. Fauci. And there was all the stuff with the Democratic Party, with all the human trafficking. And it filled a lot of the Jeffrey Epstein case. There was a lot of documents in regard to that.

During our conversation, it was clear that this person was sincerely concerned about the well-being of children, and antisemitic or even partisan considerations did not play a role in her thinking. At the time she started down the QAnon and COVID-skepticism rabbit holes, she said she was still a Democrat. Although she was quite convinced of these theories at the time of our conversation, there was no indication that she had absorbed and accepted any of the antisemitic or racist ideas that were often associated with QAnon and related conspiracy theories. Another person I spoke with suggested that the conspiracy theorists gain traction because they are willing to talk about things the mainstream Republican Party and conservative movement would rather avoid, but then they undermine themselves by taking things in a crazy direction: "I think a lot of the extremist right will hit on things that the establishment right won't hit on, and that's why they have a following, but then they wrap in some more extremist rhetoric, which then becomes problematic ... They wrap it in antisemitism, or they wrap it in extremist violent rhetoric."

QAnon and related theories thankfully have a relatively low ceiling of possible support. The odds that belief in these kinds of conspiracy theories will become prevalent among Republicans is, in my estimation, very low. More concerning, however, is the large number of Republicans who believe in conspiracy theories surrounding elections. In particular, in my interviews I was alarmed by the prevalence of the belief that the 2020 US presidential election was "stolen," and that Donald Trump had been the true winner. In this instance, political elites, especially Trump himself, must take the lion's share of the blame. Polls indicate that a majority of Republicans believed fraud was widespread in that election.[39] The January 6th riots, about which most Republicans remain nonchalant, represented an unprecedented break with the tradition of peaceful transitions of power. I have yet to hear any prominent voices in conservative media reverse their earlier claims that the Democrats engaged in widespread election fraud. Conspiratorial thinking in the Republican Party on the subject of elections is a serious problem, and we

---

39 Gary C. Jacobson, "Donald Trump's Big Lie and the Future of the Republican Party," *Presidential Studies Quarterly* 51 (2021): 273–289.

should be concerned that a huge swathe of the electorate erroneously believes that the election process is no longer fair. Claims of voter fraud, even those with no supporting evidence, appear to lead to more negative attitudes toward elections and even democracy itself.[40] I am not convinced we have reached a point of crisis yet, and suspect these problems will wane when the Trump era of the GOP reaches its inevitable conclusion, but these concerns must not be ignored and I hope more elected Republicans and conservative media figures will abandon this kind of irresponsible rhetoric.

As I noted above, some commentators have correctly pointed out that the American right has always had a paranoid streak.[41] The outlandish claims associated with PizzaGate and QAnon are scarcely weirder and more implausible than Robert Welch's statements about communist subversion when the John Birch Society was at its peak of influence. It does nonetheless seem to the be the case that conspiratorial thinking is ascendant during periods when the right is dominated by populist impulses. Populism is well-suited to conspiracy theorizing because it begins from the premise that elites are corrupt and at odds with "the pure people."[42] Once one accepts the idea that politics can be viewed through such a Manichean lens, it is simply intuitive that elites are constantly conspiring to enrich themselves at the public's expense and use their misbegotten wealth on the most decadent and sometimes devilish pursuits.[43]

Although populism aims to restore power to ordinary people, populist sentiments are often disempowering. Believing that political, economic, and media elites are hopelessly corrupt and deceitful inclines people toward cynicism. It is not surprising that populism and conspiracy theorizing go together. Distrust in political elites is not necessarily unhealthy – at times, there may be very good reasons to distrust elites. This becomes a more serious problem if these attitudes lead to a diminished sense of political efficacy, eventually convincing people that democratic engagement is pointless or even counterproductive.[44] An additional problem

---

40 Florian Justwan and Ryan D. Williamson, "Trump and Trust: Examining the Relationship between Claims of Fraud and Citizen Attitudes," *PS: Political Science and Politics* 55 (2022): 462–469.
41 For a strong argument on this subject, see John S. Huntington, *Far-Right Vanguard: The Radical Roots of Modern Conservatism* (Philadelphia, PA: University of Pennsylvania Press, 2021).
42 Cas Mudde, "The Populist Zeitgeist," *Government and Opposition* 39 (2004): 543.
43 Jan-Werner Müller, "What, If Anything, Do Populism and Conspiracy Theories Have to Do with Each Other?" *Social Research: An International Quarterly* 89 (2022): 607–625.
44 Political scientists define political efficacy as "the feeling that individual political action does have, or can have, an impact on the political process, i.e., that it is worthwhile to perform one's civic duties. It is the feeling that political and social change is possible, and that the citizen can play a part in bringing about this change" (Angus Campbell, Gerald Gurin, Warren E. Miller, Sylvia Eberhart, and Robert O. McWilliams, *The Voter Decides*, [Evanston, IL: Row, Peterson, 1954], 187).

with conspiratorial thinking is that it, perhaps paradoxically, can make people more gullible when it comes to preposterous claims from untrustworthy sources – when people reject the idea that credentialed experts deserve deference, they become more likely to believe anyone who supplies information that confirms their own biases.[45]

We should not overstate the evidence for a direct, causal relationship between populist attitudes and belief in conspiracy theories. Scholars have shown that when conspiracy theorists' preferred candidate wins elections, belief in conspiracies tends to decline.[46] Other research indicates that electing populist politicians makes people feel more empowered, less cynical, and less inclined toward zero-sum thinking.[47] Of course, these studies do not tell us what happens to these voters when a populist in power is defeated in a subsequent election. I have yet to see a peer-reviewed study on this subject, but common sense and recent political headlines seem to suggest that such defeats can result in a surge in conspiratorial thinking and anti-government attitudes.

The populism question

During my talks with Republicans with lower levels of involvement and political sophistication, but who were nonetheless intensely emotional about politics, I found that frustration with elites was a common sentiment. Hostility toward the "establishment" was a consistent theme. This was especially true of fervent Trump supporters, who often believed that their president had been betrayed by self-serving and disloyal Republican leaders.

Republican elites, for their part, sometimes also expressed frustration with the angriest elements of their own base, though they tended to use more careful language. Some directly critiqued the "nuts" that made it hard to build a professional and effective party and movement. One Republican elected member of a municipal government stated that she appreciated and admired the passion and energy she was witnessing at the grassroots level, but many of these political neophytes sim-

---

45 Jan-Willem van Prooijen, Talia Cohen Rodrigues, Carlotta Bunzel, Oana Georgescu, Dániel Komáromy, and André P. M. Krouwel, "Populist Gullibility: Conspiracy Theories, News Credibility, Bullshit Receptivity, and Paranormal Belief," *Political Psychology*, 43(2022): 1061–1079.
46 Joseph E. Uscinski and Joseph M. Parent, *American Conspiracy Theories* (New York: Oxford University Press, 2014).
47 Kostas Papaioannou, Myrto Pantazi, and Jan-Willem van Prooijen, "Unravelling the Relationship between Populism and Belief in Conspiracy Theories: The Role of Cynicism, Powerlessness, and Zero-Sum Thinking," *British Journal of Psychology,* 114(2023): 159–175.

ply lacked the knowledge necessary to accomplish real change. Making a lasting difference requires working within existing institutions and understanding their rules and culture. A disorganized rabble disrupting school board meetings, for example, may be a nuisance, but can ultimately be waited out by people in positions of authority.

Another person I interviewed, a professional political consultant, thought that the GOP's populist turn did the party some good. He noted that a lot of people have been activated and brought into the fold who had previously been apolitical. These newcomers, however, had zero respect for the people who had been working in politics for years. They were unwilling to defer to expertise, but also not apparently interested in learning how to run things themselves. They simply wanted to lambaste elites of all kinds.

A conservative activist working with non-profit organizations expressed similar frustrations, noting that some people who only recently became active in politics had decided to form groups designed to promote a particular policy or ideological agenda. The problem is that they sometimes seemed to be unaware that groups promoting an identical mission already existed, do a generally good job, and have the knowledge and connections to be effective. New organizations formed during a wave of populist fervor, thrown together with relatively little research and possessing few meaningful connections to people with real power, will have little long-term impact.

A different activist, an employee at a conservative think tank, similarly critiqued the newly emboldened populist wing of the Republican Party. I Interviewed him shortly before the 2022 midterm elections. He expressed a worry that "the Red Wave" might turn into the "Red Puddle." He thought this specifically because the candidates who were most effective at tapping into Trumpian energies looked like they would be terrible candidates in a general election. More broadly, he thought populism would harm the party:

> I think populism has this reactionary quality to it, one that is inherently against leadership and against those at the higher ends of society as intrinsically bad or immoral or amoral. I think populism also has a route to tear down tradition, in the sense that those who are higher up in the tradition or those who lead the tradition are in and of themselves those who are in opposition to the populists [...]. I think populists are inherently anti-hierarchical in many ways, and I think hierarchy is essential to a healthy society.

Affective partisan polarization

Throughout this book, we have seen little evidence that, overall, the Republican Party has become more radical or right-wing on most economic or social issues.

Compelling empirical evidence that the GOP is becoming more racist, antisemitic, or homophobic is similarly hard to come by. If anything, on most questions, it seems that the Republican Party in the electorate is becoming more moderate and tolerant. On the other hand, the claim that the Republican Party in the electorate is slowly moving in a more moderate and tolerant direction seems at odds with our everyday experience of US politics. The American public, on both sides of the partisan divide, seem extremely angry about politics. How can we reconcile this?

One explanation may be that we receive an inaccurate picture of the electorate from the media. We only hear the angry voices. There is not apparently much of an audience for reasonable moderates, and only strident partisans draw audiences. Such figures thus rise to prominence on cable news and editorial pages. Social media may similarly skew our perceptions. We open X or Facebook and only see political posts from enraged ideologues, giving us the false impression that such people are the norm in the US. Ambivalent moderates, who see problems and virtues on both sides of the partisan divide, are unlikely to post online about politics every day.

This can only account for some of this finding, however, and we should not underestimate the degree to which political anger is very real. The strange thing about this anger, however, is that it can often be completely disconnected from questions of policy, or feelings of prejudice toward different racial, ethnic, or religious groups. It is true that partisanship tends to be downstream from other social identities, such as our race, religion, education level, region, or occupation.[48] Increasingly, however, partisanship in the US is becoming an important element of personal identity.[49] Our party identities are not just a standing preference for one political party over another because we prefer its policy platform. For many Americans, being a Republican or a Democrat is an important element of their sense of self. This can make elections and other partisan battles feel extremely important, even when the policy stakes are low or we have very low levels of knowledge and political sophistication. We cheer for our team, and intensely dislike the opposition. These negative emotions about partisan politics seem to be increasing.

We can see how these emotions have been changing in Figure 6.1, which shows the changes in attitudes (measured via feeling thermometers) toward different groups between 2000 and 2020. As I have already discussed, Republican feelings

48 Donald Green, Bradley Palmquist, and Eric Schickler, *Partisan Hearts and Minds* (New Haven, CT: 2004).
49 Liliana Mason, *Uncivil Agreement: How Politics Became our Identity* (Chicago, IL: University of Chicago Press, 2018).

toward most groups have actually improved over the last 20 years. The change in their views toward gays and lesbians is particularly remarkable. They now also have more positive feelings toward blacks, Hispanics, and Jews, and their feelings toward whites and big business have become slightly more negative – the latter finding may be indicative of the more populist views that have apparently been ascendant within the GOP in recent years.

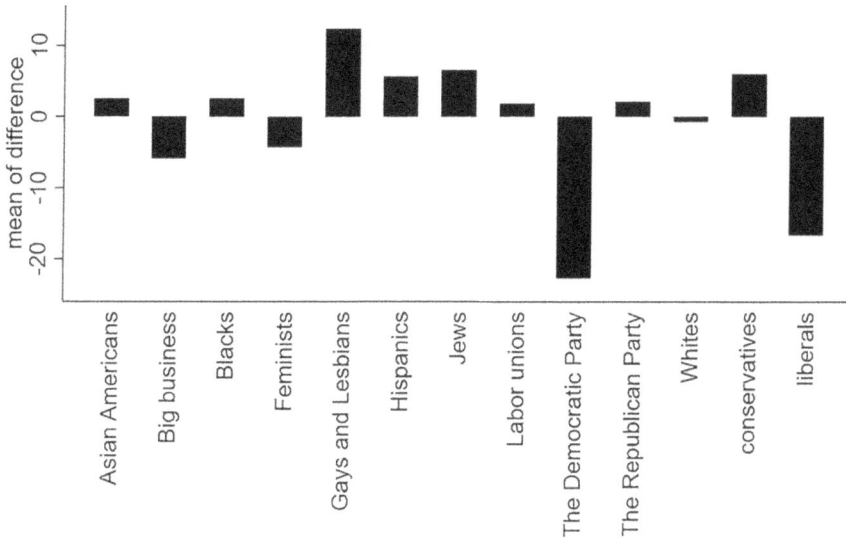

Figure 6.1: Change in Republican Feeling Thermometers for Groups, 2000–2020. Source: Cumulative ANES.

Republicans have also developed slightly more positive feelings toward their own party and toward conservatives. The biggest movement, however, has been in regard to their political and ideological enemies. Republican attitudes toward Democrats have nosedived over the last 20 years – dropping almost 23 points. Feelings toward liberals dropped almost 17 points. As I noted earlier, feelings toward feminists have also dropped. This may be because this category is often viewed from a partisan or ideological lens. It is unfortunate that the ANES no longer uses the broader category of "women" in its feeling thermometer questions, as that would likely show different results.

This is one of the more interesting recent developments in the US electorate. Republican hostility toward major minority groups is declining, yet partisan hostility continues to increase. We know, however, that partisan identity is largely shaped by our social group identities. It may be the case that Americans' other forms of prejudice and anger are increasingly being sublimated into their party identities. From the perspective of inter-group relations, this may be a positive development. All things considered, it is probably better if Republican anger is focused on Democrats as a social group, rather than, say, African Americans or immigrants. On the other hand, if our social identities and our partisan identities become very highly correlated, this may become a distinction without a difference. Henry Adams once described partisan politics as the "systematic organization of hatreds."[50] Perhaps, as US party politics has further matured, party politics has simply become a proxy for other kinds of prejudice and distrust.

Conclusion

Despite that very big caveat about growing partisan anger among Republicans, we should nonetheless welcome most of the polling data we see regarding Republican attitudes. Again, progressive Democrats can be reasonably worried the typical Republican holds positions well to the right of their own, but so much of the hand-wringing about this subject seems to disregard the direction of the trends. The claim that Republican voters have made a sharp turn to the right on questions of culture and race is simply not vindicated by the relevant data. If the current trends showing a small but discernable movement among Hispanic voters toward the Republican Party[51] continues, I suspect Republican nativism will dissipate further.

I was relieved to find relatively little evidence to support the idea that a large percentage of Republicans support the most implausible conspiracy theories, but their commitment to the lie that Donald Trump was somehow cheated in the 2020 election is concerning. The good news is that, since January 6th, 2021, we have not witnessed further widespread criminal behavior on behalf of Trump. Republicans have spent the last few years grumbling that Joe Biden sits in the White House, but grudging acceptance of this fact appears to be the norm. I remain concerned by the high levels of election denialism in the Republican electorate, a problem exacerbated by many politicians (including Trump himself) and conservative media pushing transparent lies about the 2020 election results. As I write this, the 2024 presidential election is still months away. Whatever the outcome,

---

50 Henry Adams, *The Education of Henry Adams* (New York: Houghton Mifflin, 1918), 7.

51 Ruy Teixeira, "The Evidence Mounts: Hispanic Voters are Drifting Toward the GOP," *The Washington Post*, July 5, 2023, https://www.washingtonpost.com/opinions/2023/07/05/hispanic-voters-gop-biden/.

my hope is that the result is sufficiently decisive to preclude further conspiratorial thinking about election results.

Partisan anger is a real phenomenon, deserving additional attention from scholars. The strong feelings and heated rhetoric inspired by contemporary US politics is concerning. Republicans, on average, intensely dislike Democrats, which is a problem because it makes political compromise more challenging – Republicans in Congress who pursue the path of moderation and bipartisanship may find themselves at odds with their own voters. Strong partisan feelings also make it harder for the electorate to hold politicians accountable. If partisans will never consider voting for someone from the other party, a politician in a district where the voting patterns benefit his party can expect to be reelected in perpetuity, regardless of performance in office.

Chapter 7
A center-right party in a changing America

People of every political persuasion will likely be unhappy with much of the data presented in this book. Conservative ideologues will be unhappy that most members of the public, including consistent Republican voters, are not especially conservative – at least as the conservative movement understands the term. Readers on the left may be frustrated that Republicans are still very ideologically distant from them, especially on social issues and racial attitudes. From their perspective, the slow Republican movement in a more liberal direction may be better than a lurch to the right, but it is nonetheless inadequate. As for economic issues, finding out that Republicans in the electorate are, on average, more moderate than Republicans in elected office can justifiably make progressives even more irritated with the Republican Party in government, which continuously pursues conservative economic policies that are not apparently even popular among their own voters.

I nonetheless hope that this book has shown that certain contemporary concerns about the Republican Party in the electorate have been overblown. I understand the argument that right-wing radicalism is a major threat to US democracy and must be treated as such. I nonetheless argue that hyperbole encouraging mass panic is unlikely to be helpful and may even be counterproductive. Although it is a venue that seems to reward the most radical voices, I am disturbed by the number of high-profile progressive X accounts that have no problem declaring Republicans, all Republicans, fascists, white supremacists, or even terrorists. For what it is worth, I offer the same critique to conservatives who make absurd accusations about their opponents on the left. We should remember that we have seen this kind of fearful thinking and hyperbolic rhetoric in the recent past, and its effects were not innocuous. One key lesson of the Global War on Terror is that threat inflation can be just as problematic as underestimating threats, resulting in attacks on civil liberties and the counterproductive demonization of harmless people. Although we should not overstate the dangers of partisan hyperbole, it nonetheless represents a problem.

An additional point to keep in mind is that radicalism is ultimately subjective. As I have attempted to demonstrate in this volume, Republicans have not changed very much over the last several decades in terms of their cultural attitudes and policy preferences. On many issues, they are more progressive than they used to be. Yet, Democrats are not wrong to perceive a growing ideological distance between themselves and their partisan opponents. This is because Democrats have – on average – moved left. This is particularly true when it comes to issues surrounding identity, especially regarding race, sex, gender, and immigration status;

https://doi.org/10.1515/9783111469720-007

political scientist Zach Goldberg has called this the "Great Awokening."[1] This book has little to say about trends among Democrats, as they were not my focus. No political party exists in a vacuum, however, and to understand and make predictions about trends in one party, we must know something about what is occurring on the other side. Although we find little evidence for this in the data I examined, it is possible that the Democrats' shift to the left will eventually result in a significant shift to the right among Republicans. Another possibility is the Democrats' move left will simply shift the political center of gravity in their direction, making US politics more progressive. At this point, both possibilities remain plausible. The fact that I found little evidence of a widespread right-wing backlash among contemporary Republicans does not mean we will not see one in the future.

In the decades ahead, Republican attitudes toward cultural and demographic changes will be very important to watch. The encouraging news, however, is that I see very little evidence that Republicans in the electorate are trending in a more exclusionary or prejudiced direction. This is an important finding that should be highlighted. I cannot claim knowledge about how Republican politicians and conservative media celebrities and pundits formulate their talking points and strategies, but I suspect some of their incendiary rhetoric toward certain minority groups are the result of bad information. They believe this is what their voters or audience wants to hear.

In this book, I focused on the Republican Party in the electorate. As I noted in the introduction, I have little to say in this book about the Republican Party in government, or about right-wing opinion leaders in the media. That being the case, this book should not be interpreted as a defense of the latter two groups. I have many complaints about both, but this is not the place for that editorializing. One may additionally argue that the Republican Party has not become more radically right wing because it has been a radical right-wing party for decades, and what we are seeing today is just more of the same. I disagree with that assessment, but it is an argument that this work cannot address.

Affective polarization is an undeniable problem in the US electorate. I unfortunately think it is unlikely to go away anytime soon, given that there seem to be so few incentives for political actors to reduce their irresponsible, hostile rhetoric. There is no taboo against partisan hyperbole – this makes it different from other kinds of bigotry. The most aggressive, angry partisans in politics and political media seem to be consistently rewarded, while moderates are ignored, or even viewed as traitors by their own side. I find this unfortunate, but do not have a

---

1 Zach Goldberg, "America's White Saviors," *Tablet*, June 5, 2019, https://www.tabletmag.com/sections/news/articles/americas-white-saviors.

practical solution to the problem, and can only seek to avoid this pitfall in my own writing and encourage others to do the same.

There are real and important differences between Republicans and Democrats in the electorate. On average, they have different cultural attitudes and want different things from government. We should, however, not overstate the degree to which the country is polarized. I hope that more moderate voices will be encouraged to know that the partisan divide is not the gaping chasm that many people believe it is. I anticipate that politics will remain an ugly, uncivil vocation for the foreseeable future, but this has always been the case, and I remain optimistic that the US will be able to overcome its many present challenges using the same constitutional, democratic means that have long served the country well.

References

Abrajano, Marisa and Zoltan L. Hajnal. 2017. *White Backlash: Immigration, Race, and American Politics.* Princeton, NJ: Princeton University Press.

Abramowitz, Alan I. 1995. "It's Abortion, Stupid: Policy Voting in the 1992 Election." *The Journal of Politics* 57: 176–186.

Abramowitz, Alan I. and Jennifer McCoy. 2019. "United States: Racial Resentment, Negative Partisanship, and Polarization in Trump's America." *The ANNALS of the American Academy of Political and Social Science* 681: 137–156.

Adams, Greg D. 1997. "Abortion: Evidence of an Issue Evolution." *American Journal of Political Science* 41: 718–737.

Adams, Henry. 1918. *The Education of Henry Adams.* New York: Houghton Mifflin.

Adorno, Theodor W., Else Frenkel-Brunswik, Daniel Levinson, and Nevitt Sanford. 1950. *The Authoritarian Personality.* New York: Harper, 1950.

Albrecht, Don E. 2019. "The Nonmetro Vote and the Election of Donald Trump," *Journal of Rural Social Sciences* 34: 1–32.

Albrecht, Don E. 2022. "Donald Trump and Changing Rural/Urban Voting Patterns." *Journal of Rural Studies* 91: 148–156.

Allport, Gordon. 1954. *The Nature of Prejudice.* New York: Addison-Wesley.

Almond, Gabriel A. and Sidney Verba. 1963. *The Civic Culture.* Princeton, NJ: Princeton University Press.

Alvarez, R. Michael and Tara L. Butterfield. 2000. "The Resurgence of Nativism in California? The Case of Proposition 187 and Illegal Immigration." *Social Science Quarterly* 81: 167–179.

Alvarez, R. Michael and Lisa García Bedolla. 2003. "The Foundations of Latino Voter Partisanship: Evidence from the 2000 Election." *The Journal of Politics* 65: 31–49.

Ansolabehere, Stephen and Philip Edward Jones. 2010. "Constituents' Responses to Congressional Roll-Call Voting," *American Journal of Political Science* 54: 583–597.

Banda, Kevin K. and Erin C. Cassese. 2022. "Hostile Sexism, Racial Resentment, and Political Mobilization," *Political Behavior* 3: 1317–1335

Barber, Michael and Jeremy C. Pope. 2019. "Does Party Trump Ideology? Disentangling Party and Ideology in America." *American Political Science Review* 114: 38–54.

Baylor, Christopher. 2018. *First to the Party: The Group Origins of Political Transformation.* Philadelphia: University of Pennsylvania Press.

Betz, Hans-Georg. 2019. "Facets of Nativism: A Heuristic Explanation." *Patterns of Prejudice* 53: 111–135.

Bishop, Bill. 2009. *The Big Sort: Why the Clustering of Like-Minded America is Tearing Us Apart.* New York, Mariner Books.

Bobbio, Norberto. 1997. *Left and Right: The Significance of a Political Distinction.* Chicago, IL: University of Chicago Press.

Borjas, George J. 1999. *Heaven's Door: Immigration Policy and the American Economy.* Princeton, NJ: Princeton University Press.

Bowler, Shaun, Stephen P. Nicholson, and Gary Segura. 2006. "Earthquakes and Aftershocks: Race, Direct Democracy, and Partisan Change." *American Journal of Political Science* 50: 146–159.

Bray, Mark. 2017. *Antifa: The Anti-Fascist Handbook.* Brooklyn, NY: Melville House.

Brown, Thad. 1988. *Migration and Politics: The Impact of Population Mobility on American Voting.* Chapel Hill, NC: University of North Carolina Press.

https://doi.org/10.1515/9783111469720-008

Brulle, Robert J., Jason Carmichael, and J. Craig Jenkins. 2012. "Shifting Public Opinion on Climate Change: An Empirical Assessment of Factors Influencing Concern over Climate Change in the U.S., 2002–2010." *Climate Change* 114: 169–188.

Buchanan, Patrick J. 1998. *The Great Betrayal: How American Sovereignty and Social Justice are Being Sacrificed to the Gods of the Global Economy.* Boston, MA: Little Brown.

Buchanan, Patrick J. 2004, *Where the Right Went Wrong: How Neoconservatives Subverted the Reagan Revolution and Hijacked the Bush Presidency.* New York: St. Martin's Press.

Buckley, F.H. 2022. *Progressive Conservatism: How Republicans will Become America's Natural Governing Party.* New York: Encounter Books.

Buckley, William F. 1993. *In Search of Anti-Semitism.* New York: Continuum.

Cahn, Naomi and June Carbone. 2010. *Red Families vs. Blue Families: Legal Polarization and the Creation of Culture.* New York: Oxford University Press.

Campbell, Angus, Gerald Gurin, Warren E. Miller, Sylvia Eberhart, Robert O. McWilliams. 1954. *The Voter Decides.* Evanston, IL: Row, Peterson.

Campbell, Angus, Philip E. Converse, Warren E. Miller, and Donald E. Stokes. 1960. *The American Voter.* New York: John Wiley.

Carmines, Edward G. and James A. Stimson. 1980. "The Two Faces of Issue Voting." *American Political Science Review* 74: 78–91.

Carmines, Edward G., Jessica C. Gerrity, and Michael W. Wagner. 2010. "How Abortion Became a Partisan Issue: Media Coverage of the Interest Group-Political Party Connection." *P&P: Politics and Policy* 38: 1135–1158.

Carney, Riley K. and Ryan D. Enos. 2017. "Conservatism and Fairness in Contemporary Politics." *NYU CESS Experiments Conference.*

Carr, Patrick J. and Maria J. Kefalas. 2009. *Hollowing Out the Middle: The Rural Brain Drain and What it Means for America.* Boston, MA: Beacon Press.

Chan, Nathan Kar Ming, Jae Yeon Kim, and Vivien Leung. 2022. "COVID-19 and Asian Americans: How Elite Messaging and Social Exclusion Shape Partisan Attitudes." *Perspectives on Politics* 20: 618–634.

Chapman, Simon and Philip Alpers. 2013. "Gun-Related Deaths: How Australia Stepped Off the 'American Path.'" *Annals of Internal Medicine* 158: 770–771.

Citrin, Jack. 1974. "Comment: The Political Relevance of Trust in Government." *The American Political Science Review* 68: 973–988

Citrin, Jack., Morris S. Levy, Matthew Wright. 2023. *Immigration in the Court of Public Opinion.* Hoboken, NJ: Polity Press.

Connor, W.T. 1927. "Fundamentalism v. Modernism." *Social Science* 2: 101–106.

Converse, Philip. 1964. "The Nature of Belief Systems in Mass Publics." In *Ideology and Discontent,* ed. David Apter. New York: The Free Press.

Corn, David. 2022. *American Psychosis: A Historical Investigation of How the Republican Party Went Crazy.* New York: Twelve.

Cramer, Katherine J. 2016. *The Politics of Resentment: Rural Consciousness in Wisconsin and the Rise of Scott Walker.* Chicago, IL: University of Chicago Press.

Damore, David F., Robert E. Lang, and Karen A. Danielsen. 2020. *Blue Metros, Red States: The Shifting Urban-Rural Divide in America's Swing States.* Washington, DC: Brookings Institution Press.

Davis, Nicholas T., Kirby Goidel, Christine S. Lipsmeyer, Guy D. Whitten, Clifford Young. 2019. "Economic Vulnerability, Cultural Decline, and Nativism: Contingent and Indirect Effects." *Social Science Quarterly* 100: 430–446.

De la Garza, Rodolfo O. and Jeronimo Cortina, "Are Latinos Republicans but Just don't Know it?" *American Politics Research* 35: 202–223.

Deneen, Patrick J. 2018. *Why Liberalism Failed.* New Haven, CT: Yale University Press, 2018.

Downs, Anthony. 1957. *An Economic Theory of Democracy.* New York: Harper.

Djupe, Paul A., Jacob R. Neiheisel, and Anand E. Sokhey. 2018. "Reconsidering the Role of Politics in Leaving Religion: The Importance of Affiliation." *American Journal of Political Science* 62: 161–175.

Dunlap, Riley E. and Araon M. McCright, "A Widening Gap: Republican and Democratic Views on Climate Change," *Environment: Science and Policy for Sustainable Development* 50 (2008): 26–35.

Dunlap, Riley E., Aaron M. McCright, and Jerrod H. Yarosh. 2016. "The Political Divide on Climate Change: Partisan Polarization Widens in the U.S." *Environment: Science and Policy for Sustainable Development* 58: 4–23.

Dyck, Joshua J., Gregg B. Johnson, and Jesse T. Wasson. 2011. "A Blue Tide in the Golden State: Ballot Propositions, Population Change, and Party Identification in California." *American Politics Research* 40: 450–475.

Edlund, Lena and Rohini Pande. 2002. "Why have Women Become Left Wing? The Political Gender Gap and the Decline of Marriage." *The Quarterly Journal of Economics* 117: 917–961.

Ehrlich, Sean D. and Eddie Hearn. 2014. "Does Compensating the Losers Increase Support for Trade? An Experimental Test of the Embedded Liberalism Thesis." *Foreign Policy Analysis* 10: 149–164.

Elliott-Dorans, Lauren. 2020. "The Influence of Values on Hard Issue Attitudes." *Journal of Elections, Public Opinion, and Parties* 32: 1–19.

Evans, Diana, Ana Franco, J.L. Polinard, James P. Wenzel, and Robert D. Wrinkle. 2012. "Ethnic Concerns and Latino Party Identification." *The Social Science Journal* 49: 150–154.

Fawcett, Edmund. 2020. *Conservatism: The Fight for a Tradition.* Princeton, NJ: Princeton University Press, 2020.

Fernandez, Kenneth E. and Matthew C. Dempsey. 2017. "The Local Political Context of Latino Partisanship," *Journal of Race, Ethnicity, and Politics* 2: 201–232.

Fetzer, Joel S. 2000. "Economic Self-Interest or Cultural Marginality? Anti-Immigration Sentiment and Nativist Political Movements in France, Germany, and the USA." *Journal of Ethnic and Migration Studies* 26: 5–23

Filindra, Alexandra and Noah Kaplan. 2016. "Racial Resentment and Whites' Gun Policy Preferences in Contemporary America." *Political Behavior* 38: 255–275.

Filindra, Alexandra, Noah J. Kaplan, and Beyza E. Buyuker. 2021. "Racial Resentment or Sexism? White Americans' Outgroup Attitudes as Predictors of Gun Ownership and NRA Membership." *Sociological Inquiry* 91: 253–286.

Fiorina, Morris Samuel J. Abrams, and Jeremy C. Pope. 2005. *Culture War? The Myth of a Polarized America.* New York: Pearson Longman.

Fischer, David Hackett. 1989. *Albion's Seed: Four British Folkways in America.* New York: Oxford University Press, 1989.

Frank, Thomas. 2004. *What's the Matter with Kansas? How Conservatives Won the Heart of America.* New York: Henry Holt and Company.

Freeman, Gary P. 2009. "Immigration, Diversity, and Welfare Chauvinism." *The Forum* 7: 1–16.

Frey, William H. 1987. "Migration and Depopulation of the Metropolis: Regional Restructuring or Rural Renaissance?" *American Sociological Review* 52: 240–257.

Gelman, Andrew, David Park, Boris Shor, and Jeronimo Cortina. 2010. *Red State, Blue State, Rich State, Poor State: Why Americans Vote the Way they Do (Expanded Edition)*. Princeton, NJ: Princeton University Press.

Gershkoff, Amy R. 2009. "The Marriage Gap." In *Beyond Red State, Blue State: Electoral Gaps in the Twenty-First Century American Electorate*, eds. Laura Olson and John C. Green. Upper Saddle River, NJ: Pearson Prentice Hall.

Gerson, Kathleen. 1987. "Emerging Social Divisions among Women: Implications for Welfare State Politics." *Politics and Society* 15: 213 – 221.

Ghatak, Sarah and Vincent Ferraro. 2021. "Immigration Control and the White Working Class: Explaining State-Level Laws in the US, 2005 – 2017." *Sociological Spectrum* 41: 457 – 477

Gilens, Martin. 1999. *Why Americans Hate Welfare: Race, Media, and the Politics of Antipoverty Policy.* Chicago, IL: University of Chicago Press.

Gilens, Martin and Benjamin I. Page. 2014. "Testing Theories of American Politics: Elites, Interest Groups, and Average Citizens." *Perspectives on Politics* 12: 564 – 581.

Gillion, Daniel Q. 2020. *The Loud Minority: Why Protests Matter in American Democracy.* Princeton, NJ: Princeton University Press.

Gimpel, James G., Nathan Lovin, Bryant Moy, and Andrew Reeves. 2020. "The Urban-Rural Gulf in American Political Behavior." *Political Behavior* 42: 1334 – 1368.

Goedert, Nicholas. 2014. "Gerrymandering or Geography? How Democrats Won the Popular Vote but Lost Congress in 2012." *Research and Politics* 1: 1 – 8.

Goldberg, Matthew H., Abel Gustafson, Seth A. Rosenthal, and Anthony Leiserowitz. 2021. "Shifting Republican Views on Climate Change through Targeted Advertising." *Nature Climate Change* 11: 573 – 577.

Green, Donald, Bradley Palmquist, and Eric Schickley. 2002. *Partisan Hearts and Minds: Political Parties and the Social Identities of Voters.* New Haven, CT: Yale University Press.

Haidt, Jonathan. 2012. *The Righteous Mind: Why Good People are Divided by Politics and Religion.* New York: Pantheon.

Hall, Matthew and Barrett Lee. 2010. "How Diverse are U.S. Suburbs?" *Urban Studies* 27: 204 – 237.

Hawley, George. 2011. "Political Threat and Immigration: Party Identification, Demographic Context, and Immigration Policy Preference." *Social Science Quarterly* 92: 404 – 422.

Hawley, George. 2012. "Home Affordability, Female Marriage Rates and Vote Choice in the 2000 Election: Evidence from U.S. Counties." *Party Politics* 18: 771 – 789

Hawley, George. 2013. *Voting and Migration Patterns in the U.S.* New York: Routledge.

Hawley, George. 2014. *White Voters in 21st Century America.* New York: Routledge.

Hawley, George. 2016. *Right-Wing Critics of American Conservatism.* Lawrence, KS: University Press of Kansas.

Hawley, George. 2017. *Demography, Culture, and the Decline of America's Christian Denominations,* (Lanham, MD: Lexington Books)

Hawley, George. 2017. *Making Sense of the Alt-Right.* New York: Columbia University Press.

Hawley, George. 2019. "Ambivalent Nativism: Trump Supporters' Attitudes Toward Islam and Muslim Immigration," The Brookings Institution. https://www.brookings.edu/research/ambivalent-nativism-trump-supporters-attitudes-toward-islam-and-muslim-immigration/.

Hawley, George. 2019. "Immigration Status, Immigrant Family Ties, and Support for the Democratic Party." *Social Science Quarterly* 100: 1171 – 1181.

Hawley, George. 2021. "The "Groyper" Movement in the US: Challenges for the Post-Alt-right." In *Contemporary Far-Right Thinkers and the Future of Liberal Democracy,"* edited by A. James McAdams and Alejandro Castrillon, 225–241. New York: Routledge.

Hawley, George. 2022. *Conservatism in a Divided America: The Right and Identity Politics.* Notre Dame, IN: University of Notre Dame Press.

Heersink, Boris and Jeffery A. Jenkins. 2020. "Whiteness and the Emergence of the Republican Party in the Early Twentieth-Century South," *Studies in American Political Development* 34: 71–90.

Hemmer, Nicole. 2022. *Partisans: The Conservative Revolutionaries Who Remade American Politics in the 1990s.* New York: Basic Books.

Hetherington, Marc J. 1998. "The Political Relevance of Political Trust," *The American Political Science Review,* 92: 791–808

Higgs, Robert. 1987. *Crisis and Leviathan: Critical Episodes in the Growth of American Government.* New York: Oxford University Press.

Hout, Michael and Claude S. Fischer. 2002. "Why More Americans Have No Religious Preference: Politics and Generations." *American Sociological Review* 67: 165–190.

Hout, Michael and Christopher Maggio. 2021. "Immigration, Race, and Political Polarization." *Daedalus* 150: 40–55.

Mulloy, Darren. 2021. *Years of Rage: White Supremacy in the United States from the Klan to the Alt-Right.* Lanham, MD: Rowman and Littlefield.

Huddy, Leonie, Lilliana Mason, and S. Nechama Horwitz. 2016. "Political Identity Convergence: On Being Latino, Becoming a Democrat, and Getting Active." *RSF: The Russell Sage Foundation Journal of the Social Sciences* 2: 205–228.

Hui, Iris and David O. Sears, 2017. "Reexamining the Effect of Racial Propositions on Latinos' Partisanship in California." *Political Behavior* 40: 149–174.

Hunter, James Davison. 1991. *Culture Wars: The Struggle to Define America.* New York: Basic Books, 1991.

Huntington, Samuel. 2005. *Who Are We? The Challenges to America's National Identity.* New York: Simon and Schuster.

Huntington, John S. 2021. *Far-Right Vanguard: The Radical Roots of Modern Conservatism.* Philadelphia, PA: University of Pennsylvania Press.

Jacobson, Gary C. 2021. "Donald Trump's Big Lie and the Future of the Republican Party." *Presidential Studies Quarterly* 51: 273–289.

Janoff-Bulman, Ronnie. 2023. *The Two Moralities: Conservatives, Liberals, and the Roots of Our Political Divide.* New Haven, CT: Yale University Press.

Jardina, Ashley. 2019. *White Identity Politics.* New York: Cambridge University Press.

Jennings, M. Kent, Laura Stoker, and Jake Bowers. 2009. "Politics across Generations: Family Transmission Reexamined." *The Journal of Politics* 71: 782–799.

Johnson, Ron, David Manley, Kelvyn Jones, and Ryne Rohla. 2020. "The Geographical Polarization of the American Electorate: A Country of Increasing Electoral Landslides?" *GeoJournal* 85: 187–204.

Joslyn, Mark R., Donald P. Haider-Markel, Michael Baggs, and Andrew Bilbo. 2017. "Emerging Political Identities? Gun Ownership and Voting in Presidential Election." *Social Science Quarterly* 98: 383–396.

Jost, John T., Mahzarin R. Banaji, and Brian A. Nosek. 2004. "A Decade of System Justification Theory: Accumulated Evidence of Conscious and Unconscious Bolstering of the Status Quo." *Political Psychology* 25: 881–919.

Judis, John and Roy Teixeira. 2002. *The Emerging Democratic Majority.* New York: Scribner.

Justwan, Florian and Ryan D. Williamson. 2022. "Trump and Trust: Examining the Relationship between Claims of Fraud and Citizen Attitudes." *PS: Political Science and Politics* 55: 462–469.

Kantack, Benjamin R. and Collin E. Paschall. 2020. "Does 'Politicizing' Gun Violence Increase Support for Gun Control? Experimental Evidence from the Las Vegas Shooting." *Social Science Quarterly* 101: 893–908.

Kaufmann, Eric and Matthew J. Goodwin. 2018. "The Diversity Wave: A Meta-Analyis of the Native-Born White Response to Ethnic Diversity." *Social Science Research* 76: 120–131.

Keith, Bruce E., David B. Magleby, Candice J. Nelson, Elizabeth A. Orr, Mark C. Westlye, and Raymond E. Wolfinger. 1992. *The Myth of the Independent Voter.* Berkeley, CA: University of California Press.

Key, V.O. 1949. *Southern Politics in State and Nation.* New York: Alfred A. Knopf.

Kinder, Donald R. and Nathan P. Kalmoe. 2017. *Neither Liberal Nor Conservative: Ideological Innocence in the American Public.* Chicago: University of Chicago Press.

Kinder, Donald R. and Lynn M. Sanders. 1996. *Divided by Color: Racial Politics and the Democratic Ideal.* Chicago: University of Chicago Press.

Kingston, Paul William and Steven E. Finkel. 1987. "Is there a Marriage Gap in Politics?" *Journal of Marriage and Family* 49: 57–64.

Kirk, Russell. 2002. *The American Cause.* Wilmington, DE: ISI Press.

Kling, Arnold. 2017. *The Three Languages of Politics: Talking Across the Political Divides.* Washington, DC: The Cato Institute.

Kono, Daniel Y. 2008. "Does Public Opinion Affect Trade Policy?" *Business and Politics* 10: 1–19.

Korey, John L. and Edward L. Lascher Jr. 2006. "Macropartisanship in California." *Public Opinion Quarterly* 70: 48–65.

Krosnick, Jon A. and Donald R. Kinder. 1990. "Altering Foundations of Support for the President through Priming," *The American Political Science Review* 84: 497–512.

Krumpal Ivar. 2013., "Determinants of Social Desirability Bias in Sensitive Surveys: A Literature Review." *Quality and Quantity* 47: 2025–2047.

Krupenkin, Masha, David Rothschild, Shawndra Hill, and Elad Yom-Tov. 2019. "President Trump Stress Disorder: Partisanship, Ethnicity, and Expressive Reporting of Mental Distress After the 2016 Election." *SAGE Open* 9: 1–14.

Kwon, Soyoung. 2023. "The Interplay between Partisanship, Risk Perception, and Mental Distress During the Early Stages of the COVID-19 Pandemic in the United States." *Psychology, Health, and Medicine* 1: 69–85.

Le, Danvy, Maneesh Arora, and Christopher Stout. 2020. "Are You Threatening Me? Asian-American Panethnicity in the Trump Era." *Social Science Quarterly* 101: 2183–2192.

Leal, David L., Matt A. Barreto, Jonho Lee, and Rodolfo O. de la Garza. 2005. "The Latino Vote in the 2004 Election." *PS: Political Science and Politics* 38: 41–49.

Lee, Heysung. 2021. "'Easy' and 'Hard' Issues: Attitude Extremity and a Role of the need to Evaluate." *Social Science Quarterly* 102: 2930–2941.

Leiner, Dominik Johannes. 2019. "Too Fast, too Straight, too Weird: Non-Reactive Indicators for Meaningless Data in Internet Surveys." *Survey Research Methods* 13: 229–248.

Levendusky, Matthew. 2009. *The Partisan Sort: How Liberals Became Democrats and Conservatives Became Republicans.* Chicago, IL: University of Chicago Press.

Levin, Ines, Alexandra Filindra, and Jeffrey S. Kopstein. 2022. "Validating and Testing a Measure of Antisemitism on Support for QAnon and Vote Intention for Trump in 2020." *Social Science Quarterly* 103: 794–809.

Lewis, Andrew R. 2014. "Abortion Politics and the Decline of the Separation of Church and State: The Southern Baptist Case" *Politics and Religion* 7: 521 – 549.

Lewis, Andrew R. 2017. *The Rights Turn in Conservative Christian Politics: How Abortion Transformed the Culture War.* New York: Cambridge University Press.

Margolis, Michelle. 2018. *From Politics to the Pews: How Partisanship and the Political Landscape Shapes Religious Identity.* Chicago. IL: University of Chicago Press.

Mason, Lilliana and Julie Wronski. 2018. "One Tribe to Bind Them All: How Our Social Group Attachments Strengthen Partisanship." *Political Psychology* 39: 257 – 277.

Mason, Lilliana. 2018. *Uncivil Agreement: How Politics Became Our Identity.* Chicago, IL: University of Chicago Press.

MacDonald, David. 2021. "Political Trust and Support for Immigration in the American Mass Public." *British Journal of Political Science* 51: 1402 – 1420

Major, Mark. 2012. "Objective but Not Impartial: Human Events, Barry Goldwater, and the Development of the 'Liberal Media' in the Conservative Counter-Sphere." *New Political Science* 34: 455 – 468.

Major, Mark. 2015, "Conservative Consciousness and the Press: The Institutional Contribution to the Idea of the 'Liberal Media' in Right-Wing Discourse." *Critical Sociology* 41: 483 – 491.

Masuoka, Natalie. 2006. "Together They Become One: Examining the Predictors of Panethnic Group Consciousness Among Asian Americans and Latinos." *Social Science Quarterly* 87: 993 – 1011.

Matzko, Paul. 2020. *The Radio Right: How a Band of Broadcasters Took on the Federal Government and Built the Modern Conservative Movement.* New York: Oxford University Press.

Mayhew, David R. 1974. *Congress: The Electoral Connection.* New Haven, CT: Yale University Press.

McAlexander, Richard J. and Johannes Urpelainen. 2020. "Elections and Policy Responsiveness: Evidence from Environmental Voting in the U.S. Congress." *Review of Policy Research* 37: 39 – 63.

McCarty, Nolan, Howard Rosenthal, and Keith T. Poole. 2006. *Polarized America: The Dance of Ideology and Unequal Riches.* Cambridge, MA: MIT Press.

McDonnell, Joshua. 2020. "Municipality Size, Political Efficacy and Political Participation: A Systematic Review." *Local Government Studies* 46: 331 – 350.

McKee, Seth C. 2008. "Rural Voters and the Polarization of American Presidential Elections." *P.S.: Political Science and Politics* 41: 101 – 108.

Mettler, Suzanne and Trevor Brown. 2022. "The Growing Rural-Urban Political Divide and Democratic Vulnerability." *The ANNALS of the American Academy of Political and Social Science* 699: 130 – 142.

Miller, Arthur H. 1974. "Political Issues and Trust in Government: 1964 – 1970." *American Political Science Review* 68: 951 – 972.

Miller, Steven V. 2018. "Economic Anxiety or Racial Resentment? An Evaluation of Attitudes Toward Immigration in the U.S. from 1992 to 2016." *Immigration Research*,1: 1 – 29

Mills, C. Wright. 1956. *The Power Elite.* New York: Oxford University Press.

Monroe, Alan D. 1998. "Public Opinion and Public Policy, 1980 – 1993." *Public Opinion Quarterly* 62: 6 – 28.

Mudde, Cas. 2004. "The Populist Zeitgeist." *Government and Opposition* 39: 543.

Muller, Edward N. 1972. "A Partial Test of a Theory of Potential for Political Violence." *American Political Science Review* 66: 928 – 959.

Müller, Jan-Werner. 2022. "What, If Anything, Do Populism and Conspiracy Theories Have to Do with Each Other?" *Social Research: An International Quarterly* 89: 607 – 625.

Munger, Kevin. 2022. *Generation Gap: Why the Baby Boomers Still Dominate American Politics and Culture.* New York: Columbia University Press.

Napier, Jaime L. and John T. Jost. 2008. "Why are Conservatives Happier than Liberals?" *Psychological Science* 19: 446–572.

Nash, George. 1976. *The Conservative Intellectual Movement in America Since 1946.* New York: Basic Books.

Neiheisel, Jacob R. 2016. "The 'L' Word: Anti-Liberal Campaign Rhetoric, Symbolic Ideology, and the Electoral Fortunes of Democratic Candidates." *Political Research Quarterly* 69: 418–429.

Newman, David B., Norbert Schwarz, Jesse Graham, and Arthur A. Stone. 2019. "Conservatives Report Greater Meaning in Life Than Liberals." *Social Psychology and Personality Science* 10: 494–503.

Norquist, Grover. 2008. *Leave Us Alone: Getting the Government's Hands off Our Money, Our Guns, Our Lives.* New York: HarperCollins.

Olson, Mancur. 1965. *The Logic of Collective Action: Public Goods and the Theory of Groups.* Cambridge, MA: Harvard University Press.

Oser, Jennifer, Amit Grinson, Shelley Boulianne, and Eran Halperin. 2022. "How Political Efficacy Relates to Online and Offline Political Participation: A Multilevel Meta-Analysis." *Political Communication* 39: 607–633.

Page, Benjamin I. and Robert Y. Shapiro. 2003. "Effects of Public Opinion on Policy," *The American Political Science Review* 77 (1983): 175–190; Paul Burstein, "The Impact of Public Opinion on Public Policy: A Review and an Agenda." *Political Research Quarterly* 56: 29–40.

Palm, Risa Gregory B. Lewis, and Bo Feng. 2017. "What Causes People to Change their Opinion about Climate Change?" *A,nnals of the American Association of Geographers* 107: 883–896.

Papaioannou, Kostas, Myrto Pantazi, and Jan-Willem van Prooijen. 2023. "Unravelling the Relationship between Populism and Belief in Conspiracy Theories: The Role of Cynicism, Powerlessness, and Zero-Sum Thinking." *British Journal of Psychology,*114: 159–175.

Park, Hong Min and George Hawley. 2020. "Determinants of the Opinion Gap between Elites and the Public in the United States." *The Social Science Journal* 57: 1–13.

Parker, Victoria A., Matthew Feinberg, Alexa Tullett, and Anne E Wilson. 2021. "The Ties that Blind: Misperceptions of the Opponent Fringe and the Miscalibration of Political Contempt." Working paper. https://www.researchgate.net/publication/355012770_The_Ties_that_Blind_Misperceptions_of_the_Opponent_Fringe_and_the_Miscalibration_of_Political_Contempt

Paul, Darel E. 2019. *From Tolerance to Equality: How Elites Brought America to Same-Sex Marriage.* Waco, TX: Baylor University Press.

Peterson, Johnathan C., Kevin B. Smith, and John R. Hibbing. 2020. "Do People Really Become More Conservative as They Age?" *The Journal of Politics* 82: 600–611.

Quadagno, Jill. *The Color of Welfare: How Racism Undermined the War on Poverty.* New York: Oxford University Press.

Raychaudhuri, Tanika. 2018. "The Social Roots of Asian American Partisan Attitudes." *Politics, Groups, and Identities* 6: 389–410.

Raychaudhuri, Tanika. 2020. "Socializing Democrats: Examining Asian American Vote Choice with Evidence from a National Survey." *Electoral Studies* 63: 102–114.

Reid, Shannon E. and Matthew Valasik. 2020. *Alt-Right Gangs: A Hazy Shade of White.* Berkeley, CA: University of California Press.

Rendon, Joshua J., Xiaohe Xu, Melinda Lundquist Denton, and John P. Bartkowski. 2014."Religion and Marriage Timing: A Replication and Extension." *Religions* 5: 834–851.

Reny, Tyler T., Loren Collingwood, and Ali A. Valenzuela. 2019. "Vote Switching in the 2016 Election: How Racial and Immigration Attitudes, Not Economics, Explain Shifts in White Voting." *Public Opinion Quarterly* 83: 91–113

Rho, Sungmin and Michael Tomz. 2017. "Why Don't Trade Preferences Reflect Economic Self-Interest?" *International Organization* 71: 86–108.

Rigueur, Leah Wright. 2015. *The Loneliness of the Black Republican*. Princeton, NJ: Princeton University Press.

Riley, Emmitt Y. and Clarissa Peterson. 2020. "I Can't Breathe: Assessing the Role of Racial Resentment and Racial Prejudice in Whites' Feelings toward Black Lives Matter." *National Review of Black Politics* 1: 496–515.

Robin, Corey. 2013. *The Reactionary Mind: From Edmund Burke to Sarah Palin*. Oxford University Press, 2013.

Rodden, Jonathan A. 2019. *Why Cities Lose: The Deep Roots of the Urban-Rural Divide*. New York: Basic Books.

Rosemary L. Al-Kire, Michael H. Pasek, Jo-Ann Tsang, Wade C. Rowatt, "Christian No More: Christian Americans are Threatened by their Impending Minority Status," Journal of Experimental Social Psychology 97(2021): 104223

Rothschild, Mike. 2021. *The Storm is Upon Us: How QAnon Became a Movement, Cult, and Conspiracy Theory of Everything*. New York: Melville House.

Ruffini, Patrick. 2023. *Party of the People: Inside the Multiracial Populist Coalition Remaking the GOP*. New York: Simon and Schuster.

Savage, Michael. 2005. *Liberalism is a Mental Disorder*. Nashville, TN: Nelson Current.

Scala, Dante J. and Kenneth M. Johnson. 2017. "Political Polarization along the Rural-Urban Continuum? The Geography of the Presidential Vote, 2000–2016," *The ANNALS of the American Academy of Political and Social Science* 672: 162–184.

Schaller, Tom and Paul Waldman. 2024. *White Rural Rage: The Threat to American Democracy*. New York: Random House.

Schlenker, Barry R., John R. Chambers, and Bonnie M. Le. 2017. "Conservatives are Happier than Liberals, but Why? Political Ideology, Personality, and Life Satisfaction." *Journal or Research in Personality* 46: 127–146.

Schoen, Robert and James R. Kluegel. 1988. "The Widening Gap in Black and White Marriage Rates: The Impact of Population Composition and Differential Marriage Propensities." *American Sociological Review* 53: 895–907.

Schrieber, Ronnee. 2012. *Righting Feminism: Conservative Women and American Politics*. New York: Oxford University Press.

Schwartz, Christine R. and Hongyun Han. 2014. "The Reversal of the Gender Gap in Education and Trends in Marital Dissolution." *American Sociological Review* 79: 605–629.

Shapiro, Robert Y. 2011. "Public Opinion and American Democracy." *Public Opinion Quarterly* 75: 982–1017

Shipan, Charles R. and William R. Lowry. 2001. "Environmental Policy and Policy Divergence in Congress." *Political Research Quarterly* 54: 245–263.

South, Scott J. 1993. "Racial and Ethnic Differences in the Desire to Marry." *Journal of Marriage and the Family* 55: 357–370.

Sowell, Thomas. 2007. *A Conflict of Visions: Ideological Origins of Political Struggles*. New York: Basic Books.

Stenner-Day, Karen and Mark Fischle. 1992. "The Effects of Political Participation on Political Efficacy: A Simultaneous Equations Model." *Australian Journal of Political Science* 27: 282–305.

Thompson, Jack and George Hawley. 2021. "Does the Alt-Right Still Matter? An Examination of Alt-Right Influence between 2016 and 2018." *Nations and Nationalism* 27: 1165–1180

Tichenor, Daniel. 2002. *Dividing Lines: The Politics of Immigration Control in the United States.* Princeton, NJ: Princeton University Press.

Tolbert, Caroline J., David P. Redlawsk, and Kellen J. Gracey. 2018. "Racial Attitudes and Emotional Responses to the 2016 Republican Candidates." *Journal of Elections, Public Opinion and Parties* 28: 245–262.

Tyson, David W. 2009. *Courage to Put Country above Color: The J.A. Parker Story.* Washington, DC: Lincoln Institute for Research and Education.

Uscinski, Joseph E. and Joseph M. Parent,. 2014.*American Conspiracy Theories.* New York: Oxford University Press.

Van Prooijen, Jan-Willem Talia, Cohen Rodrigues, Carlotta Bunzel, Oana Georgescu, Dániel Komáromy, and André P. M. Krouwel. 2022. "Populist Gullibility: Conspiracy Theories, News Credibility,
Bullshit Receptivity, and Paranormal Belief." *Political Psychology* 43: 1061–1079.

Vandeweerdt, Clara, Bart Kerremans, and Avery Cohn. 2016. "Climate Voting in the U.S. Congress: The Power of Public Concern." *Environmental Politics* 25: 268–288

Weisberg, Herbert F. 1987. "The Demographics of a New Voting Gap: Marital Differences in American Voting." *Public Opinion Quarterly* 51: 335–343.

Weisman, Jonathan. 2018. *(((Semitism))): Being Jewish in America in the Age of Trump.* New York: St. Martin's Press.

White, Ismail K. and Chryl N. Laird. 2020. *Steadfast Democrats: How Social Forces Shape Black Political Behavior.* Princeton, NJ: Princeton University Press.

White, John Kenneth. 2024. *Grand Old Unravelling: The Republican Party, Donald Trump, and the Rise of Authoritarianism.* Lawrence, KS: University Press of Kansas.

Will, George. 2019. *The Conservative Sensibility.* New York: Hachette Books.

Williams, Daniel K. 2010. *God's Own Party: The Making of the Christian Right.* New York: Oxford University Press.

Wojcik, Sean P., Arpine Hovasapian, Jesse Graham, Matt Motyl, and Peter H. Ditto. 2015. "Conservatives Report, but Liberals Display, Greater Happiness." *Science* 347: 1243–1246.

Wong, Janelle, S. Karthick Ramakrishnan, Taeku Lee, and Jane Junn. 2011. Asian American Political Participation: Emerging Constituents and their Political Identity. New York: Russell Sage Foundation.

Wong, Janelle and Sono Shah. 2021. "Convergence Across Difference: Understanding the Political Ties That Bind with the 2016 National Asian American Survey." *RSF: The Russell Sage Foundation Journal of the Social Sciences* 7: 70–92.

Ybarra, Vickie D., Lisa M. Sanchez, and Gabriel R. Sanchez. 2016. "Anti-Immigrant Anxieties in State Policy: The Great Recession and Punitive Immigration Policy in the American States, 2005–2012." *State Politics and Policy Quarterly* 16: 313–339.

Yudkin, Daniel. Stephen Hawkins, and Tim Dixon. 2019. *The Perception Gap: How False Impressions are Pulling Americans Apart.* New York: More in Common.

www.ingramcontent.com/pod-product-compliance
Lightning Source LLC
Chambersburg PA
CBHW022317280326
41932CB00010B/1128